# THE HAND OF DESTINY

## FOLKLORE AND SUPERSTITION FOR EVERYDAY LIFE

"For when we think fate hovers o'er our heads,
  Our apprehensions shoot beyond all bounds,
  Owls, ravens, crickets seem the watch of death;
  Nature's worst vermin scare her godlike sons."
                    DRYDEN and LEE'S *Œdipus* (Act IV, Sc. 1).

# THE HAND OF DESTINY
# FOLKLORE AND SUPERSTITION

## FOR EVERYDAY LIFE

## C.J.S. THOMPSON

BELL PUBLISHING COMPANY
NEW YORK

*Publisher's Note:* The modern reader may be surprised
to discover certain old-fashioned and British styles
of punctuation and spelling, but these have been retained
in order to convey the flavor of the original edition.

This 1989 edition is published by Bell Publishing Company,
distributed by Crown Publishers, Inc.,
225 Park Avenue South, New York, New York 10003

Printed and Bound in the United States of America

Library of Congress Cataloging-in-Publication Data

Thompson, C. J. S. (Charles John Samuel), 1862–1943.
    The hand of destiny : folk-lore and superstition of everyday life
/ by C.J.S. Thompson.
        p.     cm.
    Reprint.
    Includes index.
    ISBN 0-517-67581-1
        1. Folklore.   2. Superstition.   3. Witchcraft.   I. Title.
GR65.T5 1989
398'.41—dc19                                        88-13762
                                                         CIP

ISBN 0-517-67581-1
h g f e d c b a

# CONTENTS

6 CONTENTS

# FOREWORD

What corner are the bay leaves in?
Fetch them, Thestylis! Where are the love charms?
Bind the goblet with a loop of the finest purple wool
so that I may place a spell upon the despicable man
   who is my lover.
He did not come to me for eleven days, the fool,
nor did he know if I was dead or alive,
and that monster didn't even knock at my door.

Simaetha's spell,
from *Idylls 2* of Theocritus (c 316–c 260 B.C.)

Some say destiny is shaped like a hand, with distinctive, separate fingers—paths reaching upward from the stable center of the palm. Others believe in a magic circle, the wheel of fortune whose infinite spokes radiate in all directions to form an endless series of possibilities. But where does causality begin, and who is in command?

Since the dawn of time and the awakening of consciousness in mankind we have sought to explore and control our own destinies. Perhaps the easiest and most familiar place to begin is in our everyday lives; hence folklore and superstition, and the variants and analogues of these, are inextricably bound to our history and culture, Eastern or Western, whoever and wherever we are.

Questions of human curiosity are naturally rich in personal history. Whether or not we believe in the sayings and the spells, we perceive the past through our legends and lore, and sense, for a moment, the presence of previous generations with similar feelings and needs.

You don't have to be superstitious to take pleasure in reading *The Hand of Destiny*. Like Simaetha, the Greek enchantress of Theocritus's *Idylls*, the book casts its spell with magic herbs and rhymes, and binds us fast to a fascinating collection of curious customs, beliefs, and practices from ancient Babylon through the beginning of the twentieth century. Here, among many other offerings, is folklore about the color of the eyes and the meaning of an itching nose; how loaves of bread and tools were marked against the influence of evil spirits; charms and cures derived from plants; interpretations of numbers; and the uses of amulets and gemstones.

What better guide is there for this mystical journey than C.J.S. Thompson (1863–1943), whose lifelong explorations into the history of magic, medicine, alchemy, and pharmacy yielded a wealth of illuminating books, among these *The Hand of Destiny*? Bearing testimony to Thompson's breadth of knowledge and boundless curiosity for things seen and unseen, this volume records the history of folklore and superstition of generations past for generations to come.

Lois Hill

*New York*
*1988*

# THE HAND OF DESTINY

## CHAPTER I

### THE FOLK-LORE OF BIRTH AND INFANCY

FROM time immemorial there appears to have been a general belief that some unseen hand or power controlled man's destiny. He imagined himself hedged about by spirits of doubtful goodwill or of definite evil intent, and he seems to have instinctively sought some means to protect himself from the terrors of the unseen. Fear has ever been part and parcel of our nature, and in this dread of the unknown we have the basis of many of the superstitions which have grown up round human life, from the cradle to the grave.

Astrology, the oldest of the sciences, taught that man's life and destiny from his birth to his death were influenced by the heavenly bodies. The stars were the abodes of the gods and by their study his fortune might be directed, success in life might be attained and ill avoided.

From this arose many of the superstitious beliefs that have come down to us from the lore of the past, for superstition in one form or another dwells beneath the surface of most human hearts. Although people of the present day no longer believe in magic, and many are sceptical of miraculous occurrences which used to be accepted as part of religion, many of the superstitious traditions of ages long ago still survive. The average individual of to-day is often, consciously or subconsciously, beset by fears of occult powers which he cannot explain, and though he believe in nothing else, he still believes in what is commonly called good or bad luck. Many people thus attempt, by some material substance or object, to attract the good and protect themselves from the harmful, hence the deep-rooted faith in charms, amulets and mascots, which may said to be almost universal.

The study of the folk-lore which surrounds human life has in recent years been receiving greater attention, its object being to collect and classify, where possible, the survivals of popular beliefs and traditions and to trace their original source. Much of their meaning has been lost in the passage of time, and modern education is fast sweeping away every vestige of many of the interestng old customs, which in bygone days held such a prominent place in social and domestic life ; therefore, their record, in time to come, will doubtless prove of great value to the student of the folk-lore surrounding the human race.

Around every stage of life, a variety of customs and superstitions are clustered, that have been bequeathed to us from early times, and although many of them now appear meaningless, yet they were the natural outcome of the meagre knowledge and primitive conceptions which then prevailed.

From the moment of birth, there were many influences which were believed to affect the future fortune and character of the child. Thus, down to the Middle Ages, the planets and stars were supposed to have an important influence on human life and so, at the advent of the infant, an astrologer was usually

called in to take the position of the heavenly bodies
and cast the horoscope at the true moment of birth,
when the baby first cried.

This once done, the parents were enabled to guard
against the many evils that might assail the child as
it grew up, as well as gather information regarding its
future career.

If the child was born when the planet Mercury

AN ASTROLOGER AT THE BIRTH OF A
CHILD
*From a woodcut.* 1618.

was in the ascendant, a happy and prosperous life
was foretold, while on the other hand, if Saturn or
Mars prevailed, a short and sorrowful future was
indicated.

Certain parts of the human body were commonly
believed to remain in a sympathetic union with it
after the physical connection had been severed. The
navel cord and the placenta or afterbirth, in particular, were supposed to be thus associated, a belief

that is to be found all over the world both among civilised and uncivilised races. So intimate was the union conceived to be, that the fortunes of the child for good or evil throughout life were often supposed to be bound up with one or other of these portions of his body.

If his navel cord or afterbirth was preserved and properly treated, it was believed that he would be prosperous, whereas if it be injured, or lost, he would suffer in the future accordingly.

Some of the curious customs prevailing among uncivilised races are interesting in this connection. Thus, among the Maoris, when the cord has dropped off, the child is carried to a priest to be named, but before doing so, the cord is buried in a sacred place and a young sapling planted over it. Ever afterwards this tree as it grows is considered a sign of life for the child.

Frazer states that the natives of Central Australia make a necklace of the cord, which is placed round the child's neck to facilitate its growth and avert disease. In some parts of Fiji, the navel cord of a male child is planted together with a coconut and the child's life is supposed to be intimately connected with that tree.

In some countries the afterbirth is buried under a stone at the threshold of the house, with the object of preventing evil spirits from entering and doing ill to the infant.

The natives of Bali, an island to the east of Java, firmly believe that the afterbirth is the child's brother or sister, and they bury it in the courtyard in the half of a coconut from which the kernel has not been removed. Among the Chinese, it is customary to store the afterbirth in " a felicitous spot under the salutary influences of the sky or moon—deep in the ground, so that the child may have long life."

In many countries in Europe also the belief is still held that a person's destiny is bound up with his navel cord and afterbirth.

In Germany, the father is enjoined to preserve it carefully so that the child shall live and thrive and be free from sickness.

It is customary in Yorkshire when a mare foals, to hang up the afterbirth in a tree, particularly a thorn tree, in order to secure luck to the animals.

In some parts of the world to-day, the navel cord and afterbirth are regarded as living beings, the brother or sister of the infant, or as the material object in which its guardian spirit or part of its soul resides, they are therefore preserved with the utmost care less the life of the child should be endangered by their injury or loss.

Many strange and curious traditions are associated with the caul, a thin membrane which is sometimes found covering the head of an infant at birth. It was deemed especially lucky and betokened good fortune in the future life of the child.

Some of the superstitions connected with it are of remote antiquity and their origin is unknown, but there is evidence that many were prevalent in the days of the Roman Empire.

Ælius Lampridius, in his life of Antonine surnamed Diadumenus, says, that he was so called from having been brought into the world with a band of membrane round his forehead in the shape of a diadem, and that he enjoyed a perpetual state of felicity from this circumstance during the whole of his life and reign.

Roman midwives, however, made no scruple of

selling the caul, and their best market was said to be the Forum, where they got high prices for it from the lawyers. The Roman lawyers prized it and wore it over their chests in the belief that by so doing they would gain their suits. Others sold it for use in magical rites, but in the Councils of the early Christian Church the superstitions associated with it were denounced and St. Chrysostom inveighed against them in many of his homilies.

Lampridius also recounts how the Empress Cesonia Celsa presented the Emperor Macrinus with a son who was born with a caul.

The monk's cowl and the caul both refer to the covering of the head and are probably derived from the same source. For a boy to be born with a caul was said to foretell that he would afterwards wear the judge's coif; on the other hand, says Collin de Planey, " when a child is born with a caul our fathers used to be sure it was a visible sign that Providence was calling him or her to the religious life, and they hardly ever failed in the absence of other proofs of vocation to shut the child up in a convent."

According to Grose, the health of the person born with a caul could in after life be judged by its condition—whether dry and crisp or relaxed and flaccid. It was believed that so long as the child, from whom the caul had been taken, enjoyed good health the caul experienced the same and remained dry and flexible, but on the caul-born person suffering from any sickness or disease, the membrane also underwent a change which daily became more apparent, either becoming totally crisp or regaining its former flexibility, according as the individual became better or grew worse.

In some families, cauls became hereditary and

were handed down from father to son and were regarded by their respective owners with as much superstition as if the person who had been born with it was still living.

In early times, midwives used to profess to tell the fortune of the newborn child by inspection of the caul and if it was red they declared it portended good fortune, but if it was of leaden hue, it foretold evil.

Lemnius states that if the caul be of a blackish colour it is an omen of ill-fortune to the child, but if of a reddish one it betokens everything that is good.

Ambrose Paré, the famous French surgeon of the sixteenth century, appears to have had some belief in the superstition, for alluding to the caul he writes : " Many times it happeneth, that the infant commeth into the world having his head covered or wrapped about with a portion of the secundine or tunicle wherein it is enclosed, especially when by the much strong and happy striving of the mother he commeth forth together with the water wherein it lyeth in the wombe and then the mydwives prophesie or foretell that the child shall be happy because hee is borne as it were with a hood on his head. But I suppose that it doth betoken health of body both to the infant and also to his mother, for it is a token of easie deliverance."

That cauls of newborn babies were highly valued and eagerly sought for in the sixteenth century, is substantiated by L'Etoile who relates that he saw two priests, " the one a procurer, the other a sorcerer, fighting with their fists in the church of the Holy Ghost for one of these cauls and that the procurer proved himself the stronger in so much that the caul remained with him."

In the seventeenth century, the caul was often called the " Silly-how," of which Sir Thomas Browne writes in his *Pseudodoxia Epidemica*. " Great conceits," he says, " are raised of the involution or membranous covering commonly called the Silly-how that sometimes is found about the head of children upon their birth and is therefore preserved with great care, not only as medical in diseases but effectual in success concerning the infant and others, which is surely no more than a continued superstition."

The well-known French expression, "*être né coiffée*," used to describe a lucky man, indicates that he was born with a caul. Thus in Brittany and other parts of France, where the lucky caul is preserved as a talisman, the young men who possess it do not forget to carry it with them on the day when they draw for the conscription.

In some parts of England it is called the " holy " or " fortunate hood," on account of its preservative associations, and the greatest care is taken that it should not be lost or taken away after the birth of a child who is fortunate enough to be born with one, for fear of death or sickness.

Apart from this, its principal property was its reputed power of preservation from drowning, and this did not alone affect the child born with it, but anyone who possessed and carried it on his person.

The presence of a caul on board ship was believed to prevent danger of shipwreck, and they have therefore always been highly prized by sailors who were ready to become purchasers for large sums.

Their value in the eighteenth century may be judged from advertisements culled from some newspapers of the time. Thus, in the *Morning Post* for August 21st, 1779, the following appears : " To the

Gentlemen of the Navy and others going long voyages to sea. To be disposed of, a CHILD'S CAUL. Enquire at the Barlet Buildings, Coffee House in Holborn. N.B.—To avoid unnecessary trouble the price is Twenty Guineas."

Some years later, we find in *The Times* for February 20th, 1813, " A Child's Caul to be sold in the highest perfection. Enquire at No. 2 Church Street, Minories. To prevent trouble, price £12."

There are frequent allusions to its supposed powers by writers of the sixteenth century. Thus in Ben Jonson's *Alchemist* (Act I, Sc. 2) we have Face saying to Dapper :

" Yes and that
You were born with a Cawl o' your head,"

and again in Digby's *Elvira* (Act V) Don Sancho observes :

" Were we not born with Cauls upon our heads ?
Think'st thou, chicken, to come off twice arow
Thus rarely from such dangerous adventures ? "

Although the price of cauls has much depreciated in these days, at the time of the German submarine campaign against merchant shipping during the Great War, they were eagerly sought for by sailors in the neighbourhood of the London Docks and were occasionally advertised at prices varying from £15 to £30.

The superstition was ridiculed by Hood in his ballad of " The Sea Spell," in which the jolly mariner loosed his sail against the wind and turned his boat to sea in the face of the gathering storm, confiding in the caul which he carried.

" But still that jolly mariner
Took in no reef at all ;
For in his pouch confidingly
He wore a baby's caul."

In spite of this, however, the boat capsized and the mariner was drowned for neither did heaven hear his cry nor the ocean heed his caul.

Another tradition connected with the caul was, that it protected the child from being secretly carried off and exchanged by some envious witch or fairy for its own ill-favoured offspring and so being a " changeling," a belief that survived to recent years in the Isle of Man.

" Changelings," says Martin Luther, " Satan lays in the place of genuine children that people may be tormented with them. He often carried off young maidens into the water."

The " changeling " is frequently mentioned by writers in the sixteenth century and among others by Shakespeare. Thus Puck, in *Midsummer Night's Dream* (Act II, Sc. 1) says of Titania's boy :

> " She never had so sweet a changeling."

And again in *The Winter's Tale* (Act III, Sc. 3) the Shepherd on discovering the babe, Perdita, tells the clown :

> · " It was told me I should be rich by the fairies,
> This is some changeling."

As a preventive of this supposed danger to the child, it is customary in the North of England to sometimes hang a carving-knife from the head of the cradle with the point towards the infant's face.

In the Western Highlands, in order to regain the lost child, should it have been taken away, parents are recommended the following device : " Place the changeling on the beach below highwater mark when the tide is out, paying no heed to its screams, and the fairies, rather than allow their offspring to be drowned by the rising waters, will convey it away and restore the child they have stolen. The sign that this has been done is the cessation of the child's cries."

In Ireland, it was customary to place the child supposed to be a changeling on a hot shovel or torment it in some way. But the real safeguard against the wickedness of the fairies is generally believed to be baptism which should be performed as soon as possible after birth, as after the rite the baby is believed to be immune from the danger.

In some parts of the North of Scotland, the sap of the ash is given to newborn children because, in common with the rowan, it is believed to possess the property of resisting the attacks of fairies, elves and witches.

A method of divining the sex of a child before birth, was to hang up over the front door of the home, the last thing at night before it was expected, a shoulder of mutton-bone stripped clean of flesh. The first person who entered the house on the following morning, either male or female, exclusive of members of the household, was said to indicate the sex of the child.

The belief in astrological influence on birth still survives in some parts of the country in connection with the day of the week on which the child is born.

An old rhyme current in Cornwall runs :

" Sunday's child is full of grace,
  Monday's child is full in the face,
  Tuesday's child is solemn and sad,
  Wednesday's child is merry and glad,
  Thursday's child is inclined to thieving,
  Friday's child is free in giving,
  Saturday's child works hard for a living."

There is, however, a general belief that Sunday is the most lucky day for a birth, and the old fortune-tellers used to predict great riches, long life and happiness to a child born on the Sabbath. In addition to this good augury, in Sussex, it is said that a child born on Sunday will never be drowned or hanged.

The hour of birth also had its significance, and in some counties it was believed that a child born at " chime hours," viz., three, six, nine or twelve, would be clairvoyant. If born in leap year either it or its mother would die within the course of the year.

In Weybridge, Surrey, some years ago, there was a curious saying common among the old villagers, when more boys than girls were being born in the village, that " the lions are roaring." The origin of this saying was obscure until the land was being excavated to make the Brooklands race track, when remains of cages and iron bars were discovered. It then transpired that many years previously, the animals from the Zoo at the Tower of London, after it was closed, were removed to a piece of land near Weybridge where they remained in captivity until most of them died.

Many of the old traditions associated with child-birth have been treasured by midwives for centuries and were doubtless handed down from one to another for generations.

Thus, it was a common idea that a child should go up in the world before it goes down. Therefore, on leaving the mother's room for the first time, it was considered absolutely necessary that it should be carried upstairs before going down, otherwise it would always remain low in the world and never afterwards rise to distinction or gain riches. When the mother's room was on the top floor, the nurse overcame the difficulty by placing a chair near the door, on which she stepped before leaving the room.

In Yorkshire, it was customary to always place a new-born infant first in the arms of a young girl before anyone else was allowed to handle it. This custom is said to have had its origin in the ancient belief that the Virgin Mary was present at the birth of St. John the Baptist and was the first to receive him in her arms.

Some mothers believe it unlucky to allow a baby to sleep on " the bones of the lap," a superstition founded on some degree of truth, for it is undoubtedly better for a child to be supported throughout its whole length than permit its head or legs to hang down, as it might do if it were sleeping on the knees.

There is another common tradition that a baby and a kitten cannot thrive together in the same house, and should a cat have kittens at the time of the infant's birth, they should either be destroyed at once or given away.

In former times, nurses had a great prejudice against weighing a baby from a superstitious conviction that if it was weighed, it would bring ill-luck and the child would never thrive afterwards. It was considered equally unlucky to rock a baby's cradle when it was empty, and the Highlanders believed it to be an omen of death. On the other hand, according to an old Sussex rhyme, it was regarded as a sign of fecundity. Thus :

> " If you rock the cradle empty
> Then you shall have babies plenty."

In some parts of Wales it is forbidden for a woman

during pregnancy to weave or spin, for if she did so her child would live to be hanged with a hempen rope. There was also a common belief that birth during the night indicated that the child would see visions, ghosts and phantoms, and the belief that it is unlucky to give a baby a name that had been borne by a dead brother or sister is general throughout the country.

Some curious customs connected with fire were formerly practised in the North of Scotland on the birth of a child. In Orkney, it was thought necessary to " Sain " infants by fire soon after birth. In order to carry out this rite, a large rich cheese had to be made before the baby was expected, which after the birth was cut into pieces and distributed among the matrons who had gathered in the house. The mother and child were then " Sained," which was performed by whirling a lighted fir-candle round the bed three times, after which all evil influences were held to be averted.

Another method of carrying out the rite of " Saining " was to draw the bed into the middle of the floor, after which, the nurse waved an open Bible round it in the name of the Trinity, three times for the mother and three times for the child.

It is still customary in Scotland to place the new-born babe in a cloth and hold it over a basket of provisions, then convey it thrice round the crook of the chimney ; while in the North of England, it is usual to put a little salt or sugar into the infant's mouth for luck the first time it is taken to another house.

In the mining districts, the cradle is held as sacred and in no case of distraint for debt may it be taken and sold.

During the early life of the child it is natural that many traditions and superstitions should have become associated with the troublesome period of teething.

In Lancashire, it is regarded as a misfortune if the first tooth should make its appearance in the upper jaw, as it is said to be an indication that the child will not thrive.  For a baby to be born with teeth is thought to be even a greater evil.

Shakespeare alludes to this in *Henry VI*, Part III (Act V, Sc. 6), when the Duke of Gloster in describing the peculiarities connected with his birth relates that :

> " The midwife wondered and the women cried
> ' O Jesus bless us, he is born with teeth ! '
> And so I was, which plainly signified
> That I should snarl and bite and play the dog."

To assist children in cutting their teeth it is still customary to place necklaces of beads made from peony roots around their necks, a practice which dates from the seventeenth century.

In the time of Charles II, these necklaces which were sold under various names had a great vogue. The virtues of one called " The most famous Miraculous Necklace for easing children in breeding and cutting teeth without pain," were thus extolled by one Major John Choke.  " The best time to put them on," he states, " is when they are over two months old and to wear them until they have bred all their teeth and none are troubled with the Evil (scrofula) or Falling Sickness " (epilepsy).  Another, called " Dr. Paul Chamberlain's Anodyne necklace," by means of which he declared a " secret harmony and sympathy was created between the necklace and the Human Body," was very popular in the eighteenth century.

These beads cut from peony roots had a much earlier origin for we find they were originally recommended by Oribasius, a Roman physician who flourished in the fifth century, to be worn round the neck of a child to prevent Falling Sickness, and the tradition was handed down from that period. Like any other hard substance given to infants to bite when teething, they doubtless assisted them during this troublesome time.

In some parts of the country, people have a great dislike to throwing away the cast milk teeth of young children in the belief that should any be accidentally found and gnawed by an animal, the child's new tooth would exactly correspond with that of the animal which had bitten the old one. In Lancashire, it is customary when the tooth falls out, to throw it on the fire while repeating the words :

> " Fire ! Fire ! burn bone ;
> God send me my tooth again."

In some districts the tooth is first wrapped in paper with a pinch of salt before being thrown on the flames.

This relic of sympathetic magic dates from a very early period when it was believed that if the tooth of a child was found by a witch, she was able to " ill-wish " it if she so desired.

Similar superstitions were attached to the nail parings that were also employed by witches in working spells.

There was a belief common in some parts of Wales, that if a child's nails were cut with any steel instrument before it was three months old, when it grew up it would become a thief, and in England, it was considered imprudent to cut the baby's nails until it was a year old and then they should be bitten off or the child might grow up to be " light-fingered " or dishonest.

Special attention had also to be paid to the day of the week on which the operation was to be carried out, for according to an old rhyme :

" Better a child had ne'er been born,
Than cut his nails on a Sunday morn."

In Northumberland, there is a tradition that if the first parings of a child's nails are carefully buried under an ash tree it will turn out to be an excellent singer, a connection which it is difficult to understand. There is also a belief that a child's future career in the world is indicated from the white specks that sometimes appear on the nails, for Melton tells us, that " to have yellow speckles on the nailes of one's hand is a great signe of death," and Burton, in his *Anatomy of Melancholy*, states, that "a black spot appearing on the nails is a bad omen."

The hand of the child is not without its traditions, and in some counties the right hand of a baby is allowed to remain unwashed for the first few months after its birth so that " it may better be able to gather riches." Should a child be born with its hand open it is believed to indicate that it will be of a bountiful disposition in the future.

In Scotland, great attention is paid as to which hand a child uses when taking up for the first time a spoon to eat its food. If it should happen to be the left, it is said that he or she will be unlucky all through life.

There was an old tradition common in some parts of the country, that parents, in order to ensure long life to their children, should pass them through the bent branches of a maple tree. Similar occult power is attributed to the ash, a tree which for centuries has been associated with witchcraft and magic. In Wales, it is customary to draw rickety or weakly infants through a cleft in the trunk. In Cornwall, this charm is carried out by inserting a large knife into the trunk of a young ash about a foot from the ground, by means of which a vertical opening is made for about three feet. Two men then forcibly pull the parts asunder and hold them so, whilst the mother passes the child through the cleft three times. After this has been done, to complete the cure, the infant has to be washed for three successive mornings in the dew from the leaves of the " charmed " ash.

There is an idea common in some parts of the country, that cats may suck the breath of infants and so cause their death. This may have arisen from the fact that cats are fond of lying in cradles when they can get the chance, and the possibility of suffocating the baby occupying it was not a remote one.

In the North of England, it is considered unlucky to walk over the graves of " unchristened children," and the person who does so is liable to contract a fatal disease which is known as " grave-scab."

Henderson states, " This complaint comes on with a trembling of the limbs with hard breathing after which the skin burns as if touched with a hot iron." The fatal nature of the disease is alluded to in the following lines :

> " And it ne'er will be cured by doctor on earth,
>     Tho' every one should tent him, oh !
>     He shall tremble and die like the elf-shot eye,
>     And return from whence he came, oh ! "

The only remedy for this mysterious complaint was to " wear a sark " prepared as follows : " The lint must be grown in a field which shall be manured from a farmyard heap that has not been disturbed for forty years. It must be spun by Habbitrot, the Queen of Spinsters, it must be bleached by an honest bleacher in an honest miller's mill dam and sewed by an honest tailor." On donning this garment the sufferer was said to at once recover and regain his health.

In Devonshire, there is a similar superstition associated with the graves of still-born children, but it is thought to be lucky to place a still-born child in an open grave as it was believed to be a sure passport to heaven for the next person buried there. There is a tradition, which still survives in some parts of the country, which dates back for at least three thousand years to the early Assyrians, that if a mother continually frets and pines after her baby when it is dead, its spirit cannot rest and will come back to earth again.

This, like many other traditions associated with childhood, may appear to be senseless and meaningless, but it should be remembered that they are often survivals of primitive culture and are therefore interesting as having been handed down to us from the far distant past.

# CHAPTER II

## THE FOLK-LORE OF CHILDHOOD

THERE is a common belief which dates from early Christian times, that a child never thrives until it is first baptised, so when a baby is born alive and yet unlikely to survive, every effort is usually made to have the rite performed without delay.

In early times it was believed that so long as a child remained unbaptised it was at the mercy of ill-disposed fairies and subject to other evil influences. Thus, baptism was supposed to be infallible in protecting a child from the " evil eye."

It is thus alluded to in the *Satires of Persius*: " Look here ! A grandmother or superstitious aunt has taken baby from his cradle and is charming his forehead against mischief by the joint action of her middle finger and her purifying spittle, for she knows right well how to check the ' evil eye.' "

Almost every trouble and ailment was attributed to the " evil eye " and many curious charms were employed to counteract its effects in childhood.

In Lancashire, it was customary to spit three times in the child's face while turning a live coal in the fire and saying, " The Lord be with us." Near Burnley, it was customary to draw blood from above the mouth, and in other districts lucky or holed stones were hung behind the door. Should a child become thin, to counteract the evil influence it was

taken before sunrise to a blacksmith of the seventh
generation and laid on his anvil. The smith would
then raise his hammer as if he were about to strike
the hot iron, but only to bring it down gently on
the child's body. This rite had to be repeated three
times, after which the baby was believed to be freed
from the influence and would thrive in the future.
There is an ancient tradition that should a child die
before baptism its spirit was doomed to wander
about in ruined or deserted places or flit restlessly
around its parents. Such children in some countries
were believed to change into the will-o'-the-wisps
that hover over wild and marshy lands.

Many curious customs are associated with baptism
in Scotland, where the water used at the service was
regarded as a preservative against witchcraft, and
the child's eyes were bathed with it, so that in after
life it might be incapable of seeing ghosts.

To make sure of baptism being altogether propitious, it was considered most important that the
person entrusted with the care of the child should
be known to be lucky. The chosen one was generally
provided with a piece of bread and cheese which she
presented to the first person she met as an offering
from the child. If that person readily accepted and
partook of the gift, it was considered a good omen,
but if it was refused she regarded it as wishing
evil to her charge. It is thought to be a lucky omen
if a child cries at its baptism, as it is that when the
baby thus screams and kicks, the evil spirit is leaving
it, but on the other hand its silence indicates that
it may be too good for this world.

In some parts of the Highlands, a child is supposed
to take the character of the person after whom it is
named and so in families where a child is called after

some relative, which is frequently the case, the choice of a name is considered to be very important.

Moresin states that in some districts in Scotland, it is customary either before or after the child is christened, to pass it three or four times over a flame saying and repeating thrice, " Let the flame consume thee now or never." This was believed to be an effectual method of preserving the infant from the power of evil spirits.

In Sussex, it is considered unlucky to divulge a child's intended name before baptism and the water sprinkled on its head at the font must on no account be wiped off.

Feasting, after the christening ceremony, was formerly common in all parts of the country. In Oxfordshire, it was customary for every woman to bring a cake and the first one was presented to the clergyman. At Wendlebury and other places, the women bring their cakes at a " Gossiping " and give a large one to the father of the child which they call a " rocking cake."

Cowel says, " It was a good old custom for god-fathers and god-mothers every time their god-children asked them blessing, to give them a cake, which was a ' God's-Kitchell,' and it is still a proverbial saying in some places, ' Ask me a blessing and I will give you some plum-cake.' "

The gift of presents to the child in the form of silver cups and spoons by their sponsors at christenings, goes back to the sixteenth century. Ben Jonson in his *Bartholomew Fair*, alludes to a " couple of Apostle Spoons and a cup to eat Caudle in," and Shipman in 1666 commenting on the failure of the old custom of giving Apostle Spoons after a christening says :

> " Especially since gossips now
> Eat more at christenings than bestow.
> Formerly when they us'd to troul
> Gilt bowls of sack, they gave the bowl ;
> Two spoons at least ; an use ill kept ;
> 'Tis well now if our own be left."

Stow, writing in 1631, states, " At this time and for many years before, it was the custom for god-fathers and god-mothers generally to give plate at the baptisme of children (as spoons, cupps and such like " ; and another writer of the period observes, " The god-mother hearing when the child's to be coated, brings it a gilt coral, a silver spoon and porringer and a brave new tankard of the same metal. The god-fathers come too, the one with a whole piece of flower'd silk, the other with a set of gilt spoons."

These spoons were called " Apostle spoons " because the figures of the Twelve Apostles were chased or carved on the tops of the handles. Rich sponsors sometimes gave the whole dozen, while others in poorer circumstances would give four or even one, generally choosing the figure of a saint in honour of whom the child received its name.

Thus, Beaumont and Fletcher in the *Noble Gentleman* remark :

> " I'll be a gossip. Bewford,
> I have an old Apostle Spoon."

These gifts of silver and sometimes gold are supposed to have had their origin in the offerings of the Three Kings to the Holy Child after His birth in the manger at Bethlehem.

Another christening gift that still remains in favour is that of the coral and bells, which is generally suspended from the necks of infants to assist them in cutting their teeth. It was supposed to have a two-fold property, for the bells when shaken were said to frighten evil spirits away and the coral was considered a protection against witchcraft.

Considerable lore is associated with red coral which has come down to us from Roman times and in some countries it is still believed to be all powerful in averting the effect of the " evil eye."

Reginald Scot in his *Discovery of Witchcraft* observes, " The Coral preserveth such as bear it from fascination or bewitching and in this respect they are hanged about the children's necks."

Coral was also said to change colour and look pale when the wearer of it was in ill-health.

An allusion to this property is made in the *Three Ladies of London*, written in 1584 :

> " You may say Jet will take up a straw,
>     Amber will make one fat,
>     Coral will look pale when you be sick, and
>     Chrystal will stanch blood."

Coles in his *Adam in Eden* says, " Coral helpeth children to breed their teeth, their gums being rubbed therewith " ; while Plat remarks, " It preserves them from the falling sickness. It hath also some special sympathy with Nature, for the best coral will turn pale and wan if the party that wears it be sick, and comes to its former colour again as they recover health."

Certain superstitions are associated with the rite of Confirmation. Thus, in Norfolk, it is considered unlucky to be touched by the bishop's left hand, while in Devonshire, where a similar idea prevails, the lucky hand is also supposed to be the right one. In some of the northern counties it is said that those girls touched with the left hand are doomed to a life of spinsterhood.

There is a curious belief prevalent in the eastern counties that the bishop's blessing at Confirmation has certain healing properties. There is a story told in this connection, that at one Confirmation at which Bishop Bathurst officiated, an old woman was observed eagerly pressing forward to the church and on being asked if she was going to be confirmed, she replied, " I have been bishopped seven times and intend to be again as it is so good *for rheumatism.*"

The old belief in guardian angels watching at the bedside during the night, is perpetuated in some verses still taught to children in the northern counties. At the close of their prayers they say :

> " Matthew, Mark, Luke and John,
> Bless the bed that I lie on ;
> Four corners to my bed
> Four angels at its head.
> One to watch, two to pray,
> And one to bear my soul away.
> God within and God without,
> Sweet Jesus Christ all round about ;
> If I die before I wake,
> I pray to God my soul to take."

In Lancashire, the following variation of the verse is said which is believed to date from Puritan times :

> " Matthew, Mark, Luke and John,
> Hold the horse that I leap on.
> Matthew, Mark, Luke and John,
> Take a stick and lay upon."

Another curious survival of the power of prayer in healing is common in Lancashire, where before swallowing a dose of medicine a child is taught to say :

> " Pray God, bless it,
> Grant it may do me good."

There are some curious charms perpetuated by children with respect to the weather. Thus we have the child's appeal for rain to cease in the couplet often repeated :

> " Rain, rain go away
> Come again another day."

This is said to have come down from a period of great antiquity. In some districts children are also taught to make a charm to cause a rainbow to vanish, by placing a couple of twigs crossways on the ground which they call " crossing out the rain-blow." A variation of the charm in certain counties, is to make a cross of two sticks and to lay four pebbles, one at each end of it. The Lancashire boys have a saying respecting the reflection of the sun's beams on a ceiling, which they allude to as " Jack-o'-lantern," or refer to it as " Jack-a-dandy beating his wife with a stick of silver."

The Medical Officer of Health for Carmarthenshire called attention to a curious superstition prevalent in his district some few years ago. It consisted in making an incision in a certain part of the cartilage of a child's ears as a cure for all kinds of " back-wardness."

This operation, which he stated is usually per-formed during the waxing of the moon, was generally carried out by a woman to whom the art had been handed down hereditarily. Children were brought to the practitioners by scores for many miles round, and the custom, which still survives, if not at first successful, is repeated on the child pending a cure.

It will be seen from the few examples given that the folk-lore associated with childhood is full of interest, and sometimes the simplest nursery rhyme has been found of help in tracing the affinity of certain races.

# CHAPTER III

## THE FOLK-LORE OF LOVE AND COURTSHIP—LOVE CHARMS AND PHILTRES

LIKE other important events in human life, love and courtship are associated with innumerable superstitions, customs, charms and omens, many of which are still believed and carried out.

The desire to know something of the hidden future still persists, especially with the maiden who is ever anxious to ascertain her destiny in marriage. She will consult the fortune-teller to gain some idea of the kind of husband that is in store for her, or she performs some charm or divination in order to obtain the sought for knowledge. Afterwards, she may use various occult methods to retain her lover's affection and to prevent others from alienating him from her.

Certain days in the year are regarded as more propitious than others for love-divinations, and of these, " All Hallow-e'en " has ever been the most popular. From early times, the thirty-first day of October has been supposed to be the time when supernatural influences most prevail, and many and curious are the charms carried out at the midnight hour. Of these only a few can be mentioned here, for they are sufficiently numerous to fill a volume.

In love-charms, birds, animals, insects and plants often play a part, while nuts and apples also take a prominent place in the operations. Roasting chestnuts and apple-ducking have come down to us from

Roman times, when every year at the end of October or beginning of November, a festival was held in honour of Pomona, the goddess of fruits, which chiefly meant at that time nuts and apples.

In some parts of the country, if a girl eats an apple while looking in a mirror on " Hallow-e'en " it is said she may see her future husband glancing over her shoulder. The leaves of the yarrow, called " nose-bleed," are used to tickle the inside of the nostrils, and the following lines repeated :

> " Green 'arrow, green 'arrow, you bear a white blow,
> If my love love me, my nose will bleed now ;
> If my love don't love me, it 'ont bleed a drop,
> If my love do love me, 'twill bleed every drop."

Some cut the common bracken fern just above the root in order to ascertain the initial letter of the future husband's or wife's name, while the blowing of the fluffy seeds from a dandelion stalk is another favourite form of divination. The number of puffs that are required to blow every seed off are said to indicate the number of years that must elapse before the person is married.

Burning nuts is a favourite method of divination with young people. They name the boy and girl to each particular nut as they lay them in the fire ; and accordingly as they burn quietly together or start from beside one another, the course and issue of the courtship will be. To ascertain if their lovers will be faithful, it is necessary to place three nuts upon the bars of the grate at the same time naming the nuts after the lovers. If a nut cracks or jumps, the lover will prove unfaithful or if it begins to blaze and burn, he is said to have a regard for the person making the trial. Should the nuts named after the girl and her lover burn together, they will be married.

Another form of divination carried out with peascods is thus described by Gay :

" As peascods once I pluck'd, I chanc'd to see
One that was closely fill'd with three times three ;
Which, when I cropp'd, safely home convey'd,
And o'er the door the spell in secret laid ;
The latch mov'd up, when who should first come in,
But in his proper person—Lubberkin."

In country places, girls catch a lady-bird and throw it into the air while repeating the words :

" Fly, Lady Bird, North, South, East or West
Show me where lives the one I like best."

A snail was also thus used in love-divination. To ascertain a lover's name or his constancy, it was placed on the hearth where it was believed to mark in the ashes the initials of the lover's name. It was thus Hobnelia tested the love of her Lubberkin according to Gay :

" Upon a gooseberry bush, a snail I found,
For always snails near sweetest fruit abound.
I seized the vermin, home I quickly sped,
And on the hearth the milk-white embers spread ;
Slow crawled the snail, and, if I right can spell,
In the soft ashes marked a curious L."

According to an old writer, a common " Hallowe'en " custom was to steal out unperceived at midnight and sow a handful of hemp-seed and repeat now and again, " Hemp-seed I sow thee ; and him or her that is to be my true love come after me. Look over your left shoulder and you will see the person invoked in the attitude of pulling hemp."

In Devonshire, the charm is usually worked on St. Valentine's Day as according to tradition it was the day on which birds chose their mates. To carry it out, the girl had to go into a churchyard at midnight with some hemp-seed in her hand, which, after she had walked round the church a certain number of times, she scattered on either side as she returned home.  It was supposed that her true lover would be seen taking up the hemp-seed she had sown, attired for the marriage ceremony in a *winding sheet*.

To work another charm, five bay leaves were gathered, four of which the girl was to pin at the four corners of her pillow and the fifth in the middle. If afterwards she dreamt of her lover, it indicated that she would be married in the course of the year.

To know whether her lover would prove true to her or not, it was customary for a girl in the Highlands to go blindfold into the kail-yard and pull up the first kail-stalk she met with.  As the stalk was large or small, straight or crooked, was indicative of the size and shape of her future husband.  The stalk was then placed over the door till next morning, when as it was found to incline to the right or the left, so she would know whether her lover would prove true to her or not.

In the Orkneys, a girl will take a clue of blue worsted at twilight and mount on the kiln, which is attached to every farm, while she calls out, " Wha halds on my clew's end," and her lover should appear at the right moment, seize it and give the right reply.

Another Highland divination charm is performed by taking a live coal out of the fire and putting it into water.  It is then placed under a piece of turf till the following morning, when if it is found broken in half and if a hair be found, its colour is said to be that of the hair of the future husband.

In the Isle of Man it is said that if a girl will eat a salt herring, bones included, without drinking or speaking, then go to bed backwards, she will see in her dreams her future husband coming towards her bringing her something to drink.

It is common knowledge in country places, that objects which are to be used as charms must always be *stolen* and never bought, so in cabbage divination, a girl must pull up at night from her neighbour's garden, in the name of the devil, a good-sized cabbage. On bringing it home it was to be hung over the door by which the future husband might enter.

Many of the charms associated with " Hallow-e'en " are of a ghostly character, thus, it is customary in certain districts for a girl to go into the garden at midnight and pluck twelve sage leaves, under the belief that she will see the shadowy form of her future husband approaching her from the opposite end of the garden.

In some parts of Lancashire, at the hour of midnight, it is believed that if a girl walks round a churchyard twelve times she will see the ghostly shape of her future husband approaching her.

Among other customs that linger in the northern counties is one in which girls and boys meet on " Hallow-e'en " and gather round a large bowl of water placed on a table. Each one is then told to secretly think of the name of a sweetheart and write it on a slip of paper. The slips are then enclosed in pellets of clay or soil and dropped into the bowl. The piece of paper which comes to the surface first bears the name of the one who will be married before any other present.

Another method of divination is carried out with

three dishes. One is filled with clean water, the second with dirty water and the third remains empty. A youth or maiden is then blindfolded and led to the table, and according to the dish into which they dipped their hands they would marry either a maid, a widow or widower, or remain single.

On the night of November 30th, St. Andrew's Day, many superstitious customs are carried out in Scotland. A girl anxious to know what colour her future husband's hair will be, is told that at midnight she must take hold of the latch of the door and call out three times, " Gentle love, if thou lovest me, show thyself ! " She is then to open the door a few inches, make a sudden snatch out in the dark, when she will find in her hand a lock of her future husband's hair. To carry this out successfully the girl must be quite alone in the house and make the trial unknown to anyone.

Another custom is for two girls to sit in a room by themselves from midnight till one o'clock in the morning without speaking. During this time each must take as many hairs from her head as she is years old, and having put them into a linen cloth with some of the herb called " true love," as soon as the clock strikes one, she must turn every hair separately, saying :

" I offer this my sacrifice,
To him most precious in my eyes.
I charge thee now come forth to me,
That I this minute may thee see."

Luther says, that " on the coming of the feast of St. Andrew the young maidens in his country, strip themselves naked, and in order to learn what sort of husband they shall have, they recite a prayer."

Naogeorgus also observes :

" To Andrew all the lovers and the lustre wooers come,
Beleeving, through his ayde and certain ceremonies done,
(While as to him they presentes bring and conjure all the night
To have good lucke) and to obtain their chiefe and sweete
    delight."

St. Agnes, the patroness of virgins, who suffered martyrdom under the Emperor Diocletian in the year 306, also had her devotees, who on the anniversary or eve of January 21st, the day dedicated to her, practised several forms of divination in order to discover their lovers.

Ben Jonson thus alludes to one, thus:

" And on Sweet St. Agnes' night,
Please you with the promised sight,
Some of husbands, some of lovers,
Which an empty dream discovers."

Aubrey directs that on St. Agnes' night, "you should take a row of pins and pull out every one, one after another, saying a Pater Noster, sticking a pin in your sleeve if you will dream of him or her you shall marry."

In some of the northern counties girls are accustomed to repeat :

" Fair St. Agnes, play thy part,
And send to me my own sweetheart,
Nor in his best nor worst array,
But in the clothes he wears every day ;
That tomorrow I may him ken
From among all other men."

St. Mark's eve was also associated with lovers' charms and according to the lines :

" On St. Mark's eve at twelve o'clock,
If the fair maid will watch her smock,
To find her husband in the dark
By praying unto good St. Mark."

It was said that if a maid would watch in the church porch all night on the eve of the vigil of St. John, she would see her future husband or her lover's wraith pass by.

Several charms were worked by girls on Midsummer eve, and it was customary in some districts to gather the herbs St. John's wort, trefoil and some sprigs of rue, and set them in clay on pieces of slate in their houses, which they called the " Midsummer men."

If the herbs died away by morning it foretold that the maid and her lover would never come together. Another custom was for the girl to walk out of doors backward and gather a white rose which she was to place between two sheets of white paper. If the rose was not looked at and if it kept fresh till Christmas Day, it was then to be worn and the future husband would be sure to come along.

It was commonly believed that if a maid took a mouthful of water from a well and walked three times round the well afterwards, without swallowing or spilling the water, she would soon be married ; or if she placed a wish-bone above the door, secretly, the first single man who entered the house would be her future husband.

In some parts of the country there was formerly a strong belief in love-omens from dreams. In Shropshire there was a saying :

> " A Friday night's dream on Saturday told,
> Is due to come true be it never so old."

In Gloucestershire there is a similar tradition but differently expressed :

> " Friday night's dream mark well ;
> Saturday night's dream ne'er tell."

A dream on Friday night was also regarded as auspicious in Norfolk, as alluded to in the following lines :

> " Tonight, tonight, is Friday night,
> Lay me down in dirty white ;
> Dream whom my husband is to be ;
> And lay my children by my side
> If I'm to live to be his bride."

For a betrothed girl, to dream of balls and dancing was said to be an augury of good luck.   Thus, those

> " Who dream of being at a ball,
> No cause have they for fear,
> For soon will they united be
> To those they hold most dear."

Friday has always been regarded as a good day of the week for love omens, and in Norfolk it was customary for a girl to scatter the seeds of the butter-dock on the ground half an hour before sunrise on a Friday morning, in a lonesome place.   While strewing the seeds it was necessary to say :

> " I sow, I sow !
> Then my own dear,
> Come here, come here
> And mow, and mow."

After repeating this incantation, she would then probably see her future husband a short distance away mowing with a scythe.   She must, however, show no signs of fear at the apparition, for should she cry out he will immediately vanish for ever.

There is some curious lore associated with knots which dates back to early times.   Thus, the Babylonians, four thousand years ago, believed that a three-fold cord on which twice seven knots were tied, when fastened round the head, would cure headache.

This has survived in a love-charm which is performed by girls with a piece of wool or silk, if while making each knot in it they repeat this incantation :

> " This knot I knit
> To know the thing I know not yet ;
> That I may see
> The man that shall my husband be ;
> How he goes and what he wears
> And what he does all days and years."

A similar charm in which knots played a part was for girls before sleeping in strange beds to tie their garters nine times round the bed-posts, making as many knots in them before so doing and repeating the following lines :

> " This knot I knit, this knot I tie,
> To see my lover as he goes by,
> In his apparel and array
> As he walks in every day."

A writer of the seventeenth century says, " Yet I have another pretty way for a maid to know her sweetheart. Take a summer apple of the best fruit. Stick pins close into the apple to the head, and as you stick them, take notice which of them is the middlemost and give it what name you fancy. Put it in thy left-hand glove and lay it under thy pillow on Saturday night when thou gettest into bed, then clasp thy hands together and say these words :

> ' If thou be he that must have me
> To be thy wedded bride,
> Make no delay but come away,
> This night to my bedside '."

Love-philtres, potions and powders as a means of inspiring and securing the affections of the male sex, have been known and used by women from a

period of great antiquity, and even at the present
day the practice has not died out.

Not only in country places but in London and
other large cities, women still make mysterious
compounds and perform charms with incantations
to influence the affections of the
opposite sex.

The Babylonians, over three
thousand years ago, made love-
charms from the brain of the
*hoopoe* mixed into a cake, and
believed that the bones of a frog
if buried for seven days and then
exhumed would, when thrown into
water, indicate love or hatred.

The ancient Egyptians employed
hair, feathers, snake's skin and
" the blood of the mystic eye," in
working their love-charms.   The
last named is supposed to indicate
dragon's blood which for ages has
been believed to be an effective
ingredient in charms for provoking
love.   The substance we now call dragon's blood is
a gum-resin obtained from the *Pterocarpus indicus*, a
tree indigenous to the East Indies, which is usually
employed as a colouring agent for varnishes and
stains.

PUTTY FIGURE OF
A MAN
Used as a love-charm,
Herefordshire.
*Pitt-Rivers Museum.*

Dragon's blood still survives as an ingredient in
certain love-charms which are generally performed
by women on " All Hallow-e'en."   It is not only
used as a method of attraction but also by those
who are jealous of their lovers and desire to win
back their affections.   To do this, the powdered
dragon's blood is wrapped in a piece of paper and

thrown on the fire while the following incantation is
repeated :

"  May he no pleasure or profit see,
   Till he comes back again to me."

As a charm to attract a lover, dragon's blood,
quicksilver, sulphur and saltpetre are mixed together
and thrown on a bright fire, while a similar incantation is said and a wish made for the person desired.
It was thus used by wives who had quarrelled with
their husbands and desired to win them back and
also by young women wanting sweethearts.

Love-philtres were commonly sold in ancient
Rome by old women and midwives, and in the time
of the first Emperors a law was passed deeming
them a poison.  Much importance was attached to
the ingredients used in their composition and some
of them, besides being obnoxious, were undoubtedly
poisonous.

Plutarch records that Lucullus, the Roman
General, lost his reason through a love-potion, and
according to Suetonius, Caius Caligula became insane
from the effects of a love-philtre which had been
administered to him by his wife Caesonia, while
Lucretius is also said to have fallen victim to a
love-charm.

Hairs from a wolf's tail, the bones from the left
side of a toad which had been eaten by ants,
pigeon's blood, hippomanes or a piece of flesh
found in the head of a newly foaled colt, and the
entrails of various animals, were among some of the
least disgusting ingredients used in love-philtres.

In some countries, a lizard drowned in wine and
dried in the sun then reduced to powder, was
regarded as an infallible love-charm.  It was rendered more effective if the woman who compounded

it pricked her finger and allowed a few drops of her blood to fall into it.

In the eighteenth century, the skeleton of a toad reduced to powder and mixed with the food of a faithless swain was believed to be effectual in restoring his wandering affections, and a much more dangerous substance, *Cantharides* or Spanish fly, was occasionally employed in love-powders. It is to this Hobnelia alludes in the following lines from Gay's *Shepherd's Week* :

> " Straight to the 'pothecary's shop I went,
> And in Love-Powder all my money spent ;
> Behap what will, next Sunday after prayers,
> When to the alehouse Lubberkin repairs
> These golden flies into his mug I'll throw
> And soon the swain with fervent love shall glow."

In a manuscript written in the sixteenth century now in the Bodleian Library, there are the following recipes :

" To cause a woman to love.

" Take of ye left foote of a wolffe ground to powder and take the marrow of it. And she shall not forsake thee."

" To know a woman's minde and secrette

" Take ye hed of a white pidgeon or of a turtle dove. Burn ye blood and yre hed to powder. And let it be thorough colde mingle it wyth qualitie of stone hony. Anoynt ye brestes of a woman and thou shalle know all her mynd and what secrettes thou shalt have of her."

Certain flowers were also in request as love-charms, a favourite being the pansy, which Oberon told Puck to gather and place on the eyes of Titania

in order that on awaking she should fall in love with
the first object she might meet :

> " Fetch me that flower—the herb I showed thee once ;
> The juice of it on sleeping eyelids laid
> Will make a man or woman, madly dote
> Upon the next live creature that it see."

Verbena was reputed to possess the power of
attracting a lover, and a loaf in which cumin seeds
were placed was believed to answer the same
purpose.    Sweet basil when worn by a love-sick
maiden was supposed to attract a likely swain, and
the mandrake, according to Gerard, " hath been
thought, the root serveth to win love."

Sometimes the root of the male-fern was used in
love-powders, allusion to whch is made in the
following lines :

> " 'Twas the maiden's matchless beauty
> That drew my heart a-nigh ;
> Not the fern-root potion,
> But the glance of her blue eye."

Lastly, a charm in which salt played a part may be
mentioned.    The salt-spell as it was called, was made
by throwing salt on the fire on three successive
Friday nights while repeating the words :

> " It is not the salt I wish to burn,
> It is my lover's heart to turn ;
> That he may not rest nor happy be
> Until he comes and speaks to me."

# CHAPTER IV

## THE FOLK-LORE OF BETROTHAL AND MARRIAGE

THE gift or interchange of a ring or a piece of gold or silver on betrothal is a custom which dates back to at least the early centuries of the Christian era, for Tertullian, who flourished in the third century, tells us that a golden ring was in his time sent to the intended bride as a pledge.

" It was also anciently very customary, to break a piece of gold or silver in token of a verbal contract of marriage and promises of love," says a writer of the sixteenth century, " one half whereof was kept by the woman while the other remained with the man."

Thus, prior to the general use of the wedding ring, a bent or broken coin was sometimes used as a bond of union. The oaths sworn and prayers breathed over them were supposed to impart a mystic value to the pieces and to endow them with virtues of a curative nature and with influence over evil spirits.

A belief in the properties of a crooked sixpence or coin in which a hole has been bored, is still regarded by the rustic maid and her swain as a bond of union, as expressed in the couplet :

" Witness this piece of sixpence, certain token
Of my true heart and your false promise broken."

So Manxalinda upbraided Moore of Moor Hall on the eve of the knight's fight with the dragon of Wantley.

49

The interchange of rings between lovers is alluded to by Shakespeare in *Twelfth-Night* thus :

> " A contract of eternal bond of love,
> Confirm'd by mutual joinder of your hands,
> Attested by the holy close of lips,
> Strengthen'd by interchangement of your rings."

Joint-rings made with two or three hoops were common between lovers in the sixteenth century, and the Gimmal ring, as it came to be called, was sometimes inscribed with the names of the betrothed couple or a suitable motto or posy.

Dryden alludes to the custom in his play *Don Sebastian*, 1690, in the following words :

> "A curious Artist wrought 'em
> With joynts so close as not to be perceived ;
> Yet are they both each others counterpart.
> (Her part had Juan inscrib'd, and his had Zayda.
> You know those names were theirs ; ) and, in the midst,
> A heart divided in two halves was plac'd.
> Now if the rivets of those Rings, inclos'd
> Fit not each other, I have forg'd this lye ;
> But if they join, you must for ever part."

Sometimes the Gimmal ring consisted of two hoops, and on betrothal a finger of the contracting persons was placed in each to indicate that the bond of union was a mutual one. Others were made with three hoops turning upon a hinge, the centre bearing two hearts and on each of the others a hand, so that when the three were brought together they formed one ring, the two hands being clasped over the hearts.

Herrick in his *Hesperides* thus alludes to a ring of this kind :

> " Thou sent'st to me a true-love knot, but I
> Returned a ring of gimmals, to imply
> Thy love hath one knot, mine a triple tye."

Vaughan in his *Golden Grove* (1608), mentions a curious French betrothal custom and says the " Antient Frenchmen had a ceremonie that when they would marrie, the Bridegrome should pare his nayles and send them unto his new Wife which done they lived together afterwards as man and wife."

Another style of betrothal ring took the form of a true lover's knot entwined which had a dual significance, for it was one which was not easily untied and was also two knots in one :

> " That Gordian knot,
> Which true lovers knit ;
> Undo it you cannot,
> Nor yet break it."

Following the Gimmal ring came the betrothal or engagement ring set with a precious stone, the choice of which, at one time, was considered of importance for considerable lore was associated with jewels.

Every month in the year was believed to be under the influence of one or more precious stones. Thus, the diamond, most valuable of all, symbolising innocence, was the stone for April ; the amethyst, sincerity, for February ; the emerald, success in love, for May ; the garnet, truth and constancy, for January ; the bloodstone, courage and presence of mind, for March ; the agate, health and long life, for June ; the carnelian, a contented mind, for July ; the sardonyx, conjugal felicity, for August ; the chrysolite, antidote to melancholy, for September ; the opal, hope, for October ; the topaz, fidelity, for November, and the turquoise, prosperity, for December.

It was said that whoever was touched with any

stone set in a silver ring would be immediately
reconciled to an enemy. A pale sapphire set in gold
and engraved with a figure and the half of a fish
would procure any desire, while a carnelian set in a
silver ring was believed to ensure the wearer against
harm or loss and to gain the friendship of many.

The diamond, in addition to its other properties,
was regarded as an antidote against satanic tempta-
tion, while the ruby made the wearer courageous
and brave. The topaz gave protection from poisons,
the amethyst was a preventive of drunkenness, the
turquoise acted as a charm against the " evil eye "
and the emerald promoted piety.

In some countries the turquoise is still a favourite
stone for a betrothal ring, for it is supposed to prevent dissensions arising between husband and wife
and to give warning of danger or illness by changing
colour. According to an old couplet it is

> " A compassionate turquoise that doth tell
> By looking pale, the wearer is not well."

Fenton, in his *Wonders of Nature*, in 1569, says,
" The Turkeys (turquoise) doth move when there is
any peril prepared to him that weareth it," and
Shylock, in the *Merchant of Venice* (Act III, Sc. 1),
is made to exclaim :

> " Thou torturest me Tubal : it was my turquoise ;
> I had it of Leah when I was a bachelor ;
> I would not have given it for a wilderness of monkeys."

Much interesting lore is attached to rings, which
in early times were regarded as symbols of power.
The ring formed a seal by which all orders were
signed and all things of value secured. The delivery
of it was a sign or signet, that the person to whom it
was entrusted was admitted to the highest friendship

and trust. It is easy, therefore, to understand how it came to be regarded as of such importance in the ceremony of marriage.

At one period not only was the ring given but the keys of the house were also handed over by the husband to his bride.

In ancient times rings of iron were generally used on marriage, but later the gold ring came into vogue and eventually formed part of the unwritten law of the land.

In the Middle Ages, rings made of rushes were sometimes used in the wedding ceremony especially among the poorer classes, but this practice came to be greatly abused by the celebration of mock marriages.

The Bishop of Salisbury writing in 1217, thus refers to it : " Let no man put a ring of rush or any other material upon the hands of young girls by way of mock celebration." Ayscough also alludes to the custom of marrying with a rush ring and says it is as common in other countries as in England, but " was scarce ever practised except by designing men."

In the *Winchester Wedding* there is a verse which runs :

> " Pert Stephen was kind unto Betty,
> And blithe as a bud in the spring ;
> And Tommy was so unto Katy,
> And wedded her with a rush ring."

" The wedding ring should be of gold," says Dean Cowler in the seventeenth century, " for gold signifyeth how noble and durable our affection is, and the form is round to imply that our respects or regards shall never have an end."

Although the circle of gold still and always will

hold its accustomed place in the marriage ceremony, it is not absolutely necessary to constitute a legal marriage. The use of a ring is enforced by the rubric of the Church of England, but in cases of emergency, a curtain ring or even a church key, has been used as a substitute.

At the marriage between the Duke of Hamilton and one of the Misses Gunning, who were the reigning beauties in the time of George II, a bed-curtain ring was used in the absence of the usual ring. According to the story, the duke had obtained the lady's consent to marriage after a brief courtship and was so impatient to have the ceremony performed that he saw Dr. Keith, who, however, refused to officiate without a licence or a ring. The duke swore that he would send for the archbishop and at last persuaded the frightened clergyman to perform the ceremony at Mayfair Chapel. But even then a wedding ring was not forthcoming in the hurry, and a bed-curtain ring which was produced by the sexton was slipped over the bride's finger instead.

In Puritan times, an attempt was made to abolish the ring on the grounds that it was only a superstitious custom of heathen origin.

Concerning this, Butler in his *Hudibras* remarks :

> " Others were for abolishing
> That tool of matrimony, a ring,
> With which the unsanctified bridegroom
> Is marry'd only to a thumb."

This refers to the wearing of a wedding ring on the thumb, a custom which Southey says, " though placed at the wedding on the fourth finger in the time of George I, it was afterwards worn on the thumb."

Among other curious lore connected with the

wedding ring is its reputation as a curative agent. Thus, for a stye on the eye it has long been customary to rub the part with a wedding ring, nine times, which is said to effect a speedy cure. A piece of bride's cake which had been passed through a wedding ring was believed to bring about an early marriage to the man or maid who ate it.

In Northumberland, a syllabub is usually prepared for the May Feast which is made of "warm milk from the cow, sweet cake and wine," and divination is practised by fishing with a ladle for a wedding ring which is dropped into it. He or she who secures it, is said to be lucky and will be the first to be married.

In the Middle Ages, rings were sometimes placed as offerings on religious statues and reliquaries, and in connection with this custom a curious story is told of a priest who besought the Pope for a licence to get married. The Pontiff is said to have granted his request on condition that the petitioner should conciliate St. Agnes, the patron saint of chastity, by placing an emerald ring on the finger of her statue in the church. To the surprise of the priest, when he came to do this, the image of the saint put forth its finger to receive it and it became so firmly fixed after he had placed it on, that it could not be removed. "Hence the priest," says the narrator, "was adjudged affianced to the saint and could wed no one else and even yet the rynge is on the fynger of the ymage."

The left hand was chosen for the wedding ring on account of the inferiority of that hand to the right and so obedience was typified. The choice of the finger is variously attributed. Sir Thomas Browne says, "It was chosen because a particular nerve, vein or artery is conveyed thereto from the heart, but as a matter of fact both the Greeks and the Romans attached peculiar virtues to this finger and it was supposed to possess certain medical or healing powers."

They stirred their medicinal preparations with it in place of a spoon, it being supposed that should any noxious ingredient be introduced into the cup, warning of the fact would be immediately given by a palpitation of the heart.

In some parts of England to-day this belief still lingers and a sore or wound is stroked by the wedding finger to aid its healing.

In selecting a day for marriage every precaution was formerly taken to avoid an unlucky day or month.

The old Roman tradition that May was an unlucky month for marriage has survived for centuries, and the ancient adage " Marry in May and you'll rue the day," is still quoted.

One of the reasons assigned for the prejudice against the " merry month " is, that the first born of such a marriage would have some physical deformity, and another is, that quarrels would soon break out between the couple.

June, on the other hand, was considered a lucky month for marriage, concerning which Ovid says :

" Resolved to match the girl, and tried to find
　What days unprosp'rous were, what moons were kind ;
　After June's sacred Ides his fancy strayed,
　Good to the man and happy to the maid."

Equal importance was attached by some to the day of the week for the wedding. Friday has always been regarded as an unlucky day for the beginning of an enterprise, which may have accounted for the prejudice against it for marriage. On the other hand, a West End registrar has recently stated that this superstition has been eradicated, and his returns showed, that nowadays, more appointments are made for marriages on Fridays, both in churches and in civil offices, than at any previous period.

In former times, Sunday was believed to be the most propitious day for a wedding. In Elizabethan dramas, the brides are usually represented as being married on Sunday, and in the *Taming of the Shrew*, Petruchio is made to say :

> " Father and wife and gentlemen, adieu.
> I will to Venice ; Sunday comes apace.
> We will have rings, and things, and fine array ;
> And kiss me, Kate, we will be married o' Sunday."

In Scotland, however, Friday was formerly considered as a lucky day and Sunday was rarely chosen for a wedding.

Concerning the choice of the day an old rhyme states :

> " Monday for wealth,
> Tuesday for health,
> Wednesday, the best day of all,
> Thursday for crosses,
> Friday for losses,
> Saturday no luck at all."

In some parts of the country the old saying survives, that he " who marries between the sickle and the scythe will never thrive."

Even the publication of the banns was not without its superstitions, for in the northern counties it is considered most unlucky for a young woman to be present in church when " her banns are called," for if so, any children she may have may be born deaf and dumb.

It is probable that some of the customs that still

survive in connection with marriage date back to an early period, and their origin is lost in antiquity.

There is an ancient myth that "a mysterious creature once lived like the wraith of a man or a fallen angel who was especially jealous when a marriage was about to take place. Even if he was not in love with the bride, he was jealous of human happiness in general and did what he could to thwart it, so every precaution was taken and means devised to guard against the malice of this malignant demon or to propitiate the deities. From him the bride hid herself by a veil and received support from her attendant maids. She carried flowers because they were the protectors of humanity and the heralds of peace, for in primitive times they were regarded as symbols of female sex energy."

The ancient Egyptians regarded the lotus as the sign of the mother, the female creator, and it was the symbol which embodied the mystery of life.

The old saying, " Blessed is the bride that the Sun shines on," may have had its origin in the Sun-god Rā unveiling his face from the clouds and smiling on the bride.

The ancient Scandinavian custom of the " Bride's Bath " survived for centuries in the custom of "feet-washing" on the eve of marriage. In some of the northern counties, on the evening before the wedding, the bridesmaids try and catch the bride and if they succeed in so doing, they struggle to get her feet into a tub of water. There they rub her feet with soot and then wash it off again in the tub with great glee. The bridegroom was similarly dealt with and he was lucky if he could dodge the girls and so prevent them from giving him a foot-bath.

It was considered unlucky for the bride to weep on her wedding day and misfortune was forecast if she or the bridegroom happened to meet a funeral on going to or leaving the church. In Lancashire, it is considered an ill-omen should a grave be open in the churchyard when a wedding is taking place.

In Sussex, when a bride returns from the church it is customary to rob her of all the pins she may have about her, for the girls believe that whoever secures one will be married in the course of the year. In other counties, the bride is warned to take every care when she removes her wreath or gown, to throw away every pin worn on the eventful day, or ill-fortune may follow.

In Yorkshire, to rub shoulders with a bride or bridegroom is considered an augury of early marriage, and in the Hull district, an engaged couple are warned " to make sure when they go to get married they don't go in at one door and out at another, as if so they will always be unlucky."

In Worcestershire, there is a similar belief and for the couple to leave the church by another door than the one by which they entered is considered to be most unlucky, for the bride, it is said, will be widowed before the year is out.

In some counties it was customary to strew the pathway to the church door with emblems of the bridegroom's calling. Thus, for a carpenter, shavings would be laid ; for a paper-hanger, slips of paper, or a blacksmith, bits of old iron. It is probable that the modern custom of forming arches of weapons or implements incident to the bridegroom's calling for the couple to walk beneath as they leave the church door, originated in this way.

There is an ancient Scottish custom, which is said

to date from the sixth century, which consists in walking round a person or an object always keeping the person on the right side. To do this was to bring down a blessing, or to perform it in the opposite direction, to invoke a curse. It was sunwise that the Celts approached a consecrated place and it was once a common practice in Scotland to carry fires, "deasil" or sunwise, round persons or property to preserve them from any malignant influence.

Therefore to ensure happiness, a bride was conducted "deasil" towards her future husband. A procession with lighted torches was made in a like manner around the cornfields in order to obtain a blessing on the crops.

"To go round a person in the opposite direction or 'withershins'," says Sir Walter Scott, "is unlucky and a sort of incantation." It was considered unlucky to step on a threshold, as from time immemorial the doorway of a house had been regarded as sacred, for it was the entrance to the dwelling which had to be guarded against demons and evil spirits. Hence the custom arose in Scotland and in the North of England of lifting the bride over the threshold sometimes called "Gaudy Loup." Its object was to prevent the "evil eye" being cast upon her.

Another curious Scottish custom was that known as "creeling" the bridegroom. A basket or creel was filled with heavy stones and fastened on his shoulders, and with this burden he was made to run until his intended wife overtook him and unfastened the creel and freed him from his load.

In the northern counties it is believed that the girl who receives a piece of cheese from the bride, that has been cut by her before leaving the table after the breakfast, will be the next to be married. It was also customary for elder sisters to dance bare-footed at the marriage of a younger one, as otherwise they would inevitably become old maids, and in some places it was considered necessary for the unfortunate elder sister to perform her dance in a hog's trough.

In some parts of Yorkshire, when a newly married couple in the country first enter their cottage after the wedding, a hen is brought and made to cackle and this is believed to bring good luck to them in future life.

A custom which died out over a century ago, was for the young men present at a wedding to strive immediately after the ceremony to see who could first pluck off the bride's garters. As this was some-times attempted before she left the altar, it became customary to tie ribbons round the leg for this purpose, for which the men eagerly strove and after-wards wore them in their hats.

Corn, in one form or another, has ever been associated with the ceremony of marriage and the wedding or bride's cake is a survival of the symbolic corn-ears originally worn by the bride. In later times they were made into cakes and scattered on the heads of the newly married couple on their return from the church.

In Scotland, it was customary to station one of the oldest inhabitants of the village near the threshold to await the bride at her new home, in order that he might throw a plateful of broken shortbread over her head, taking care that it fell outside the doorstep. This was then immediately scrambled for by the bridesmaids, for a piece of it was considered to bring good luck and a token of an early marriage.

Smollett in his *Expedition of Humphrey Clinker* (1771) describes how Mrs. Tabitha Lismahago's wedding cake was broken over her head and the fragments distributed among the bystanders, who imagined that to eat one of the hallowed pieces, would ensure the unmarried eater the delight of seeing in a vision the person who was to be the future wife or husband.

This custom survives in the practice of passing a small piece of bride's cake through a ring and placing it under the pillow to dream upon. A common custom a couple of centuries ago was to place a ring in every cake made for a wedding. It is thus alluded to in a poem written in 1799:

> " The hallowed ring, infusing magic power,
>     Bide Hymen's visions wait the midnight hour ;
>     The mystic treasure placed beneath her head,
>     Will tell the fair if haply she will wed ;
>     These mysteries portentous lie concealed,
>     Till Morpheus calls and bids them stand reveal'd ;
>     The future husband that night's dream will bring,
>     Whether parson, soldier, beggar or a king ;
>     As partner of her life the fair must take,
>     Irrevocable doom of bridal cake."

According to a manuscript in the British Museum, written in the sixteenth century, the bride and bridegroom kissed over the bride-cake and cakes were laid one upon the other upon the Bible.

These cakes or buns, which took the place of the hard, dry biscuits of an earlier period, were made of spice, currants, milk, sugar and eggs and were provided in large quantities. Some were thrown over the bride's head and fragments passed through her ring and eaten for luck or preserved to inspire prophetic dreams.

The development of these small cakes piled one on the other, into the massive and rich concoction covered with almond paste and elaborate sugar ornaments which we now call bride's-cake, is easily conceived. The latter is said to have been first introduced into England at the time of the Restoration by French cooks, and since then the bride's cake has become universal.

In Yorkshire, it was customary in former times when the bride reached her father's house to throw a plate covered with small pieces of the wedding-cake from the second-floor window, and if the plate did not break it was regarded as a most unfavourable omen for the newly married couple ; but should it be shattered into many pieces, it was considered that good fortune awaited them.

The practice of throwing rice over the bride and bridegroom on leaving the church originated in the ancient custom of carrying ears of wheat or scattering corn, symbolic of plenty, on the bride's head. In the towns, rice superseded the use of corn, just as confetti has now almost eradicated the use of rice for this purpose.

The custom of throwing the slipper or an old shoe at weddings is said to have originated in the East, where the shoe was regarded as a symbol of authority. Thus, in token of submission to her husband, the bride received a rap on the head with her husband's shoe after the marriage.

In early Jewish times, the delivery of a shoe was a sign of formal renunciation of authority over a woman, and the Romans were accustomed to throw their sandals after a wedding procession. Thus a poet says :

> " When Briton's bold
> Wedded of old
> Sandals were backward thrown,
> The pair to tell
> That, ill or well,
> The act was all their own."

With reference to this shoe-lore, it was formerly customary at Haworth in Yorkshire for every bride coming that way, either to give her left shoe or ¾d. to the forester of Cookryse by way of custom or gate lyse, a practice which was instituted by charter in the time of Edward II.

" In throwing this symbol of good luck," says an old writer, " it is well to remember that to be effective the left shoe only should be used."

> " From this thou shalt from all things seek
> Murrow and mirth and laughter ;
> And whereso'er thou move, good luck
> Shall throw her old shoe after."

# CHAPTER V

THE folk-lore of the human body as a whole is of especial interest as it reflects the many early traditions concerning life, in health and disease. When we come to examine the majority of these, however, we find that the bad influences considerably outnumber the good, and in primeval times man's greatest desire was to find protection from the attacks of the evil demons and spirits that menaced his body from without and within. If they got entrance within, they caused disease, and from without, they often cast spells on his cattle and his crops. Thus, the "evil eye," as it came to be termed, has ever been the most dreaded vehicle of spiritual malice.

The belief in its influence is practically universal and it is almost as common to-day in some countries as it was in early times.

Its origin is lost in the obscurity of the far distant past but we find allusions to it in records going back four thousand years.

The root-conception of the very earliest ages which is still held by superstitious people, is, that certain individuals have the power, whether voluntary or not, of casting a spell or producing some malignant effect upon an object or person upon which their eye may rest, especially when exercised upon victims of their displeasure.

The ancient Egyptians were in fear and dread of

65

it, and the Assyrians and Babylonians recognised its power and did all they could to avert its influence. The Greeks and the Romans were in constant terror of it and used every means known to them to protect themselves from its baleful power. They firmly believed that some malignant influence darted from the eyes of certain envious or angry persons which could penetrate the bodies of living creatures and inanimate objects.

" When anyone looks at what is excellent with an envious eye," says Heliodorus, " he fills the surrounding atmosphere with a pernicious quality and transmits his own envenomed exhalations into what is ever nearest to him."

It was fully believed, both in ancient and modern times, that by many persons, even a glance of the eye was sufficient to cause evil effects, without their consent and even against their will.

We find reference to it in the Bible in the Book of Proverbs (Chap. xxiii, verse 6), " Eat thou not the bread of him that hath an evil eye," which became an adage among the ancient Jews.

Not only human beings but domestic animals of all kinds are believed to be susceptible to the dreaded power, which was mostly exercised by women, hence the prevalence of the female name of witch in English and other languages.

Hunchbacks, dwarfs, deformed or people with squinting or different coloured eyes, are also regarded as possessors of the power, a belief common to nearly all races. Thus, Shakespeare makes Margaret say in speaking of Richard, Duke of Gloster in *King Richard III* (Act I, Sc. 3) :

"Thou elvish-mark'd, abortive, rooting hog!
Thou that was seal'd in thy nativity,
The slave of Nature and the son of hell!"

The tradition associated with the hunchback dates from very early times for the ancient Egyptian deity Bes, a deformed, hunchbacked dwarf, was venerated and his representations in faience and silver were used as charms. The belief survives in Italy to-day, where to meet a hunchback or " *gobbo* " as he is often called, is usually considered unlucky although sometimes it is thought other-wise, especially when his influence has been counteracted.

In a well-known restaurant in Rome, the writer was surprised to find a hunch-back as head waiter and the proprietor on being asked the reason declared, that he employed him as he brought good luck to the establishment. It is stated that another thus deformed man haunted the precincts of the Casino at Monte Carlo so that players might touch him for a con-sideration, in the belief that in so doing they would have good luck at the tables. Thus, the hunchback, although from time immemorial associated with the " evil eye," was also regarded as an antidote and was used as a charm against the force that emanated from the eyes of others.

HUNCH-BACK CHARM

Used to avert the "evil eye."

*Pitt-Rivers Museum.*

There is an old saying common in the North of England, " no one can say black is your eye," meaning that nobody can justly speak ill of you. Theocritus states that there were in Scythia, women called " Bithiae " having two balls or blacks in the apples of their eyes and " these, with their angry looks do bewitch and hurt not only young lambs but young children which the Irish call ' eye-bitten '."

Carden writing in the sixteenth century thus describes the symptoms by which a physician may determine that his patient has been bewitched. "He will have loss of colour, heavy and melancholy eyes, either overflowing with tears or unnaturally dry, frequent sighs and lowness of spirits, watchfulness, bad dreams and falling away of flesh." The cause of his troubles was also indicated if " a coral or jacinth ring worn by him loses its colour, or if a ring made of the hoof of an ass put on his finger grows too big for him after a few days' wearing."

In England, at one time, if a baby was seized with convulsions or the cows ceased to give milk they were said to have been " overlooked " and countless troubles were attributed to the influence of the " evil eye."

Threatened and in constant fear of this terrible unseen power, man began to seek for some antidote or method of protection from its dire effects, and from early times he has employed charms and amulets in which he had faith for this purpose. Thus for centuries the charms and amulets used in all countries against the malign influence have been innumerable.

There were those which could attract upon themselves the evil glance, while others were secretly worn beneath the clothing.

DOUBLE HORUS EYE
An amulet used to avert the " evil eye." Egypt.

It is natural from the association of the idea of sympathetic magic, that representations of the eye should, among all people, have been considered potent amulets against the evil influence. In ancient Egypt, the eye of Osiris or the " Horus eye," fashioned in blue faience or metal, was worn by the living and the dead. So numerous were the forms and shapes of the charms employed that only a few of the most important can be mentioned here.

Foremost among them were the hand and the horns which were both largely used in Europe and the East. Others took the form of the moon or crescent, the wheel, ladder, club, knife, hook, serpent, snail, lion, pig, dog, frog and lizard.

Among other charms, besides the hand and horns, which will be dealt with later, in which the Italians, especially in the neighbourhood of Naples, place great faith, is the *cimaruta* or sprig of rue which is said to be of Etruscan origin and is usually fashioned in silver.

The rue was held in high esteem in ancient times and was regarded as being sacred to Thor. It was also numbered among the plants revered by the Druids, who credited it with occult virtues and only gathered it " when the dog star arose from unsunned spots."

Sprigs of rue were worn round the neck as an amulet against fascination in early times and it was known as the " herb of grace," for it was a plant " bestowing grace and a most beneficent remedy in diseases." It was employed as an antidote for the bites of snakes and the stings of scorpions, hornets and wasps, while it also entered largely into magical rites especially as a protection against witches. In the silver charm called *cimaruta*,

*CIMARUTA* IN SILVER
Believed to be a powerful charm to avert the " evil eye." Italy.
*Pitt-Rivers Museum.*

the tips of the sprig represented are made to carry other charms in order to make it more powerful. Thus we find  clustered round it, the moon, the key, the hand and other emblems which were regarded as affording a valuable protection against the "evil eye," especially if worn on the breast.

In early times the word fascination, which in its general acceptation meant to enchant or bewitch by the eyes or looks, was used as an alternative for "evil eye," and the Romans included a deity they called "Fascinus" among their objects of worship. His phallic attribute was worn suspended round the necks of children as a charm against the "evil eye," many examples of which have been found at Pompeii. The eye of Osiris was commonly used by the Egyptians, Etruscans, Greeks and Romans and survives to-day among the Arabs and Turks.

*MANO FICA*
Used as a charm in Italy to avert the "evil eye."

In southern Italy, where belief in the "evil eye" still persists, the use of garlic or even the word that signifies that odorous bulb, is considered a sovereign preventive, but the most popular charm of all is a representation of the hand in which the thumb is doubled under the forefinger which is called *mano fica*.

"*Te faccio na fica*" is a common saying among the Neapolitans, who will take immediate steps to avoid contact with any person suspected of possessing the dreaded power should they meet one in the street.

The *mano cornuta*, in which the index and little fingers are extended, the middle and ring finger being clasped by the thumb, is also another gesture frequently used to ward off the evil influence. A large red glove filled with sand, with the thumb and two middle fingers sewn together so as to make the *mano cornuta,* is sometimes hung as a sign outside their houses by the Neapolitan laundresses.

The *mano pantea* or the hand in the attitude of sacerdotal benediction having the first two fingers and thumb extended, is said to have been used as an amulet against the " evil eye " long before the Christian era.

*MANO CORNUTA*

Italian charm to avert the " evil eye."

*Pitt-Rivers Museum.*

It was the directing hand of fate and may well be called the " hand of destiny," as it was believed not only to afford guidance and protection but also favour and blessing. Its sacred symbolism will be referred to in connection with the folk-lore of the hand, but as evidence of personal contact, its use as an amulet against fascination is generally agreed to be of great antiquity.

The *mano fica* gesture was not unknown in England, as Dean Ramsey records, that he remembered when he was a boy in Yorkshire, between 1800 and 1810, " to put the thumb between the first and second finger pointing downwards, was believed to be an infallible protection against the evil influence of one particularly malevolent and powerful witch."

The custom of blackening the eyebrows and the darkening of the eyelids common in the East, is said to have been originally done as a charm against the " evil eye," for the blackening of the eyelids was believed to be a protection against the darts that shot from the eyes of others and protection also from casting the baleful emanations oneself.

Curiously enough, in England, at the time of the epidemic of the Black Death, even a glance from the eyes of a person suffering from the disease was thought sufficient to give the infection to those on whom it fell. The carrying of salt in the pocket was believed by the Jews to be a protection against the effects of the " evil eye " and in Somersetshire, in order to avert the influence from cattle, the following charm was carried out.

" Take a handful of salt in your right hand and strew it over the backs of the beasts. Begin at the head of the near side and go to the tail and from the tail to the head up the off side and as you let it out of your hand say these words: ' As thy servant Elisha healed the waters of Jericho by casting salt therein, so I hope to heal this my beast, in the name of God the Father, God the Son, and God the Holy Ghost. Amen.' "

Another method was to take a small wooden milk-cog bound by three hoops and place a silver coin in it. " Then take it to a ford where the living and the dead pass." Three spoonfuls from water above the ford and three spoonfuls from below are placed in the cog and as each spoonful is being lifted the Trinity is to be invoked.

When the house is reached the cog is passed three times round the chimney-chain, sunwise. The water is then placed in a ladle and passed three times round the head of the " ill-wished " person and each time a mouthful of the water has to be drunk and the Trinity invoked. The water is then gently emptied out of the ladle and if the coin is found to stick to the bottom, it is considered to be a clear case of " evil eye " and a cure is sure to follow.

A similar charm is said to be common in Scotland,

where to avert the influence " gold and silver water " is made by putting a sovereign and a shilling in water, after which it is sprinkled over the person in the name of the Trinity. To protect cattle, a small piece of the wood of the mountain-ash was bound to the animal's tail, but to ensure it being effective, it had to be tied with a piece of black cloth and held in position by some yards of blue yarn. Sometimes it was bound round the cow's horns and at others round its neck.

In the Highlands, where belief in the " evil eye " still lingers, " when anyone was said to be ' ill-wished,' they grew sick, had no great pain but began to feel tired and drowsy. They grew thinner and thinner every day until at last they became mere bones.

" When under the influence, cows ceased to give milk and other cattle had accidents which destroyed them, while fisherman caught very little and ruin threatened the household."

In Essex, Gloucestershire and Herefordshire, according to Mrs. Charlotte Mason, many super-stitions connected with the " evil eye " still survive. In the first-named county, a man known as " Cunning Murrell " was renowned as a " witch breaker " in recent years. His remedy was to put cuttings of the bewitched person's hair, finger and toe nails into a bottle, which was placed either in the copper fire or buried under the " grunsill " of the door. He possessed a glass by means of which he was supposed to be able to see through a wall.

As a precaution and to prevent the use of hair that had been cut from a person being used by witches, it was customary to spit on it. To spit three times was a common charm against the " evil eye " and in Somersetshire they say, " Nif you do meet wi'. anybody wi a north eye, spat dree times."

To counteract the effect of the " evil eye " in some of the northern counties, it was customary for a woman to "take off her shift over her head, turn herself three times from right to left, then, while holding the garment open, to drop a burning coal through it three times before putting it on again."

Children were believed to be especially susceptible to the evil effect of fascination, an idea which may have arisen from the fact of pretty children attracting from strangers more attention than others.

In order to ascertain whether a child be fascinated or not, three oak apples were to be dropped into a basin of water placed under its cradle, the person who drops them observing the strictest silence. If they floated the child was believed to be free, but if they sank it was said to be affected. Another method was to take a slice of bread, cut with a knife marked with three crosses and allow both it and the knife to lie on the child's pillow for a night. If marks of rust appeared on the blade in the morning, it was a sign that the child was fascinated. If on licking a child's face with your tongue a salt taste was perceived, this also was an infallible proof that it had been " ill-wished."

Among other objects inimical to the " evil eye " mention should be made of the horns and claws of animals. Charms in the form of horns are commonly worn in Italy, while horns, painted red, the witches' colour, are frequently to be seen fixed over the doors of butchers' shops.

Tiger's claws or boar's tusks with a lobster claw, mounted in silver, are favourite amulets.

In Turkey, the " evil eye " of an enemy or infidel

is still dreaded. Quotations from the Qur'an are painted on the outsides of many houses, silvered balls of glass are suspended from the ceilings in the rooms or placed in the garden and the horses are often covered with blue charms designed to attract

HIPPOCAMPUS OR SEA-HORSE
Used as a charm in Italy to avert the "evil eye."
*Pitt-Rivers Museum.*

attention and divert the sinister influence. When a child is born, it is immediately laid in the cradle and loaded with amulets and a small piece of soft mud, well-steeped in a jar of water, is stuck upon its forehead to ward off the effects of the "evil eye." The malignant influence is feared at all times and supposed to affect people of all ages, especially those who by their prosperity may be the objects of envy. At one time, a Turkish woman on seeing a stranger look eagerly at her child, would spit in its face and sometimes at herself in her own bosom in order to avert ill-effects of the hateful glance.

Some of the remedies resorted to in the Middle Ages to counteract the effects of the "evil eye" have a definite meaning, thus, the skin of a hyaena's forehead, fantastic as it seems, was doubtless used on account of that animal's association with fascination. The eye of the hyæna was believed to have this peculiar power and even its shadow was sufficient to stop a dog from barking. It is stated that an attack from a hyæna if it approaches on the right hand is peculiarly dangerous, but if from the left, it may be beaten off without much trouble. The belief in its powers of fascination is common in Palestine to-day.

Other curious charms were, licking a child's forehead first upward then across and lastly up again, which was in fact making the sign of the cross on it with saliva. Another, was to draw water from a well, silently, and throw a lighted candle into it in the name of the Trinity, then washing the person's legs in this water and throwing the remainder behind his back in the form of a cross. Hanging the key of the house over a child's cradle or some coral washed in the font in which it was baptised, were other remedies. A piece of looking-glass was frequently used to avert the evil glance, on account of its ability to catch the eye's attention and so to attract it from the person. The custom of a mother giving a child some grotesque doll or animal, probably originated in the same idea, viz., that of attracting the eyes to the doll and so away from the child, who thus may escape their harm.

The hare was believed to possess the power of fascination, so it is easy to understand how its paw, or that of a rabbit, came to be used as a counter-charm to the " evil eye " and was carried in order to bring good luck.

There can be no doubt that there are people who by means of their eyes have an extraordinary influence over others for good or evil, and many instances could be cited of this peculiar power, akin to fascination, which men are able to cast over women.

It is in this power we probably have the origin of the firmly rooted belief in the influence of the eye which is common to every race throughout the world.

# CHAPTER VI

## THE FOLK-LORE OF THE HAND

THE folk-lore of the hand, that member of the body which we employ more than any other for most actions whether ordinary, religious or magical, is both extensive and significant.

From remote times, the hand has been regarded as a symbol of power and in Semitic usage an attack by a ghost on a human being was called " the Hand of the Ghost."

In the Highlands of Scotland, where many ancient traditions still survive, invocation by the hand of a father and grandfather meant invocation of their power.

The phrase, " God's hand," is taken to mean " His power " in the Bible and in the Qur'an, and the fact that it is universally used as an instrument of blessing shows that it bears a relation to the supernatural.

As the hand signifies power, we find that gods and heroes are often represented with several arms and hands as shown in Hindu mythology and religious art. In Buddhist sculpture, the downcast hand signified renunciation as represented in the gigantic figure of Buddha at Kyaikpun. In ancient Egypt, the symbolism is found as early as 1570 B.C., for in a stone carving of that period, the Rā, the sun's disk is represented with numerous rays each terminating in a hand.

In later Jewish times, each of the fingers of

77

God's hand were regarded as having a special meaning, and the taking of a judicial oath was made by holding up the right hand. The right hand was considered more important than the left and the Arabs to-day will not allow the left hand to touch food, as the left is regarded as unlucky.

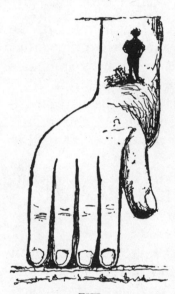

THE
HAND OF RENUNCIATION
The gigantic downcast hand of the
four-faced Buddha at Kyaikpun,
near Pegu

Among the early Greeks and the Etruscans, the hand formed a symbol of significance and the Romans used it as a special ornament on many household ornaments as instanced in their handles and knockers for doors.

As a sacred symbol, it was constantly reproduced in early Christian art in mosaics and carvings, and a representation of the hand is to be found on a bas-relief in a tomb in the catacombs of Rome which is dated 359.

It was employed to represent the first person of the Trinity and is often depicted as emerging from clouds, which were supposed to conceal the brightness of the invisible Almighty " which no man could behold and live."

There are many varieties in the form and position of this Divine hand and when superimposed on a cross, it was regarded as one of the most remarkable of all the composite charms employed against the " evil eye."

It is sometimes represented as sending down rays of light, thus expressing the Divine beneficence shed upon the earth or on a person. At others, it is shown in the act of blessing and depicted in two positions called the Greek and Latin benedictions.

In the Greek attitude, the middle finger is bent and the thumb crossed upon the third finger, thus forming the first Greek letter of the name of Christ. In the Latin position, the two first fingers are extended while the other two are bent inwards, an attitude frequently seen depicted in later pictures of the Saviour.

The significance of the open hand is almost universal, its obvious meaning being to avert or to ward off and so to protect. How instinctively we throw up our open hand, palm outwards, as a gesture prompted by surprise at any harmful appearance or to ward off a threat short of actual violence. Like the hand of the policeman extended to hold up traffic, it is naturally used to stop the approach of any person or undesired thing, a symbol which even the most ignorant cannot fail to understand.

The open hand was largely used as an amulet in Oriental countries as a charm to avert the " evil eye," which is variously called the " Hand of the Prophet " or the "Hand of Fatima." Hand-shaped charms representing a variety of gestures, and holding some other protective or covered with symbols, are still widely employed for the same purpose.

The custom of wearing jewelled rings on the hand probably arose from magical reasons, as each precious stone was supposed to possess special virtues or properties which it conferred on the wearer.

The large bronze hands that have been discovered,

several of which are described by Montfaucon, are believed to be of late Roman or early Christian origin. In some of them, the thumb and first two fingers are outstretched and the other two closed, while a serpent is entwined round the wrist, the head of which looks out in the direction of the thumb or fingers. In a specimen in the British Museum, which is about eight inches long, the two first fingers are extended and the others closed. These hands must have had a special significance as charms as they are covered with amulets in order to render them more powerful.

On the back of the last-named example there is a frog which was commonly used as an amulet against the " evil eye." Here also is the serpent symbolising eternity and perpetual union, and the ram's head on the palm signifying divinity with the horns of virtue. The crocodile was an Egyptian amulet to avert evil and the pine-cone on the tip of the thumb, which was of Babylonian origin, was believed to possess similar power, for in Roman times the pine tree was sacred to Zeus and an attribute of Serapis.

In some countries, the hand was regarded as a symbol of justice, as in the one surmounting the staff that was used in France at coronations which is preserved in the Treasury at St. Denis. For this reason it was also carried in processions and on certain occasions at opening ceremonies. The uplifted hand was used to command silence, while in religious rites, as in confirmation and ordination, the laying of the hand on the head signified blessing, as if it communicated some unseen power to the person on whom it was laid.

From time immemorial, the touch has been used for magical purposes and the person with the evil touch was dreaded, just as the one with the healing touch was reverenced and besought by the suffering.

From the time of Edward the Confessor, the touch of the kings of England was believed to heal those suffering from scrofula which on this account came to be called " the King's Evil."

The practice of " healing by touch " can be traced back to a very early period and was probably a survival of a rite performed by the priest-physicians of ancient Egypt and Babylonia. The Emperors Constantine, Vespasian and Hadrian, cured by their hands and the Edda shows us that King Olaf performed a similar solemnity.

It is thought to have originated from the ancient belief that certain individuals were born with superior powers to those possessed by their fellows. Monarchs were exalted above others on account of the supposed distinctive excellence imparted to them at birth by the ruling signs and planets. It was but natural, therefore, that their subjects believed them capable of imparting this influence by a glance of the eye or a touch of the hand. In a similar way the belief arose in the healing power of the hand of the Lord's anointed, a belief that is deeply rooted in the human mind.

Edward the Confessor, from whom the hereditary right is said to have descended to all his successors to the English throne, according to William of Malmesbury, was the first to exercise it on a young woman who was afflicted with " overflowing humours in her neck," and also on a cripple much diseased, whom he is said to have carried on his back to St. Peter's Church in Westminster, " whereupon he was immediately cured of all his maladies."

Shakespeare makes several allusions to the King's

healing power and in *Macbeth* (Act IV, Sc. 3), Malcolm is made to say in reply to Macduff's question as to the disease :

> " 'Tis called the evil :
> A most miraculous work in this good king ;
> Which often, since my here-remain in England,
> I have seen him do."

From the time of Henry VII, a gold coin was given to each person " touched " which afterwards became generally known as the " touch-piece " and was generally preserved with great care and worn as an amulet. Queen Elizabeth is said to have made the sign of the cross on the scrofulous swellings, as did also James II, but Charles I and Charles II performed the rite by stroking the affected part. The latter king excelled all his predecessors in the practice of the rite, for he touched thousands of people every year and in 1682 they numbered 8500.

The touch of a dead man's hand was believed to possess peculiar healing virtues, especially that of a felon who had been hanged, while the hand of a suicide was applied to cure a wen.

In a Roman Catholic Church in Ashton-in-Makerfield, there is preserved with great care in a white silk bag, the hand of a dead man to which wonderful curative virtues are attached. It is said to be that of one Father Edmund Arrowsmith, who was executed at Lancaster in 1628 for apparently no greater offence than that of being true to his faith.

After his execution, one of his friends cut off his right hand which was kept for many years at Bryn Hall in Lancashire but was afterwards removed to Ashton-in-Makerfield.

This " Holy hand," which has been regarded with veneration in Lancashire for centuries, is believed to remove tumours and restore the use of their limbs to those paralysed or crippled by rheumatism. At one time, pilgrims used to come from all parts of the country to seek healing from the touch of the " Holy hand."

There is a weird story told by Grose, of the use made by robbers of a dead man's hand when they wished to enter houses at night without fear of opposition.

He states that its properties were wrung from criminals, who confessed while under torture how they procured and prepared it.

" The Hand of Glory " as it was called, was said to stupefy those to whom it was presented and to render them motionless, insomuch that they could not stir or move. It was used as a candlestick to carry a specially prepared candle, which when lighted, deprived the persons whom it was brought near of the power of speech or the use of their limbs. The candle was made as follows : " Take the hand severed from the body of a man who had been hanged and exposed on the highway ; wrap it up in a piece of a shroud, in which let it be well squeezed to get out any blood that may remain in it, then put it into an earthen vessel with Zimat, saltpetre, salt and long-pepper ; leave it fifteen days and afterwards take it out and expose it in the sun till thoroughly dry, and if the sun is not sufficient, put it in an oven heated with fern and vervain, then mould it into a candle with the fat of a hanged man, virgin wax and Sesame from Lapland."

The " Hand of Glory " is said to have been used

by a gang of Irish thieves who attempted to commit a robbery on the estate of a Mr. Napper of Lough-screw in County Meath, as late as January 13th, 1831.

According to a report in a newspaper of that date, " The men entered the house armed with a dead man's hand with a lighted candle in it, believing in the superstitious notion that a candle placed in a dead man's hand will not be seen and will prevent those who may be asleep from awaking. The inmates, however, were alarmed and the robbers fled leaving the hand behind them."

From Roman times, the washing of the hands in public was significant of removing all possibility of guilt and in Cornwall, until comparatively recent times, washing the hands was used as a token of innocence with regard to any crime.

The power and sensitiveness of the hands of some people are very extraordinary and many possess that degree of personal magnetism that they can thus relieve pain of nervous origin, but even the touch of the hands of others is at once repellent and obnoxious to us.

It has been said, that no members of the body are so eloquent as the hands and between them and the brain there is a mysterious link. The very clasp of the hand given by some persons, at times conveys to us an idea of their character and their sincerity or otherwise.

The finger-tips of the hands of some people afflicted with blindness are so sensitive, that they have almost a visual sense and can even distinguish colours. A case is recorded of a man who was quite blind who declared that he could tell any colour that he touched and could distinguish a white handkerchief from a coloured one when it was placed in his hands.

Milligen, in his work on *The Passions*, states that in the hospital for the blind in Paris, *Les Quintz*, " there was a pensioner who by the touch of a woman's hands and nails and their odour, could infallibly assert if she were a virgin. Several tricks were played upon him and even wedding rings were placed on the fingers of young girls but he was never at fault."

According to more popular lore, a large, thick hand signifies one who is not only strong but stout ; a little slender hand, one who is weak and timid ; a long hand with lengthy fingers, one who is not only apt for mechanical artifices but generally ingenious. Short hands are said to denote foolishness and " fit for nothing " ; a hard, brawny hand, dullness and rudeness ; a soft hand, one who is witty but effeminate, and a hairy hand, one who is luxurious.

Long finger joints are said to signify covetousness, and frequent gesticulations with the hands, to indicate loquacity and a volatile nature.

Short and thick fingers are said to mark a person as intemperate and silly, but when long and thin they denote wit. If the fingers crook upward liberality is denoted but if downward niggardliness. Long and crooked nails signify brutality or fickleness in character, but nails that are very short, pale and sharp, subtlety and guile.

The itching of the palm of the right hand is supposed to signify that it will shortly receive money, whereas if the left hand be irritable, it is an indication that before many days money will have to be paid away.

There is an old Suffolk rhyme that runs :

> " If your hand itches,
>     You're going to take riches ;
>     Rub it on wood,
>     Sure to be good ;
>     Rub it on iron,
>     Sure to come flying ;
>     Rub it on brass,
>     Sure to come to pass ;
>     Rub it on steel,
>     Sure to come to a deal ;
>     Rub it on tin,
>     Sure to come agin."

A moist hand is said to denote an amorous disposition, while a dry hand is characteristic of age and debility, as Shakespeare makes the Lord Chief Justice say to Falstaff in *Henry IV*, Part II (Act I, Sc. 2) :

" Do you set down your name in the scroll of youth, that are written down old with all the characters of age ? Have you not a moist eye ? A dry hand ? A yellow cheek, a white beard, a decreasing leg ? "

# CHAPTER VII

## THE FOLK-LORE OF THE FACE AND FEATURES

**B**ESIDES the power of the eye in fascination already considered, some curious lore has come down to us from early times concerning that organ.

The colour of the eyes has ever been an attractive theme for poets and writers and few romances have been written in which the shade of the eyes of the heroine has not been described.

Blue eyes appear to have always been the admiration of the poets as instanced in Longfellow's *Masque of Pandora* :

> " O lovely eyes of azure,
> Clear as the waters of a brook that run
> Limpid and laughing in the summer sun."

Shelley also in *Prometheus Unbound*, sings of " eyes of deep blue boundless as heaven," while Keats avers that
> " Dark eyes are dearer far
> Than those that mock hyacinthus bell."

Dark blue eyes are said to be most common among persons of delicate, refined or effeminate natures. Light blue, and still more grey eyes, are associated with the hardy and strong, while greenish eyes have generally the same characteristics as the grey, but hazel eyes are said to be indicative of a masculine mind and one that is vigorous and profound.

The folk-lore of the eye has thus been described :

> " Black eyes most dazzle at a ball,
> Blue eyes most please at evening fall,
> The black a conquest soonest gains,
> The blue a conquest best retains ;
> The black bespeaks a lovely heart,
> Whose soft emotions soon depart ;
> The blue a sturdier frame betray,
> Which burns and lives beyond a day ;
> The black the features best disclose,
> In blue my feelings all repose ;
> Then each let reign without control,
> The black all mind, and blue all soul."

## An old rhyme common in Lincolnshire runs :

> " Black eye—beauty,
> Black eye—steal pie.
> Grey eye—greedy gut,
> Brown eye—love pie."

Black-eyed girls were once credited with being deceitful while those with grey eyes, according to an ancient saying, were said to be greedy :

> " Grey-eyed, greedy,
> Brown-eyed, needy,
> Black-eyed never likin
> Till it shame a' its kin."

The itching of the right eye has been considered a lucky omen from ancient times especially in connection with lovers.

Concerning this tradition Theocritus writes :

> " My right eye itches now and I shall see my love."

There is also an old saying that " when the right eye itches the person affected will shortly cry, but should it be the left eye they will soon laugh."

The power of the eyes in expressing love, hatred and passion has been appreciated from early times. Shakespeare thus alludes to it in *Titus Andronicus*

(Act II, Sc. I), when Aaron speaks of Tamora as :

> " . . . fettered in amorous chains—
> And faster bound to Aaron's charming eyes
> Than is Prometheus tied to Caucasus."

In former times there was a prejudice against people whose eyebrows met across the nose, as they were believed not only to be unlucky but also deceitful.  Hence the couplet :

> " Trust not the man whose eyebrows meet,
> For in his heart you'll find deceit."

The modern fashion of thinning and training the eyebrows now so frequently practised by girls, is by no means new, as in the sixteenth century a writer tells us, that " a female eyebrow ought to be delicately and nicely pencilled."  Dante says of his mistress's eyebrow that it looked as if it were painted, and describes it as "polished and dark as though the brush had drawn it," while Mamillius in *The Winter's Tale* (Act II, Sc. I) exclaims :

> " Black brows, they say,
> Become some women best, so that there be not
> Too much hair there, but in a semicircle,
> Or a half-moon made with a pen."

Over three hundred years ago, physiognomists sought to prove that the form of the ear was an index to character, and Michael Scott in his *De Secretis Naturae* declared that " Those whose ears are uncommonly long, are vain, bold and foolish people, incapable of work."  Phrenologists of the last century concluded that small and thin ears denoted delicacy and refinement in character, and that people with abnormally large, thick ears were usually of a sensual and coarse nature.  Thin and angular ears were said to denote bad temper and cruelty, while long or prominent ears were believed to indicate a person with musical tastes.

A tingling of the right ear is said to indicate that someone is speaking favourably of the one who feels it, but the same sensation in the left ear implies the reverse.

Thus, in *Much Ado About Nothing* (Act III, Sc. 1) Beatrice says to Ursula and Hero who had been talking of her :

" What fire is in mine ears ? Can this be true ? "

Pliny also observes : " When our ears tingle, someone is talking of us in our absence."

Sir Thomas Browne associates the idea with the belief in guardian angels who touch the right ear or the left according as the conversation is favourable or not to a person.

Nathaniel Home writing in 1650 says, " If the ears tingle it is a signe they have enemies abroad that doe or are about to speake evill of them, so if the right eye itcheth, then it betokens joyfull laughter."

There is an old Scottish saying : " Right lug, left lug, whilk lug lows. If the left ear they talk harm ; if the right, good " and Herrick in his *Hesperides* thus alludes to the tradition :

" One eare tingles ; some there be
That are snarling now at me.
Be they those that Homer bit,
I will give them thanks for it."

Ears with small lobes or ears without, are said to be sometimes indicative of imperfect mental development, while ears with large pendulous lobes denote intellect and wisdom, and in support of this assertion both Aristotle and Homer are stated to have had ears of the latter type.

The nose, that prominent organ of the face, has long played a notable part in folk-lore and physiognomists go so far as to assert that it is an index to character. Certainly it varies considerably both in size and shape and its effect on the voice is well known.

Aristotle clearly defined the changes in the voice at puberty, and in ancient times the amputation of the nose was a common punishment for adulterers and adultresses detected in the act.

Astrologers believed that there was an intimate relationship between the organs of generation and the nose, a belief which is not without some foundation.

Both Wellington and Napoleon are said to have been believers in the shape of the nose as an indicator of character, and chose men to fill important military positions from the size and formation of their nasal organs.

Noses with prominent nasal bones, according to physiognomists, are believed to indicate firmness, intelligence and trustworthiness, while noses with a receding nasal bone denote obstinacy, irritability and pugnacity. Thin, pointed noses indicate a jealous and uncertain disposition, and the nose with the upturned end denotes a bright and lively nature.

When the nose itches it is said to foretell the visit of a stranger before many hours have passed by, a tradition to which Dekker thus alludes in the *Honest Whore* :

"We shall ha' guests to-day my nose itcheth so."

Melton observes, that "when a man's nose itcheth it is a signe he shall drink wine, but if his lips itch, he shall kisse somebody." In the North of England, when the nose itches it is regarded as a sign that the person will either be crossed, vexed or kissed by a fool.

Bleeding of the nose also has its traditionary lore and Grose declares that, " one drop of blood from the nose commonly foretells death or a very severe fit of sickness ; three drops are still more ominous," yet according to other writers, " one drop of blood from the left nostril is a sign of good luck."

Curiously enough, nose-bleeding was also reckoned to be a sign of love as instanced by Boulster in his *Lectures*, who remarks, " Did my nose ever bleed when I was in your company ?  And poor wretch, just as she spake this, to show her true heart, her nose fell ableeding."

Shakespeare alludes to nose-bleeding as an omen of ill in the *Merchant of Venice* (Act II, Sc. 5) when he makes Launcelot exclaim, " It was not for nothing that my nose fell ableeding on Black-Monday last at six o'clock."

A blue vein in prominence across the nose of a child was believed in some of the western counties to presage an early death.

The popular saying of " paying through the nose," implying extortion, is said to have originated in a poll-tax levied by Odin which was called in Sweden a " nose tax," on account of a penny being charged per nose or poll.

The consideration of the lore of the nose naturally leads to the traditions associated with sneezing, some of which may be traced back to an early period. In the classic days of Greece and Rome we are told of the lucky sneeze of Telemachus, and Aristotle observes that people in his time considered a sneeze as divine. Because it was deemed a good omen, it was usual to salute the sneezer, a custom which the Greeks are said to have derived from Prometheus who stole celestial fire to animate his newly-made figure of clay.

According to the legend " as the fire permeated its frame, the figure sneezed which caused Prometheus to invoke blessings on it." Sneezing to the right was believed to be propitious but sneezing to the left augured bad luck.

According to Ross in his appendix to *Arcana Microscomi*, " Prometheus was the first that wish't well to the sneezer, when the man he had made of clay fell into a fit of sternutation upon the approach of that celestial fire which he stole from the Sun. This gave origine to that custome among the Gentiles in saluting the sneezer."

St. Austin says, that the custom of blessing persons when they sneeze goes back to the pre-Christian era, and that the ancients were wont to go to bed again if they sneezed while putting on their shoe.

Considerable importance has always been attached to a baby's first sneeze, which is attributed to a common idea that no idiot ever sneezed or could sneeze, so that the child's sneeze signified that its mentality was normal.

In Scotland, a new-born babe is said to be in " the fairy spells " until it sneezes, after which all danger is past.

There was a saying in the western counties, that if you :    " Sneeze on Sunday morning fasting,
You'll enjoy your true love to everlasting."

In the Midlands, grandmothers still exclaim, " God help you ! " when they hear a child sneeze, and there is a popular belief that to sneeze three times before breakfast augurs that one will receive a present of some kind during the day.

If the cat sneezes it is considered an evil omen and a sign that colds will be prevalent in the house.

The cheek has its own folk-lore, and when it itches it is considered an ominous sign. Thus, if the right cheek burns, someone is speaking to the person's advantage, but if it is the left, it is to their disadvantage.

The following charm is sometimes repeated by a person whose cheek suddenly burns :

> " Right cheek ; left cheek ; why do you burn ?
> Cursed be she that doth me any harm ;
> If she be maid, let her be staid ;
> If she be a widow, long let her mourn ;
> But if it be my own true love—burn, cheek, burn."

Ravenscroft in his *Canterbury Guests* thus alludes to the tradition : " Why, all the while I was last in your company, my heart beat all on that side you stood, and my cheek next you, burnt and glowed."

With regard to the lore of the feet, a flat-footed person is generally supposed to have a bad temper, while the itching of the foot denotes that its owner will shortly be undertaking a strange journey.

The sensation commonly known as the foot " going to sleep," was in former times said to be charmed away by crossing the feet with saliva.

When the division between the toes is incomplete and they are partially joined, they are popularly called " twin toes " and are said to be a sign of good luck.

To meet a person with splay-feet was considered unlucky, a tradition to which Machin thus alludes in *The Dumb Knight* (1663) :

> " Sure I said my prayers, ris'd on my right side,
> Wash'd hands and eyes, put on my girdle last ;
> Sure I met no splea-footed baker,
> No hare did cross me, nor no bearded witch,
> Nor other ominous sign."

Moles, those little black excrescences which may be disfiguring or otherwise when they appear on the face, are considered lucky or the reverse, according to their position on the body.  A mole on the throat is said to be a sign of good luck, but one on the left side of the forehead near the hair is believed to be unlucky.  A mole either on the chin, ear or neck, is said to be an indication of riches, but one on the breast signifies poverty.

Lupton in his *Thousand Notable Things* adds considerably more to the lore of moles of which but a few examples need only be mentioned.  He declares that a mole on the feet and hands of a woman denotes many children ;  on the right arm and shoulder of a man, great wisdom, on the left, debate and contention ;  on the stomach, strength ;  on the nose of man or woman, great lechery ;  on the ankles or feet, modesty in men and courage in women ;  on or about the knees, riches and virtue ;  on a woman's left knee, many children, while a mole on the thighs denotes great poverty and infelicity.

The following quaint rhyme is common in Nottinghamshire :

" I have a mole above my right eye,
    And shall be a lady before I die ;
    As things may happen, as things may fall,
    Who knows but that I may be Lady of Bunny Hall."

Another popular saying in the Midlands is :

" If you've got a mole above your chin,
    You'll never be beholden to any of your kin."

# CHAPTER VIII

## FOLK-LORE OF THE HAIR, NAILS AND TEETH

THE hair, which in former times was often described as the " crowning glory of the daughters of Eve," has played a part in the lore of the supernatural from the age of mythology.

We cannot picture the gorgon Medusa without her wild snaky locks or Lilith without her golden tresses.

From the fact that it is one of the most indestructible parts of the human body and intimately connected with the person, it was frequently employed in magical rites and witchcraft.

The sudden loss of the hair was deemed to be unlucky and was said to forecast the loss of children, health and property. It was considered imprudent to throw hair away, from the belief that if hair was left about, the birds might build their nests with it, which would be a fatal thing for the person from whose head it had fallen. If a magpie for instance should use it, it was said to augur that the person's death would be sure to happen within a year and a day.

But although it was generally considered unlucky to burn hair, in some parts of the country it was customary to throw hair on the fire to draw various omens from the way in which it burned. Thus, should it slowly smoulder away, it was considered an omen of death, but if it burnt brightly, it was deemed a sign of longevity and the brighter the flame the longer the person's life would be.

In Devonshire, when the hair grows low on the forehead and retreats up the head above the temples, it is considered an indication that the person will have a long life.

There is an idea common in all parts of the country that persons who have much hair on their arms are born to be rich, but abundance of hair on the head is supposed to indicate a lack of brains, hence the saying, " Bush natural, more hair than wit."

In Yorkshire, when a woman's hair grows in a low point on her forehead, it is commonly supposed to presage widowhood and is called the " widow's peak."

The colour of the hair is believed to be often indicative of the person's character and disposition. Black and dark brown hair are said to be a sign of strength, while fair hair is associated with a timid and effeminate person. Curly hair is believed to be a sign of good temper and equable disposition, while straight and lank hair is said to indicate cunning and slyness.

Red hair has always been associated with a hot-tempered and choleric disposition, although when women have hair of a ruddy hue it is said to inspire love and passion.

It is significant that some of the most beautiful women in history have had hair of this colour. Cleopatra who enslaved Antony and had lovers innumerable and Helen of Troy, whose loveliness was renowned, had red hair. There were also Aspasia, Phryne, and Xantippe, whose golden and copper locks inflamed the hearts of their admirers, while in later times we have our own Queen Elizabeth, Catherine of Russia, Anne of Austria, Madame de Maintenon and Madame Recamier.

Auburn or copper-coloured hair for which the women of Venice were at one time famous, has always attracted the artist's eye and admiration and excited the envy of their less favoured sisters

Titian loved to paint the women he depicted with hair of a rich chestnut hue, which even to-day is regarded by some as a mark of great beauty.

But although its beauty among women may be generally acknowledged, a certain prejudice or odium appears to have been always attached to red hair. There is an old tradition that Judas Iscariot had hair of this colour, to which Shakespeare makes allusion in *As You Like It* (Act III, Sc. 4) where Rosalind says of Orlando : " His very hair is of the dissembling colour," to which Celia replies, " Something browner than Judas's."

Some early writers state their belief, that the dislike to red hair in this country originated from the aversion felt to the red-haired Danes who invaded our shores and wrought devastation in the early centuries, after which it is said a red beard was held in contempt and regarded as an infallible token of a vile and cruel disposition.

Persons having what is described as " yellow hair " were not regarded with favour in the sixteenth century. Thus, in the *Merry Wives of Windsor* (Act I, Sc. 4), Simple, when asked, says of his master, " He hath but a little wee face, with a little yellow beard, a cane-coloured beard."

This is supposed to refer to the tradition that Cain, the murderer of his brother, had a yellow beard.

That the dyeing of beards as well as hair was common in Shakespeare's time may be judged from Bottom's exclamation in *Midsummer-Night's*

*Dream* (Act I, Sc. 2). Perplexed as to what beard he should wear in performing his part before the Duke, he says :

"I will discharge it either in your straw-colour beard, your orange-tawny beard, your purple-in-grain beard or your French-crown-colour beard, your perfect yellow."

The old and popular tradition that the hair may turn white by sudden fright, great anxiety or violent distress, has often been doubted, although there are many well-authenticated cases on record.

An old French chronicler in describing the torture of Damiens who attempted to assassinate King Louis XV of France, states, that under the ordeal his hair literally stood on end and then quite suddenly turned white, and the sudden bleaching of the hair of the ill-fated Marie Antoinette when her flight from France was checked at Varennes, may be regarded as an historical fact.

There is also a tradition that the hair of King Charles I became white in a single night when he attempted to escape from Carisbrooke Castle, and likewise the hair of Ludwig of Bavaria, when on learning of the innocence of his wife whom he had caused to be put to death on a suspicion of infidelity.

Shakespeare alludes to the tradition in *Henry IV*, Part I (Act II, Sc. 4), when Falstaff in his speech to Prince Henry says : "Thy father's beard is turned white with the news;" and we have also Byron's reference in the *Prisoner of Chillon*, "whose hair turned white in a single night."

In the biography of the late Canon Hughes of Barmouth, North Wales, it is stated that his hair turned white in one night owing to the shock he suffered when the tower of St. John's Church,

Barmouth, collapsed during a storm. Another case occurred when H.M.S. *Doteral* was blown up in the Straits of Magellan in 1881, and the hair of a young engineer who was saved, was found to have turned white from the shock.

In cases recorded in more recent times, there is one of a young woman who had beautiful chestnut-coloured hair, who met with a serious accident and had to have her leg amputated. Within two or three days afterwards, her hair turned snowy white with the exception of one strand which remained its natural colour.

Another instance which is vouched for as being authentic, was that of a sailor who fell from the forecastle of his ship to the bottom of a dry dock in Malta. When picked up dead his hair was found to have turned white.

The lore of the finger nails seems chiefly to be connected with their cutting. Thus, says Sir Thomas Browne, " to cut the nails upon a Friday or a Sunday is accounted unlucky by people in many places. The set and statutary times of paring nails and cutting of hair is thought by some a point of consideration, which is perhaps but the continuation of an ancient superstition. To the Romans it was piacular to pare their nails upon the Nundinae, observed every ninth day, and was also feared by others on certain days of the week."

Gaule in his *Mag-astromancers* says, " that long nailes and crooked, signe one brutish, ravenous unchaste ; very short nailes, pale and sharpe show him false, subtle, beguiling ; and so round nailes libidinous ; but nailes broad, plain, thin, white and reddish are the tokens of a very good wit."

The importance of the day on which nails were

cut is mentioned by Thomas Lodge in his *Wit Miserie* (1596) when in alluding to one of his characters he says, " Nor will he paire his Nailes White Munday to be fortunate in love." In *Albumazar*, a comedy written in 1634, we have the lines :

" He puls you not a haire, nor paires a Naile,
Nor stirs a foote, without due figuring
The horoscope."

There is an old rhyme common in some parts of the country with reference to the days on which the nails should be cut, that runs as follows :

" Cut them on Monday, you cut them for health ;
Cut them on Tuesday, you cut them for wealth ;
Cut them on Wednesday, you cut them for news ;
Cut them on Thursday, a pair of new shoes ;
Cut them on Friday, you cut them for sorrow ;
Saturday, see your true love to-morrow ;
Sunday, the devil will be with you all the week."

Certain superstitions are attached to the spots which sometimes appear on the nails. Melton says, " that to have yellow speckles on the Nailes of one's hand is a great signe of death," a tradition which is also referred to in Reed's *Old Plays*, where it is stated,

" When yellow spots do on your hands appear,
Be certain then you of a corse shall hear."

Richard Burton in his *Anatomy of Melancholy* tells us that a black spot appearing on the nails is a bad omen, but such little white spots especially on the nails of children are believed in the northern counties to indicate good luck, and are popularly called " gifts."

There are but few traditions connected with the teeth, although to dream about them was supposed to be a warning that sorrow of some kind was at hand, while it was considered even more unlucky to dream of one's teeth falling out.

Large teeth were believed to indicate physical strength, while teeth that are small and regular were supposed to denote persons who were naturally accurate and methodical in their habits. Teeth set far apart were believed to be a sign of prosperity and to indicate one's future happiness in life.

The custom of throwing teeth which have fallen out into the fire, is a relic of sympathetic magic and originated in the early belief that if they fell into the hands of some witch or evilly disposed person, they might work ill or cause misfortune to the individual to whom they once belonged.

Practitioners in Voodooism, in order to carry out a death-curse against an individual, procure a nail-paring or some hairs of the victim or a fragment of his clothing that has been worn next to the skin ; then place it in a handkerchief with some corrosive substance. They believe that as these substances decay, so will the body of the person from whom they were obtained.

They take care that the victim knows what is being done so it preys on his mind. " Sometimes he makes frantic searches to find the handkerchief and dies from exhaustion ; at others he is found at the bottom of a cliff apparently having committed suicide."

# CHAPTER IX

## THE FOLK-LORE OF APPAREL

LIKE other things pertaining to our everyday life, some curious lore is associated with our apparel and other articles of dress we are accustomed to wear.

Concerning clothes in general, there is a well-known custom, especially common in the northern counties, that new clothes should be worn on Easter Day. Hence the couplet :

> " At Easter let your clothes be new,
> Or else be sure you will it rue."

This custom probably originated from an idea prevalent in ancient times that at Eastertide, everything old and dirty should be renewed for the festival. In a manuscript of the *Liber Festivalis* in the Cotton collection written in 1422, it is stated, " Of the houce at the Astur that hath bene all the wynter brente wyt fuyre and blakud with smoke, hit schal this day bene arayed with grene rusches and swete floures strowde alle aboute, schewyng a heyghe ensaumpal to alle men and wommen that ryzte os thei machen clene the houce alle with ine bering owte the fyre and strawing thare flowres, ryzte so ze schulde clanson the houce of zoure sowle."

After all things dirty and fouled with smoke had been cleansed and cleared away, it was customary to put on fine things and deck the fireplace with fair and fresh flowers, so that all would be bright

on Easter, or " Godde's Sondaye," as it was sometimes called.

In the North of England, many women and girls
still buy new hats to wear at church or chapel on
Easter Sunday, and country folk will journey to the
nearest market town to buy at least some new
article of dress to adorn themselves, as otherwise,
they say, the birds, notably rooks, will spoil their
clothes.

A similar custom prevails in Lancashire with
regard to Whitsuntide, where it is said if something
new is not worn on Whit-Sunday, one will have no
luck for a year.

But superstitions regarding apparel vary and
what is considered unlucky in some counties is
thought to be the reverse in others.

In Sussex, if you have a rent in your coat mended
on your back it is said, " you will come to want,"
while in Suffolk, they declare that " you will be
ill-spoken of."

In some parts of the country, when putting on a
new coat or dress for the first time, one must always
take care to place a little money in the right-hand
pocket, as this is said to insure some always being
there afterwards, but if by mistake the coins are
put in the left-hand pocket, one will never have a
penny as long as the garment lasts.

In connection with the Easter-day custom of
wearing new clothes, it is worthy of note that in the
north, there is a belief that if one would secure
good luck with any article of costume it must be
worn for the first time in church.

To put on any article of clothing accidently inside
out is regarded by some as an omen of luck, but it is
necessary to wear the reversed portion of attire

wrong side out till the usual time comes to take it off if one wishes the luck to hold, otherwise the good fortune is immediately lost.

This belief is said to have originated from a story told of William of Normandy, who when arming himself prior to the battle of Hastings happened to put on his shirt of mail the wrong way. The by-standers noticing that he had donned it back to front, at once took it as an ill-omen for the day, but William assured them that the augury was a good one and betokened that he was to be changed from a duke to a king.

There is an idea common in some parts of the country, that clothes that have belonged to one who has died never last very long afterwards and that as the body decays, so in the same degree do the clothes and linen that belonged to the deceased person. This notion is said to have given rise to the saying well known in Essex that " the clothes of the dead always wear full of holes."

According to another tradition, rings that have been worn by a deceased relative or friend should never be given away out of the family, or they will surely bring bad luck to the recipient.

In Dorsetshire it is believed that if a man accidently burns the tail of his coat or a woman the edge of her skirt, during a visit to a friend's house, it is a proof that they will repeat their visit.

In the northern counties, if one puts a button or hook into the wrong hole when dressing in the morning, it is regarded as a warning that some misfortune will happen during the course of the day, and in Northamptonshire it is believed that domestics who go to their situations in black clothes will never stay the year out.

It is customary among women in some districts, to always turn their aprons before the new moon so that they may have good luck during the ensuing month. In Yorkshire, when the apron of a married woman accidentally falls off, it is regarded as a sign that something is coming to vex her, but if the same incident happens to an unmarried girl, it is an indication that she is thinking of her sweetheart.

Several superstitions are associated with women's clothes and if a girl's petticoats were noticed to be longer than her skirt, country folk used to say, it was " a sign that her mother did not love her so much as her father." This idea may have arisen from the idea that the mother had not attended to her daughter's dress as was her duty.

The word petticoat has long been associated with certain flowers in some country districts, thus, a poppy is said to have a red petticoat and a green gown, and the daffodil a yellow petticoat and a green gown. We have an instance of these quaint fancies in the old rhyme :

" Daffadown-dilly is come up to town,
    In a yellow petticoat and a green gown."

Stockings, although they were not commonly worn until Elizabethan times, have also some quaint lore associated with them.

In former days it was considered a matter of great importance by women as to which foot they put their stocking on first when dressing in the morning, for the luck of the day was supposed to depend on this circumstance. To put the left foot stocking on first was regarded as a sign of coming misfortune, and to put a stocking on wrong side out was deemed unlucky and the bad luck would continue if an attempt was made to reverse it.

In some parts of the country, it is customary with girls on a Friday night, to draw their left stocking into the right one while saying the following rhyme :

" This is the blessed Friday night,
I draw my left stocking into my right ;
To dream of the living, not the dead,
To dream of the young man I am to wed."

Stockings are associated with several old marriage customs and formerly when a bride retired to rest on her wedding night, it was usual for her bridesmaids to lay her stockings across, as this act was supposed to ensure her future prosperity.

The rite of " flinging the stocking " on the wedding night, was another early custom referred to by several writers of the seventeenth century.   One tells us, that the young men took the bride's stockings and the girls those of the bridegroom, each of whom sitting at the foot of the bed, threw a stocking over their heads endeavouring to make it fall upon that of the bride or her spouse.  If the bridegroom's stockings thrown by the girls fell upon his head, it was a sign that they themselves would soon be married ;  and a similar prognostic was taken from the falling of the bride's stockings thrown by the young men.

Sack Posset was the usual nightcap given to the bridal couple, and according to another writer, " the Sack Posset must be eaten and the stocking flung, to see who can first hit the bridegroom on the nose."

" The stockings thrown, the company gone,
And Tom and Jenny both alone."

A variation of the rite mentioned, was for one of the girls instead of flinging the stocking at the bride, to throw it full in the bowl which held the Sack Posset and this was regarded as the time to take the Posset away, "which done they last kiss round and so depart."

An eighteenth-century poet thus describes the custom in verse :

> " Then come all the younger folk in,
> With ceremony throw the Stocking ;
> Backward, o'er head, in turn they toss'd it,
> Till in sack posset they had lost it.
> Th' intent of flinging thus the hose
> Is to hit him or her o' th' nose ;
> Who hits the mark, thus o'er left shoulder,
> Must married be ere twelve months older."

Allan Ramsay, alluding to the rite in his poems in 1721, says :

> " The bride was now laid in her bed,
> Her left leg Ho was flung ;
> And Geordy Gib was figen glad,
> Because it hit Jean Gun."

The old custom, still common among children, of hanging a stocking on their bed on Christmas Eve so that they may receive gifts from Santa Claus, is supposed to have arisen from the presents brought by the Wise Men at the Nativity.

Garters played a part in several old customs and were sometimes used by girls in their love-divinations on Midsummer Eve.

The maiden anxious to have a peep of her future husband had to sleep in a county different from that in which she usually lived, and on going to bed, had to take care to knit her left garter about her right stocking, while repeating the following lines and at every pause knitting a knot :

> " This knot I knit
> To know the thing I know not yet ;
> That I may see
> The man that shall my husband be ;
> How he goes, and what he wears,
> And what he does all days and years."

After this was carried out, it was believed that the wished-for one would appear to her in a dream carrying with him some symbol of his calling.

Shoes, especially when they are old, have ever been popular objects of superstition, and frequent allusions are made to them in the works of old writers as being regarded as symbols of good fortune. Thus, Beaumont and Fletcher in *The Honest Man's Fortune*, observe :

> " Captain, your shoes are old ; pray put 'em off,
> And let one fling 'em after us."

Ben Jonson in his *Masque of the Gypsyes* also remarks :

> " Hurle after an old shoe,
> I'll be merry whate'er I doe."

The putting of the left shoe accidentally on the right foot or the right on the left, was thought to be the forerunner of some unlucky accident as Butler mentions in his *Hudibras :*

> " Augustus, having b' oversight
> Put on his left Shoe 'fore his right,
> Had like to have been slain that day
> By soldiers mutin'yng for pay."

In some parts of the country it is customary for girls, on going to bed, to place their shoes at right angles to one another in the form of the letter T, while repeating the following rhyme :

> " Hoping this night my true love to see
> I place my shoes in the shape of a T."

"Among Jewish customs," says Leo Modena, "some observe the ceremony when dressing themselves in the morning, to put on the right stocking and right shoe first without tying it. Then afterwards, to put on the left shoe and so return to the right ; that so they may begin and end with the right one, which they account to be most fortunate."

There is a rhyme well-known in Suffolk respecting the wearing of shoes, which runs :

" Tip at the toe ; live to see woe ;
Wear at the side ; live to be bride ;
Wear at the ball ; live to spend all ;
Wear at the heel ; live to save a deal."

A charm to cure cramp practised in the northern counties, is to lay the shoes across on the floor after taking them off, a custom which also applies to Suffolk, where it is usual for sufferers from cramp, to put their shoes in the form of a cross every night by the side of the bed, and a leaf of tansy if placed in one of them is believed to be a protection against an attack of ague.

In the Norfolk villages, when a girl goes to seek service or a new situation, it was customary to throw an old shoe after her at the same time wishing that she may be successful.

In some seaport towns, it was formerly a regular custom to throw a shoe after a ship when she was leaving port. When vessels employed in the Greenland whale fisheries left Whitby, it was at one time the custom for the wives and friends of the sailors to throw old shoes at the ships as they passed the pier-head. In Swansea a similar custom prevailed, and the friends of the seamen on throwing the shoes used to wish good luck to the crew on their voyage.

Various explanations have been offered from time to time as to the origin of the custom of throwing a shoe after a bridal couple or attaching one to their carriage when leaving on their honeymoon.

Some believe it was intended to symbolise an assault on the bridegroom for carrying off the bride and a survival of the old ceremony of opposition to the capture of the bride. Others state it had its origin from the fact, that the shoe in former times was the symbol of the exercise of dominion and authority by the father or guardian, and the receipt of the shoe by the bridegroom was a sign that the authority had been transferred to him.

Among the Hebrews in early times, the receiving of a shoe was an evidence and symbol of asserting or accepting dominion or ownership, whereas the giving back of the shoe signified resignation.

According to an old rhyme :

> " When Britons bold
> Wedded of old,
> Sandals were backward thrown,
> The pair to tell
> That ill or well
> The act was all their own."

In Yorkshire, the custom of shoe-throwing was called " thrashing," and it was said the older the shoe the greater the luck would be that followed. It was formerly customary in Kent, after the departure of the wedded couple, for the single women to be drawn up in a row and the bachelors likewise. This being done, an old shoe was thrown as far as possible which the girls ran for, the winner being considered to have the best chance of marriage. She then threw the shoe at the bachelors, when the first who recovered it was believed to have the same chance of matrimony.

With reference to the shoe as a symbol of authority, there was formerly an ancient ceremony in Ireland when electing a person to any office to throw an old shoe over his head.

In the majority of the superstitions associated with the throwing of a shoe, however, it is employed as the bearer of a wish for good luck, and as John Heywoode wrote in 1598, " Now, for good lucke, cast an olde shoe after mee."

There is a belief in Scotland that to place a pair of boots on the table portends death to the wearer, or should a pair of bellows be laid on a table after using them, it may be followed by " a possible cessation of the person's breath who placed them there."

Several curious customs and ceremonies are associated with gloves.

In early times, as well-known, the mailed glove was used as a token of a challenge to fight or battle ; probably as a symbol of the prowess of the hand of its owner. It was also given by way of delivering or investiture in sales of lands and goods. A glove hung up in a church was regarded as a public challenge and when thrown down in front of a person it was intended as a direct challenge to combat.

In the fourteenth and fifteenth centuries, when gloves were of much greater value than they are now, the gift of a pair was the ordinary reward to a person who had performed some service, and to make them more valuable, a glove was sometimes lined with money, from which custom the term " glove-money " still survives.

Another survival was the presentation of gloves at weddings and funerals, a custom which has now practically died out.

In the northern counties, if a woman wakes a man whom she discovers asleep in his chair with a kiss, she can claim a pair of gloves as a gift from the sleeper.

Sir Walter Scott alludes to this custom in the

*Fair Maid of Perth*, when Catherine steals from her chamber on St. Valentine's morn and catching Henry Smith asleep, gives him a kiss. " Thou knowest," she remarks, " the maiden who ventures to kiss a sleeping man wins of him a pair of gloves."

The custom probably had its origin in the ancient custom of choosing a lover or a valentine when the object of affection was coy.

The sentiment is expressed in the following verses, written in 1696 :

> " Shall only you and I forbear
> To meet and make a happy pair ?
> Shall we alone delay to live ?
> This day an age of bliss may give.
>
> But ah ! when I proffer make,
> Still coyly you refuse to take ;
> My heart I dedicate in vain,
> The too mean present you disdain.
>
> Yet since the solemn time allows
> To choose the object of our vows ;
> Boldly I dare profess my flame
> Proud to be yours by any name."

The saying " right as my glove," common in some parts of the country, is said to be derived from the practice of pledging the glove as the sign of unbroken faith in a person.

A reference to " glove-money " is made in a story told of Sir Thomas More, who when he was Lord Chancellor of England, happened to decide a case in favour of a lady named Croaker. As a mark of her gratitude, she sent him as a New Year's gift, a pair of gloves lined with forty angels, but the Chancellor returned the money with a message, saying, " Mistress, since it were against good manners to refuse your New Year's gift, I am content to take your gloves, but as for the lining, I utterly refuse it."

In Tudor times, it was customary for rural bride-grooms to wear gloves in their hats as emblems of good husbandry, and at a later period, in some places, it was usual to hang a pair of white gloves on the pews in church of unmarried villagers who had died young, a custom that was perpetuated in the use of white ribbons and reins for horses at the funeral of a child.

White gloves are still presented to a judge at a maiden assize, a custom which is said to have originated in a Saxon law which forbade the judge to wear gloves while sitting on the Bench. The gift of a pair of gloves, there-fore, to a judge or magistrate who had no cases to try, was a sign that he need not con-tinue on the Bench and so might wear gloves.

At the Restoration, it was customary for Bishops upon their consecration, to present a pair of gloves to the Arch-bishop and to all who had been invited to the banquet which usually followed.

WOODEN SIGN USED AS A SIGNAL FOR THE OPENING OF CHESTER FAIR IN THE SEVEN-TEENTH CENTURY.

From an early period it has been customary in several towns in England where annual fairs are held, to announce the opening by hoisting a large glove upon the end of a pole which is only taken down at the conclusion of the fair. This ancient practice still survives at Portsmouth, Chester, Southampton, and other places. Hone, in de-scribing the Lammas Fair at Exeter, thus alludes to it, " The charter for this fair is perpetuated by a glove of immense size, stuffed, and carried through the city on a very long pole decorated with ribbons, flowers and attended with music, parish beadles and the nobility.  It is afterwards placed on the top of the Guildhall and then the Fair commences ;  on the taking down of the glove the fair terminates."

An allusion to what was probably the origin of this custom is made in *Speculum Saxonicum*, in which it is recorded, that " No one is allowed to set up a market or mint without the consent of the ordinary or judge of that place ;  the king ought also to send a glove as a sign of his consent to the same." The glove therefore was the " king's glove," which may be considered as the earliest form of Royal Charter or the original Sign Manual.

The " biting of the glove," like the " biting of the thumb," was considered as a sign of derision or a method of picking a quarrel, and on the Scottish border was regarded as a pledge of deadly vengeance. Sir Walter Scott thus alludes to the act in the *Lay of the Last Minstrel :*

> " Stern Rutherford right little said,
> But bit his glove, and shook his head."

# CHAPTER X

## THE FOLK-LORE OF FOOD

IN considering the folk-lore associated with various common articles of food, one naturally first turns to bread, the making and baking of which, in former times, was a regular household practice. In country places few houses or cottages were without their bread-ovens specially built of brick or stone for baking the " Staff of Life."

After the dough is ready, many a country house-wife still marks the sign of the cross upon her loaf before placing it in the oven. In some parts of the country, butchers will similarly mark a shoulder of mutton or lamb after taking off the skin, a survival of an old custom of protecting the food from the injurious influence of witchcraft. Iu some parts of Scotland, craftsmen were formerly in the habit of making a cross on the handles of their tools for a similar reason, as they believed they would so be rendered safe from the pranks of mischievous elves in the night.

In some parts of England, if a loaf of bread accidentally comes in half while an unmarried woman is cutting it, this either augurs that she will not be married during the ensuing year or there will be a quarrel of some kind in the family. In certain districts, women also have a superstitious objection to turning a loaf upside down after cutting it, but the reason for this is not clear.

In England before the Reformation, as it is still

customary in some French churches on Sundays at Mass, bread was hallowed and distributed amongst the congregation. This bread was originally the surplus of the element provided for the Holy Eucharist by the offering of the people, and after a money offering had been substituted, the custom of blessing and distributing among the people of what remained of the Holy Bread was continued as an outward token of the love and charity they ought to have one for another.

BAKING BREAD
*From a manuscript of the fifteenth century.*

This Holy Bread was believed by many people to have the power of driving away evil and bringing health, and as Bishop Ridley says, it " was received to obtain health of mind and body."

Herrick thus alludes to it in his *Hesperides :*

" Bring the Holy crust of bread,
Lay it underneath the Head,
'Tis a certain charm to keep
Hags away while children sleep."

And again :

" If ye fear to be affrighted
When ye are by chance benighted,
In your pocket for a trust
Carry nothing but a Crust ;
For that Holy piece of Bread,
Charms the Danger and the Dread."

Bread baked on Good Friday was believed to ensure the possessor preservation from accidents, ills and calamities, and at one time it was customary

to place a piece in the coffin with a body in order
that it might be " better " for the deceased.

That the marking of a piece of bread with a cross
was believed to give it power of healing is instanced
in the following old charm to cure toothache, written
in 1537 : " The charmer taketh a piece of whyte
brede and sayeth over that brede the Pater Noster
and maketh a crosse upon the brede ; then doth he
lay that piece of brede unto the toth that aketh or
unto any sore ; tournynge the crosse unto the sore
or dysease and so is the person healed."

In Shropshire, it is considered unlucky for a
woman to pass a piece of bread with a knife or fork,
so it is customary to use a skewer for the purpose,
as it is said :

> " She that pricks bread with fork or knife
>   Will never be a happy maid or wife."

There is an old superstition common in some parts
of the country, that a loaf of bread in which some
quicksilver has been placed, when allowed to float
on a river or pond in which a person is supposed
to have been drowned, will indicate the spot where
the body lies by spinning round when it reaches it.

Some quaint lore is connected with certain cakes,
and the baking of special cakes was part of a Hallowe'en custom which was carried out by girls in some
country districts called " going a souling."  To get
the cakes, the maidens had to walk to a farmhouse
and sing outside :

> " Soul, Soul, for a soul cake.
>   Pray you mistress, a soul cake."

These " soul cakes " were kept heaped on a board,
lying in layers, and were given by the farmer's wife
to the girls who sang.

The association of cakes with Saints' and other days is also interesting. Thus, we have St. Michael's bannock for Michaelmas, the seed-cake for All Hallow-e'en, the plum cake for Christmas, the spiced-bread or sugared cake for Twelfth-Night, the pancake for Shrove Tuesday, the tansy cake for Lent and the simnel cake for Easter Day.

The history of the " hot-cross bun " associated with Good Friday, is said to go back to the days of the early Greeks, who stamped cakes with a horned symbol and offered them to Astarte. The custom in England is coeval with the introduction of Christianity into this country, and the " cross bun " was later regarded as symbolical of the bread broken by our Lord at the Last Supper.

In mediæval times, the " cross bun " was believed to be endowed with peculiar sanctity and was often kept throughout the year to bring good luck to the house, or used as a charm against fire.

In some parts of the country, a small loaf of bread is baked on the morning of Good Friday, and then put by and kept till the following year to be used for medicinal purposes. A small portion grated and swallowed with water is considered a sovereign remedy for diarrhœa.

The Epiphany cake, which in the seventeenth century it was customary to make in every household, was composed of honey, ginger, pepper and flour. The housewife when making it, thrust in at random a small coin during the process of kneading, and when baked it was divided into as many parts as there were persons in the family, but portions of it were also assigned to Christ, the Virgin and the three Magi, and these were given away in alms. Whoever found the coin in his share, was saluted by all as king and being placed on a special seat was thrice lifted aloft with joyful acclamations. He was given a piece of chalk to hold in his right hand and each time he was lifted up he had to make a cross on the ceiling. These crosses were believed to prevent evil or misfortune and were much revered.

In Yorkshire, it was customary for the housewife on the eve of All Saints' Day, to make a cake for every member of the family and present them on " Cake night." In Warwickshire, the custom took the form of a seed-cake which was made at the end of wheat-seed time, and again at the end of barley and bean-seed time, a " fraise " or kind of thick pancake was made and given to the ploughmen.

There was a curious custom, common in some parts of the country in former times, for a husband who was expecting an increase in his family, to provide a large cheese and a cake which was called the " groaning cake." In Oxfordshire, the cheese was cut in the middle as soon as the child was born and so by degrees hollowed out until it formed a large ring, and through this the child was passed on the day of christening. This custom of passing a child through some circular formed object, such as the bent or cleft branch of a tree or shrub, was symbolic of rebirth, and has already been referred to. It was a rite performed for various reasons, but chiefly to ensure renewed health when the baby was weakly. A piece of the " groaning cake " was often religiously kept in the house for years, and slices of the first cut of the " groaning cheese " were in demand among young girls to place under their pillows so that they might dream of their lovers.

The chair in which a child was to be born, was formerly provided by the midwife, and often called the "groaning chair," to which a writer in 1676 thus alludes :

> " For a nurse, the child to dandle,
>   Sugar, sope, spic'd pots and candle,
>   A Groaning Chair and eke a cradle."

There is a tradition concerning the cake which it was customary to distribute on " Twelfth Night," that if any member of the family be absent when it was cut, his or her share should be carefully kept and put by. If the absentee is in good health, the cake will remain fresh, but should he or she be ill, it will become moist and in the event of death, it goes bad. A wedding ring and button placed in a " Twelfth Cake " prognosticated whether the respective recipients will remain single or get married.

Before leaving the subject of cakes, allusion may be made to that popular delicacy associated with Christmas, the mince pie.

Mince pies can be traced back to the sixteenth century, when in the time of Queen Elizabeth they were known as " Minched pies " and in the seventeenth century called " Christmas Pyes " or " Shrid pies." They are thus referred to in a verse written in 1661 :

> " Three Christmas or Minc'd pies all very fair,
>   Methought they had this motto,
>   ' though they flirt us and preach us down,
>   sub pondere crescit virtus '."

Eggs have an extensive folk-lore and the custom of presenting them as gifts, which was originally practised by the ancient Egyptians, Greeks and Romans, is of great antiquity.

By these early peoples, the egg was regarded as an emblem of the Universe and the work of the supreme Divinity. Le Brun states in 1701, that

" the Persians kept the festival of the solar New Year by presenting each other with coloured eggs. The feast of the New Year was celebrated at the vernal equinox, that is, at a time when the Christians removing their New Year to the Winter Solstice kept only the festival of Easter. Hence with the latter, the feast of eggs is no longer made at the New Year, but during Easter, hard-boiled eggs painted different colours but principally red, are the ordinary food of the season.

"Among the Christians of Mesopotamia, on Easter Day and for forty days afterwards, it is customary for the children to buy themselves eggs and stain them of a red colour, symbolic of the Blood of Christ shed at the time of His Crucifixion."

Eggs stained various colours in boiling, or sometimes gilded, are still given to children in several towns in the North of England and called " Paste " eggs, " Paste " being a corruption of Pasque (Easter). The custom prevailed in the Greek Church, and in the Ritual of Pope Paul V, for use in England, Ireland and Scotland, the following form of benediction occurs : " Bless, O Lord, we beseech thee this thy creature of Eggs, that it may become a wholesome sustenance to thy faithful servants, eating it in thankfulness to thee on account of the Resurrection of our Lord."

It is customary with some people after eating an egg to crush the shell with special care, and to omit to do this is to invite ill-luck, but why they should do it, few are able to give a reason.

Sir Thomas Browne says, " The real reason is to prevent witchcraft, lest witches should draw or prick their names therein and veneficiously mischief their person, they broke the shell."

There seems little doubt that the custom is a relic of witchcraft and in the western counties the practice is to make a hole through the bottom of the shell before throwing it away and so, according to tradition, "prevent witches using it to put to sea for the purpose of wrecking ships."

Beaumont and Fletcher in their *Women Pleased* thus allude to it :

" The devil should think of purchasing that egg-shell
To vitual out a witch for the Burmoothies."

In some parts of the country it is considered a bad omen to bring eggs into a house after dark, and the farmers' wives avoid burning egg-shells lest their hens should cease laying. It is believed to be equally unlucky to take eggs from a house or shop after dark as it is to bring them in.

There is a curious tradition in Norfolk, that the eating of the marrow from the bones of a pig will cause insanity, and in the northern counties, there is a belief that should meat shrink when it is being boiled in a pan, it presages a downfall in life, but should it swell, it is a sign that the head of the household will be prosperous in his undertakings.

The lore of the breakfast table is not without interest, and there is a widespread belief that if a person sings before that meal he will cry before supper. It is said to be unlucky to shake hands over the breakfast table and if a person on rising upsets the chair he has been sitting on, it is believed to be a sign that he or she has been perverting the truth.

Many omens, both good and evil, are gathered from the spilling of salt at table, for to eat salt with another person is said to create a mystic union which is broken and destroyed when any is spilled. Thus, to upset a salt cellar when in the act of passing

it to anyone is regarded as a sign of an impending
quarrel between the parties, while it also indicates
trouble or sorrow to the person spilling it. To
counteract the evil consequences which may follow,
it is necessary to throw a pinch of salt over the
shoulder.

Gay thus alludes to the omen in the fable of the
" Farmer's wife and the Raven " :

> " The salt was spilt, to me it fell,
> Then to contribute to my loss,
> My knife and fork were laid across."

When salt is spilt towards a person, it is considered a most unlucky omen and to betoken some
ill to the individual or one of the family. Bishop
Hall referring to the superstition in 1608 says, " If
the salt fall towards him, he looks pale and red and
is not quiet until one of the waiters have poured
wine on his lappe."

Pennant ascribes the origin of the superstition
to the fact that the Greeks and Romans regarded
salt as sacred and a repository of life itself. They
mixed it with their sacrificial cakes and used it in
their lustrations. Selden observes, that it " was
used in all sacrifices by the expresse command of
the true God, the salt of the covenant in Holy Writ,
the religion of the salt, set first, and last taken away
as a symbole of perpetual friendship. Therefore,
if it fell, usually the persons between whom it
happened thought their friendship would not be of
long duration."

The spilling of wine on the clothes was supposed
to be equally unlucky in some countries, but " If
the beere fall next a man," observes Melton, " it is
a signe of good luck." The following lines occur in a
poem written in 1708 relative to the spilling of salt :

" Wee'l tell you the reason
Why the spilling of Salt
Is seemed such a fault
Because it doth ev'ry thing season.

Th' antiques did opine
'Twas of friendship a sign,
So served it to guests in decorum,
And thought love decay'd
When the negligent maid
Let the salt-cellar tumble before them."

It was further considered unlucky to help a person to salt, as it was believed to be equivalent to wishing him misfortune, and according to the old adage, to " help one to salt," was to " help one to sorrow." In some countries, salt was used as an amulet and as a charm against the " evil eye," and Waldron in his *Description of the Isle of Man* says, " No person will go out on any material affair without taking some salt in their pockets, much less remove from one house to another, marry, put out a child or take one to nurse, without salt being mutually being interchanged."

The phrase " to sit above the salt " originated from the custom in early times of placing a large salt-cellar about the middle of the long table in the dining hall ; the places above or the upper part of the table being assigned to guests and persons of distinction, while their inferiors and servants were given seats at the lower end, " below the salt."

There are some quaint superstitions associated with knives, and in Yorkshire, especially in the neighbourhood of Sheffield, when a person receives a gift of a pocket-knife or a pair of scissors, he is expected to give the donor a small coin in exchange or it will bring him bad luck. The same applies to the giving of almost any sharp or cutting instrument in order to counteract the ill effect that is said to surely follow. The reason for the custom appears to have its origin in the idea that the sharp knife or instrument will sever friendship unless the article is bought and not given.

Melton observes, " that it is naught for any man to give a pair of knives to his sweetheart, for feare it cutts away all love that is betweene them," and the same superstition is referred to by Gay in his second Pastoral of *The Shepherd's Week :*

> " But woe is me ! such presents luckless prove,
> For Knives, they tell me, always sever love."

Anyone who crosses the blades of two knives at table courts disaster, while bread must not be toasted nor food stirred in a pot with a knife.

To drop a table knife is regarded as a sign that a visitor is coming to the house and to lay a knife and fork crosswise, is an omen that " crosses and troubles " will soon arise.

In some parts of the Highlands, the falling of a knife is said to be a sign of a visit from a woman, the falling of a fork a man, and the falling of a spoon, a fool.

A bird falling down a chimney is a bearer of good luck, and if a bee flies into a room it is thought to be a harbinger of good news.

It is considered unlucky to find a knife, while to place a knife near a sleeping child is regarded as a charm to preserve it from harm. Herrick thus refers to this superstition :

> " Let the superstitious wife
> Near the Child's heart lay a knife.
> Point be up, and haft be down,
> While she gossips in the town.
> This 'mongst other mystic charms
> Keeps the sleeping child from harms."

# CHAPTER XI

## THE FOLK-LORE OF EVERYDAY LIFE

THE many superstitions, customs and beliefs that have come down to us from past generations, in the form of traditions, rhymes and proverbs, told orally or recorded in ancient manuscripts, have gradually become interwoven with our everyday life.

They cluster round our habits and customary duties in such a way that it is difficult to avoid them, much as we may dislike to be thought superstitious. Superstition is an element in human character that may be said to be universal and cannot altogether be ignored, in spite of the advance of education and knowledge, for the psychological effect of many of these old beliefs, especially on nervous people, is undoubted.

The fear of what may follow is expressed in the well-known lines :

" How superstitiously we mind our evils !
The throwing down salt, or crossing of a hare,
Bleeding at nose, the stumbling of a horse
Or singing of a cricket, are of power
To daunt whole man in us."

Of superstitions associated with household objects in daily use there are few more portentous than those connected with mirrors. It has been suggested that the idea of the misfortunes that are generally believed to follow the breaking of a looking-glass or mirror originated in primitive times, when men saw their reflections in a pool or lake and imagined that these images were the souls or spirits of the living disporting themselves in reflecting surfaces. Hence it came to be thought that bad luck would follow the breaking of a mirror, as it might injure the soul if it is in the looking-glass at the time.

From early times mirrors have been intimately associated with magical practices, and there was an ancient custom of dipping a looking-glass into water in order to ascertain the condition of a sick person. Accordingly, as he looked well or ill in the glass when it was wet with water, so it was judged whether he would recover from the illness or not.

Black mirrors played an important part in the prognostications of magicians, and Dr. Dee, the famous astrologer of Elizabethan times, used his black mirror in foretelling the future and fortunes of those who consulted him or to discover the perpetrator of a theft. In the seventeenth century it was customary for both men and women to wear small mirrors in their hats or doublets, to avert the influence of the " evil eye."

Ben Jonson thus alludes to the custom in *Cynthia's Revels* (Act III, Sc. 1) : " Call for your casting bottle and place your mirror in your hat as I told you."

While men wore them in their hats, women carried them at their girdles or on their breasts. Thus, Lovelace makes a lady say :

> " My lively shade thou ever shalt retaine
> In thy inclined feather-framed glasse."

If a looking-glass or mirror be accidentally broken or cracked, it is generally believed that bad luck and misfortune will follow to those who dwell in the house. It is also said to be an omen that the person to whom it belongs will lose his best friend.

Cornish people declare, that " seven years of sorrow " will follow the breaking of a looking-glass, while in Yorkshire they say, " seven years of trouble but no want " will result.

In some districts it is believed to signify death to the master of the house or some member of his family, and other fatalities. In the nothern counties, it is considered to be most unlucky to see the new moon reflected in a mirror or through a window pane, and some mothers are careful to prevent their youngest child from looking in a glass until it is over twelve months old.

Holiday, writing in 1630, says, " I have often heard say that 'tis ill-luck to see one's face in a glasse by candle-light," and in Warwickshire, it is " dreaded that if one looks in a mirror in a room where a dead person lies, he may see the face of the deceased looking over his shoulder."

The practice of covering the looking-glass or removing the mirror from the chamber of death still survives in some parts of the country. This is said to be " symbolic that all vanity, all care for earthly beauty are over with the deceased, and as the invisible world trenches closely upon the visible one, a superstitious dread is felt of the face of some spiritual being seen in the mirror."

Napoleon Bonaparte is said to have been a firm believer in the superstitions connected with the looking-glass and during one of his campaigns in Italy he broke the glass over a miniature of Josephine which he carried with him. He never rested till the return of the courier he forthwith despatched to assure himself of her safety, so strong was the impression of her death upon his mind.

Certain omens are associated with clocks, and in

the North of England there is a superstition called " clock-falling," to the effect, that if a woman enters a house after her confinement and before being " churched," the house clock will fall down on its face. So strong was this belief in former times, that women would never think of transgressing this rule under any circumstances. It was also customary to stop the clock when a death took place in a house, in order, it was said, " to remind the survivors that with the deceased person time was over and henceforth the days and hours were no longer of any account to him."

It was regarded as a bad omen, if, when a person left a house he replaced the chair on which he had been sitting against the wall, the probability being that he would never visit the house again.

Beds also have their peculiar lore, and in some parts of the country it is customary to always place them parallel with the boards in the floor, for it is considered unlucky to sleep across them. It is also said to be conducive to sound sleep if the head of the bed be placed to the north and the foot to the south. There was an idea that a magnetic influence thus passed through the body from head to foot. A well-known physician once stated that when he failed by every other method to bring sleep to sick children, he had their beds placed due north and south, the head to the north, and it never failed to produce sleep.

The common phrase, " to get out of bed the wrong side," or with the left leg foremost, which is often remarked when a person comes down in the morning in a bad temper, is said to have originated in an old superstition which regarded it as unlucky to place the left foot first on the floor on getting out of bed.

Several omens are associated with the fireside, and there is a popular idea that a flake of soot hanging on the bar of the grate denotes the visit of a stranger. Thus, Cowper, in his *Winter Evening*, wrote :

" The sooty films that play upon the bars,
Pendulous and foreboding in the view
Of Superstition, prophesying still,
Though still deceiv'd some stranger's near approach."

A hollow cinder which is thrown out by a jet of gas from the coal into the room, is looked upon as a coffin and a sign of death if it be oblong in shape, but as a money-box if it be round.

In the Midlands it is believed that if the fire burns brightly after it has been stirred, it is a sign that an absent husband, wife or lover is in good spirits, or if it burns with a pale flame it is an indication of bad weather. When the coals burn with a buzzing sound it signifies that storms are at hand, while a very bright fire is said to be a sign of rain.

When a person sits musing and lost in a day-dream looking into the fire, it is supposed that some evilly-disposed individual is either fascinating him or casting a spell over him. To break the spell, some-one should take the tongs without speaking and turn the centre piece of coal in the grate right over.

To stumble up stairs is considered unlucky by some, but by others it is regarded as a sign of a wedding and prognostic of good fortune. Probably the observation that it was unlucky meant that it was lucky the person did not tumble down stairs. The superstition regarding stumbling was apparently associated with both man and beast, for Melton tells us that " If a man stumbles in a morning as soon as he comes out of dores it is a signe of ill-luck, and if a horse stumble on the highway it means the same."

" That you may never stumble at your going out in the morning," was a common saying in the seventeenth century, for it was regarded as a bad omen for the day and at the beginning of any enterprise.

Stumbling at a grave was considered as being specially ominous, and Shakespeare observes :

" . . . How oft to-night
Have my old feet stumbled at graves."

Women addicted to whistling were formerly regarded with disfavour either in or out of doors, as its practice was said to be always attended with misfortune.

The whistling woman formed the subject of several adages. Thus in Cornwall they say, " A whistling woman and a crowing hen are the unluckiest things under the sun," while the Lancastrians aver that

" A whistling wife and a crowing hen
Will frighten the devil out of his den."

In Northamptonshire there is still another variation of the adage, for it is said that

" A whistling woman and a crowing hen
Are neither fit for God nor men."

Sailors in particular are said to be greatly averse to hearing a woman whistle, and a story is told that one morning some years ago, when a pleasure steamer was leaving Scarborough, the captain stood by the gangway and stopped a girl from going on board. " Not that young lady," he said, " she whistles." Strangely enough the steamer was wrecked on her next voyage.

This superstition is said to have originated from a tradition that " a woman stood by and whistled while she watched the nails for the Cross being forged."

There was another tradition in the Roman Church, that every time a woman whistles the Virgin's heart bleeds, and the French also have an adage that " a whistling woman in a house brings misfortune."

In household duties and other matters, Friday is still regarded as an unlucky day, and in some places the housewives will not even turn a bed for fear of some misfortune happening.  In Sussex it is said, " never begin a piece of work on a Friday or you will never finish it."

Country folk in Suffolk say, if a broom is left accidentally in the corner of a room after it has been swept, it is a sign that strangers will visit the house during the day ; while in Norfolk there is a belief that if dust is swept out of the house by the front door, it is equivalent to sweeping away the good fortune and happiness of the family.

There is another curious belief common in Sussex, that empty medicine bottles should never be sold or else they will soon be required to be filled again for someone in the house : a premonition of sickness.

There are several superstitions associated with the common insects that visit our houses ; thus there is a popular belief that it is unlucky to injure or kill a spider, for says an old proverb :

> " If you wish to live and thrive
> Let the spider run alive."

In Scotland, it was believed that should anyone wilfully kill a spider, some piece of china or glass would be broken before the close of the day.  Spiders have long been supposed to bring good luck and prosperity to a house, and this belief is said to have

originated in the ancient tradition that when Christ
lay in the manger at Bethlehem, a spider came and
spun a web over the spot, thus preserving his life
by screening him from all the dangers that surrounded him.

The magicians of ancient Rome made prognostications from the manner in which the spiders spun
their webs. Pliny says, " Spynners (spiders) ben
tokens of divynation and of knowing what wether
shalfal, for oft by weders that shalfal, some spin
and weve and were higher or lower. Multytude of
Spynners is token of moche reyne."

Willsford in his *Nature's Secrets* states : " Spiders
creep out of their holes and narrow receptacles
against wind or rain. Minerva having made them
sensible of an approaching storm." The small
spiders, commonly called " money spinners," are held
by many to prognosticate good luck, if they are not
destroyed or injured, or removed from the person
on whom they are first observed. " Others," says
an old writer, " have thought themselves secure of
receiving money if by chance a little spider fell upon
their cloaths."

The presence of crickets in the house is said to
be of evil portent, although to kill one was held to
be extremely unlucky—" Perhaps," says Grose,
" from the idea of its being a breach of hospitality
this insect taking refuge in houses."

There appears to have been a general belief in
former times that the chirping of a cricket was a
sign of death. Thus Gay, in his rural prognostications of death, refers to the " Shrilling Crickets that
in the chimney cry'd," and in Dryden's *Œdipus* we
have the line : " Owls, Ravens, Crickets, seem the
watch of death ; " while another writer says,

" The voice of a cricket has struck more terror than the roaring of a lion."

White in his *Selborne* takes a kindlier view of crickets and says, " They are the housewife's barometer, foretelling her when it will rain ; and are prognostic sometimes, she thinks, of ill or good luck, of the death of a near relation or the approach of an absent lover.  By being the constant companions of her solitary hours they naturally become the objects of her superstition."

In country places, flies are said to foretell the weather, and when they swarm together and sport themselves in the sunbeams it is regarded as a good omen.

Willsford tells us that " if in the spring or summer season they grow busier or blinder than at other times, or they are observed to shroud themselves in warm places, expect then quickly for to follow either hail, cold storms of rain or very much wet weather ; if they are noticed early in autumn to repair to their winter quarters, it presages frosty mornings, cold storms with the approach of hoary winter."

There are some curious superstitions associated with pins, and it is said on seeing a pin on the ground one should always pick it up as it will bring good luck, an idea which probably arose from the fact that when a pin is urgently required one can rarely be found to hand.  According to an old rhyme :

> " See a pin and pick it up,
>   All the day you'll have good luck ;
>   See a pin and let it lie,
>   All the day you'll have to cry."

In the northern counties, it is considered unlucky to give a person a pin if it is asked for.  The usual reply is " You may take one, but mind I do not give it."

Pins were often employed in divination in " wishing

wells " in various parts of the country. Thus, if a passer-by drops a pin into the well and breathes a wish when doing so, it is said he may rest assured of its fulfilment at some future time. In some rural villages it is still customary for girls who desire to find a lover, to visit the neighbouring " wishing well" and drop in a pin while thinking of some suitable swain, in the hope that their desire will be fulfilled.

Pins or thorns also played a part in witchcraft, for by sticking them into a wax or clay figure or the heart of a calf or sheep, at the same time uttering an imprecation on the person it was aimed to injure, they caused pain or misfortune to him.

The incantation that is sometimes repeated when pins or thorns are being stuck into a calf's heart is as follows :

" It's not this heart I mean to burn,
But the person's heart I wish to turn,
Wishing them neither rest nor peace
Till they are dead and gone."

When this had been done the heart was usually secreted up the chimney.

Many omens were formerly derived from the burning of a candle. Thus in the northern counties, a bright spark in the candle-flame was said to predict the arrival of a letter, and if it dropped on the first shake, it was taken as an indication that the missive had been already posted. Love-divination by candle was practised by taking a pin and while the candle was burning, to stick it carefully into the wax taking precautions that it pierced the wick. At the same time it was necessary to repeat the following lines :

" It's not the candle alone I stick,
But my lover's heart I mean to prick ;
Whether he be asleep or awake,
I'd have him come to me and speak."

The anxious maiden had then to watch the candle patiently, for if the pin remained in the wick after the candle had burnt below the place in which it was inserted, it was a sign that the lover would be sure to come ; but should the pin drop out, it was an indication that he was faithless.

In some parts of the country to snuff out a candle accidentally was regarded as a sign of a coming marriage in the household.

There was an ancient custom, which survived until the present century, of selling by auction by inch of candle.    Time-candles appear to have been known to the Anglo-Saxons, and in this country in the seventeenth century the " bell and cry " indicated a sale by auction or, as it was called, " to sell at the candle."

Pepys refers to the custom in his *Diary* (September 3rd, 1662) : " After dinner we met and sold the Waymuth, Successe and Fellowship hulks, when pleasant to see how backward men were at first bid and yet when the candle is going out, how they bawl and dispute afterwards who bid the most first."

The custom survived in Dorchester until 1903 when the annual lease of a meadow was sold in this way.    The bidding started at £3, and the candle expired at £8 4s. od.

In ancient times, saliva was regarded as a charm against all kinds of fascination, including the " evil eye " and witchcraft.    Theocritus says, " Thrice on my breast I spit to guard me safe from fascinating charms," and Pliny remarks on its use to avert witchcraft and as a defiance or sign of the greatest contempt and aversion.    " Hence," he says, " seems to be derived the custom our Bruisers have of spitting in their hands before they begin their

barbarous diversion, unless it was originally done
for luck's sake." This custom is perpetuated by
schoolboys in the northern counties who still have a
habit of spitting on their hands before having a
tussle.

The common custom of spitting on money first
received in country markets is an ancient one, and
in some counties is called "handsel." It was said
to thus bring good luck and was put in a pocket by
itself. Misson remarks on the custom, "A woman
that goes much to market told me t' other day that
the Butcher women of London, those that sell fowls,
butter and eggs, and in general most tradespeople,
have a particular esteem for what they call ' handsel,'
that is to say the first money they receive in a
morning ; they kiss it, spit upon it and place it in
a pocket by itself. This rite is said to make it
tenacious, that it may remain with them and not
vanish away like a fairy gift or else to render it
propitious and lucky, that it may draw more money
to it."

Fasting spittle was believed to have peculiar
curative properties, and Lemnius states, it cures " all
tetters, itch, pustules and creeping sores and the
bites of venomous little beasts that have fastened
on the body as hornets, beetles and such like." To
lick a wart first thing in the morning was also one
of the recognised cures for that excrescence.

Many methods of divination or foretelling events
have been employed in the household from an early
period, and among them, that of the Bible and key,
which was used as a detection of guilt, was perhaps
one of the most common. To carry this out, a key
was placed in the Bible on a certain chapter and after
the book was closed it was tightly fastened. The

Bible and key were then suspended on a nail in the wall, and the accused person's name was repeated three times by one of those present, while another recited the following lines :

> " If it turns to thee, thou art the thief,
>     And we all are free."

When this had been done, if the key was found to have turned it was agreed that the accused person was guilty.

As late as the middle of the last century, a case came before the magistrates at Southampton in which a boy working on a collier was charged with theft, the only evidence against him being the trial by the Bible and key.  The ordeal was carried out on the vessel and the key was placed on the first chapter of Ruth, and while the Bible was turning the names of several suspected persons were called out, but on the mention of the accused boy's name, the Bible fell to the ground.  The magistrates, however, were not convinced by this evidence and he was discharged.

Another method of divination called " Dipping " was formerly practised in some parts of the country on New Year's Day.  A Bible was laid on the breakfast table in the morning and those who wished to consult it opened its pages at random, it being supposed that the events of the ensuing year would in some way be indicated in the contents of the chapter contained on the two open pages.

As a means of discovering a person guilty of theft in the household, divining by the sieve and shears was sometimes practised.  To carry this out, a sieve was held hanging by a thread or by the points of a pair of shears stuck on its rim.  On being thus held, it was said to turn, sway or fall on the mention of the thief's name.

This ancient rite, which was originally called the " Trick of the Sieve and Scissors," was practised by the Greeks for divination and is thus mentioned by Theocritus :

> " To Agrio, too, and made the same demand ;
> A cunning woman she, I crossed her hand,
> She turned the sieve and shears and told me true
> That I should love but not be lov'd by you."

Another allusion to the custom is made in *Hudibras* as follows :

> " Th' oracle of sieve and shears,
> That turns as certain as the spheres."

Divination by means of a new laid egg was thus carried out. The person anxious to be enlightened about the future, perforates with a pin the small end of an egg and allows three drops of the white to fall into a basin of water, which soon diffuse themselves on the surface into fantastic shapes. From this it is claimed that the character of a future husband or wife and a variety of particulars concerning future domestic happiness may be foretold.

The origin of the popular superstition of " touching wood " when a person has made a boastful assertion, is said by some to have come down from the times when many old churches treasured as relics pieces of the " True Cross," on which solemn oaths were taken by the person or persons concerned by placing their hands on the reliquary. By others, it is said to have arisen from the veneration in which certain trees were held on account of their association with the ancient deities. Thus, the oak was sacred to Zeus and the ash to Thor, but the cult of the oak was universal and it was reverenced by the Druids who from ancient times performed many of their ceremonies under its branches.

It has also been stated that the custom originated from St. Paul's exclamation, " God forbid that I should glory save in the Cross of Jesus Christ."

But it may be observed that in some parts of the country it is customary to " touch cold iron " instead of wood, for the same purpose.  The object in this is assigned to the wish to invoke the protection of the deity presiding over the metal.

It is most probable that the origin of touching either wood or metal was induced as a protection against the " evil eye," when a boast had been made or something said which might arouse admiration, so that no harm might follow to the person who had spoken the words.

The traditionary power of the horseshoe to avert evil and witchcraft probably had a twofold origin. First, on account of the metal of which it was composed, and second, because of its shape, which is roughly that of a crescent and therefore a lunar symbol of peculiar power.

The Romans drove iron nails into the outer walls or beams of their dwellings to avert pestilence, a custom which survived in England throughout the Middle Ages.

Mars was the God of War and iron was the metal dedicated to him.  The war-horse was supposed to be the enemy of Saturn who according to an early tradition ruled witches, therefore iron instruments of any kind came to be used to keep witches at bay.

The lunar tradition is still more ancient, and the crescent or horned moon, a symbol of the Moon Goddess, was believed to be a most powerful protection against the "evil eye" and witchcraft generally. Charms and ornaments, like the moons on the camels' necks, mentioned in the Book of Judges (Chap. viii, 21), were used by human beings and placed on animals, and we have a relic of the tradition in the brass charms still often seen decorating the harness of our horses both in town and country.

Few superstitious practices have been more persistent than the nailing of a horseshoe over the door of a house which was frequently done in the fifteenth and sixteenth centuries.

Aubrey in his *Miscellanies* says, "It is a very common thing to nail horseshoes on the thresholds of doors which is to hinder the power of witches that enter the house. Most of the houses in the West End of London have the horseshoe on their thresholds."

In Monmouth Street, probably the part of London alluded to by Aubrey, many horseshoes were to be seen on the doors in 1797, and a writer in 1813 states he counted seventeen at that time.

The practice is still common in country places where few cottages or barns are to be seen without a horseshoe nailed on the door, although many are now ignorant of the reason for the custom. Old people say the shoe must be one that has been found, and to be effective should be nailed points upwards with its own nails. The shoe cast from the near hind leg of a grey mare was believed to be specially effective, and among the good wishes common in the seventeenth century was "May the horseshoe never be pulled from your threshold."

Superstitions still persist in this country in connection with figures of idols and Oriental deities brought from the East to decorate our houses, and from time to time we hear stories of misfortunes that have happened in families to whom they belonged.

Quite recently an account was published in the Press concerning a large alabaster figure of the seated Buddha that had been sent home from India and which found a resting place on the mantelpiece of a London drawing-room. Soon afterwards, it is stated, a daughter of the house fell ill and then the master died, both of which misfortunes being attributed to the figure of the deity.

Many similar cases have been published, which show that a belief exists that some evil influence or occult force may emanate from these idols which may affect their temporary owners, and such influence will only cease when the figure is restored to the temple or place from which it was originally taken.

A letter written by an English officer recently appeared in a Sunday newspaper, in which he gives a method, in all seriousness, how such misfortunes may be averted. He says, " Possessors of articles from the East which are suspected of being ill-omened can get rid of bad luck by taking a good pinch of salt, passing it round the object three times and then throwing the salt into an open fire. But they must be careful not to look into the fire. This treatment," concludes the writer, " has never been known to fail."

The use of salt in this experiment is interesting, as from early times it has been employed in exorcising evil spirits, and it would appear that the salt attracted the wicked genius which was afterwards destroyed in the fire, and so the bad influence was removed.

# CHAPTER XII

## THE FOLK-LORE OF HEALING

THE folk-lore of healing, which includes the charms, incantations and all the armoury of witchcraft and magic with which it has been associated throughout the ages, is very extensive.

The belief of primitive man, which persists among savage races to-day, that disease was caused by evil spirits or demons that entered his body, gave rise to the methods employed for ridding himself or others from the power that caused the mischief.

The demons of disease showed their power in many ways and contorted the body in fits or convulsions, or with shivering agues and pains, and to get rid of their evil influence they had to be appeased by sacrificial offerings or frightened away. Hence the use of charms and incantations, by means of which the Babylonian and Egyptian priest-physicians in ancient times endeavoured to exorcise the cause of the trouble.

To do this, the aid of various deities was invoked with the assistance of some material substance or fumigation, as instanced in the following text inscribed on a Babylonian clay tablet which dates from about 2500 years before the Christian era:

" Come, my sorceress or enchantress,
Over a *nulukhkha-plant* shalt thou recite,
Upon the fumigation bowl which is at the head of the bed shalt thou place it, and with an upper garment shalt thou envelop the bed."

Such an incantation made by the magician was accompanied by offerings of honey, butter, dates, garlic or other substances which were generally destroyed by fire, indicating the sympathetic connection between the destruction of the ban and that of the object.

Another general incantation potent against evil spirits that afflict man and cause disease may be mentioned. It has been translated as follows :

" Sickness of the head, of the teeth, of the heart, heartache,
  Sickness of the eye, fever, poison,
  Evil spirits, evil demon, evil ghost, evil devil, evil god, evil fiend,
  Hag demon, ghoul, robber sprite,
  Phantom of night, night wraith, handmaiden of the phantom,
  Evil pestilence, noisome fever, baneful sickness,
  Pain, sorcery, or any evil,
  Headache, shivering,

  .   .   .   .   .   .   .

  Evil spell, witchcraft, sorcery,
  Enchantment and all evil,
  From the house go forth,
  Unto the man, the son of his god come not into,
  Get thee hence."

Another method of thwarting the demons from their evil purpose, was to prevent them from gaining entry to a house, and to do this charms consisting of magical herbs or objects obnoxious to them were placed over the door. Such a charm is described in the following Babylonian text :

" Fleabane (*pyrethrum*) on the lintel of the door I have hung,
    St. John's wort, caper and wheat-ears.
  On the latch I have hung
  With a halter as a roving ass."

After the Christian era, we often find Christ and the Trinity invoked in the incantations in place of the pagan deities, as instanced in the following charm " to remove a thorn," taken from an Irish manuscript of the eighth century :

" Nothing is higher than heaven, nothing is deeper than the sea. By the holy words that Christ spake from his Cross, remove from me the thorn."

At a later period, the doctrine of signatures played an important part in folk-medicine. This was based on a belief that the Creator in providing herbs for the service of man, had stamped on them in many instances an indication of their special curative powers. Thus, rhubarb and saffron on account of their yellow colour were said to cure bilious disorders ; trefoil relieved heart troubles because the leaf was shaped like a heart ; tormentilla, because it had a red root, was believed to be a remedy for flux, and Canterbury bells, on account of their long necks, were used to cure sore throat.

Judging from the many charms and incantations recorded in manuscripts from the eighth century down to the Middle Ages, epilepsy or falling sickness, ague, coughs, toothache, fevers, shingles and cramp appear to have been the most common ailments of humanity.

As might be expected, toothache seems to have been particularly prevalent and the charms for this painful malady, which from early times was believed to be caused by a worm gnawing at the root of the tooth, are innumerable.

The following may be taken as examples :

" Toothake.—I adjure thee toothake of blood, worm and rume, by the virtue of our Lord, Jesus Christ, and by the merits of Joseph his Foster father, and as he was betrothed to that blessed Virgin Mary not a husband, and a witnesse of undefiled virginitie,

soe by soe much the more suddenly depart thou
tooth ake from this person, now, and annoy them
no more, nor trouble them, nor vex them, nor appear
in their body, by the virtue of the Father, Son and
Holy Ghost by the virtue of all the Holy Names
(of) God, obey to my bidding and avoid thou tooth
ake from this person, now without any more delay."
After this had been repeated the Lord's Prayer was
to be said three times and the Creed once.

Another cure was to " go to a young oak tree,
cut a slip in the tree, cut off a bit of your hair and
put it under the rind, put your hand to the tree and
say to the tree : ' This I bequeath to the oak tree
in the name of the Father, and of the Son and of
the Holy Ghost.' "

The following quaint charm was to be written on
a piece of paper, rolled into a ball and worn round
the neck :

> " Peter and Paul sat on a marble stone,
> Jesus came to them alone ;
> ' Peter ' said He, ' What makes you quake ? '
> ' Why Lord and Master, it is the tooth ake.'
> Whoever will carry these words for my sake
> Shall never be troubled with the tooth ake."

Among other favoured cures were texts of Scrip-
ture containing some reference to teeth, as, for
example, " There shall be weeping and gnashing of
teeth." This was to be written and carried on the
person.

Another more potent remedy was to " cut the
gum with an iron nail till the blood flows, smear some
of the blood on the nail and drive it up to the head
into a wooden beam," and so long as the nail remains
in position, toothache will never again attack the
operator.

The fore and one of the hind legs of a mole suspended round the neck were believed to be an excellent charm against toothache, and another cure was to " pare your finger and toe nails, wrap the parings carefully in paper, make an incision in the bark of an ash tree and having placed the packet under the bark, close the slit again as closely as possible." Having thus grafted a part of oneself to the tree the pain was said to trouble one no more.

Among other curious cures were the pieces of human skin that were sometimes seen nailed to church doors, and washing out the mouth of a newly-baptised infant with the remaining sanctified water was regarded as a sure safeguard against teething troubles in future.

The " plant of human destiny " figures largely in the remedies for the toothache. Other medicines for an aching tooth are " the fruit of the yellow snake-wort," " the roots of the herb of the Sun-God," and " the roots of a thorn which does not see the face of the sun when growing, together with linament," all of which to induce relief must be placed upon the tooth.

A story is told of a young woman suffering from this persistent malady, who had a charm cure given her with the strict exhortation that the sealed packet was never to be opened. As the charm was marvellous in the expediency of its working, she became, like most women, curious to know the secret, and at length sought her parish priest, who with her proceeded to make an investigation. Imagine their horror upon finding the following boldly inscribed upon a scrap of paper : " Good Satan cure her, and take her for your pains ! "

Certain charms appear to have been regarded as

being equally infallible in one complaint as in
another. Thus, we find the charm for toothache in
which the apostle Peter figures, was also used to cure
ague, which was very prevalent in some parts of the
country. In Sussex, the sufferer was told to eat
seven sage leaves for seven consecutive mornings
while fasting, and another remedy was to go early
in the morning to an old willow tree and tie in one
of its branches three knots, saying at the same time,
" Good morrow, old one, I give thee cold, good
morrow, old one," which having said, turn and run
away without looking.

In Suffolk, it was believed that if you buried a
handful of salt in the ground the ague would disappear, while in Devonshire, a leaf of tansy worn in
the shoe or pills made of spiders' webs, one taken
before breakfast for three successive mornings, were
regarded as excellent remedies.

Cross oaks, or oaks growing at the junction of cross-
roads, and spiders in particular, were accredited with
the power of curing ague.

Elias Ashmole, writing in his Diary on April 11th,
1681, says : " I took early in the morning a good
dose of Elixir and hung three spiders about my neck
and they drove my ague away. Deo Gratias."

In East Norfolk, a popular remedy was to take as
much snuff of a candle as would lie on a sixpence
and after mixing it with honey, swallow it at
bedtime.

In South Wales, many curious superstitions still
survive in connection with healing, some of which
have been recorded by Professor Gwynn Jones.
He tells us, that it is still a common belief that
shingles could be cured by certain persons blowing
on the affected parts, especially if the person who

performed the cure was descended from one who had eaten the flesh of an eagle.

In connection with this, it is interesting to note, that Dr. Thomas Beddoes, a well-known physician of the last century, believed that cow's breath had a beneficial effect in chest complaints, and in some parts of the country it is still believed that the breath of cattle is a specific in cases of consumption. To live over a shed where cows or goats were kept was considered to be beneficial to those suffering from tubercular disease.

In Cardiganshire, a disease of the heart or liver is said to be cured by drinking a decoction of saffron with other ingredients and the use of a piece of yarn. The method of treatment was for the sufferer to take a piece of steel from a smithy, a packet of saffron and a pint of old ale. A piece of the yarn was soaked in the beer, after the saffron and steel had been placed in it, and was then wound around the sufferer's wrist or leg and he had to drink the beer. If, on a second visit, the yarn was found to have lengthened, the patient would recover, if otherwise, he would die.

Persons suffering from epilepsy, which was commonly called " falling sickness," were often regarded as demoniacs and many charms are recorded for its cure. One which dates from the fourteenth century was as follows :

> " Gasper with his myrrh beganne
> These presents to unfold,
> Then Melchior brought in frankincense
> And Balthasar brought in gold.
> Now he that of these holie kings
> The names about shall beare,
> The Fallyng yll, by grace of Christ,
> Shall never need to feare."

" Every man or woman bearing this writing about them with good devotion saying every day three Paternosters, three Aves and one Credo, were assured that they should not be overcome of his enemies."

Another cure for the disease was to beg thirty pence from thirty poor widows and exchange them with a clergyman for half-a-crown taken from a Communion plate. Having accomplished this, the patient was bidden to walk nine times up and down the aisle of the church, then pierce the coin and hang it round his neck.

Coins of all kinds bearing the impression of a cross were worn round the necks of persons desiring a cure for " falling sickness," and certain tokens, called the "money of St. Helena," were considered especially efficacious.

In Berkshire, a ring made from a piece of silver collected at the Communion was believed to be a cure for fits and convulsions, and another variation of the charm, was to have " a ring made of five six-pences collected from five different bachelors, to be conveyed by the hand of a bachelor to a smith that is a bachelor, but none of the persons from whom the sixpences were obtained were to know for what purpose they were to be used."

Charms for the cure of fevers are very numerous and one which dates from the fourteenth century is as follows :

" I forbid the quaking fevers, the sea-fevers, the land-fevers, and all the fevers that ever God ordained; Out of the head, out of the heart, out of the back, out of the sides, out of the knees, out of the thies ; Frae the points of the fingers to the nebs of the taes ; Out sail the fevers go, some to the ill, some to the hope ; some to the stone ; some to the stock.

In St. Peter's name, St. Paul's name, and all the saints of Heaven ; In the name of the Father, the Son, and the Holy Ghost.''

Another of the same period is directed to be written on a laurel leaf and treated as follows :

FOR FEVER

" Wryt thys wordys on a lorell lef+Ysmael+ Ysmael+adjuro vos per angelum ut soporetetur iste Homo N. and ley thys lef under hys head that he wote not thereof, and let hym ete Letuse oft and drynk Ip'e seed small grounden in a morter, and temper yt with ale.''

For typhus fever, it was customary in some parts of the country to apply the " skirt " of a sheep to the soles of the feet, while in Norfolk they employed the spleen of a cow in a like manner with the idea of " drawing " the fever from the head.

For bleeding at the nose, in Norfolk, a skein of scarlet silk placed round the neck and tied with nine knots in the front was employed as a remedy. If the sufferer was a male the silk must be put on and the knots tied by a female, or vice versa.

Another charm was to repeat the words :

" Christ that was born in Bethlehem and was baptised in fludd Jordan, and water is mild, the Child is meeke and mild, as the flood so stood so stanch thou blood of this person and bleed no more, by the virtue of the Father, Son and Holy Ghost, obey to my bidding and stanch thou blood without any more delay. This, Lord's Prayer three times over, and this three times over, and the Creed in the latter end.''

Another favourite remedy was the application of the text taken from the sixteenth chapter of Ezekiel (6 v.) : "And when I passed by thee and saw thee polluted in thine own blood, I said unto thee when thou wast in thy blood, Live."

The dying words of our Lord, " It is finished," were likewise esteemed as a cure for bleeding at the nose, the application being made by writing them in the troubled person's own blood upon his forehead.

Of the many charms to cure coughs, great faith appears to have been placed in the " Judas-ear," a fungus found growing on elder stumps. Thus :

" For the cough take Judas Eare,
With the parynge of a Peare,
And drynke them without feare,
If you will have remedy ;
The syppes are for the hyckocke
And six more for the chyckocke
Thus my pretty pyckocke
Recover by and by."

In the northern counties, another cure was to shave the patient's head and hang the hair on a bush, whence birds carried it and the "cough" to their nests. In Devonshire and Northamptonshire, the procedure was varied by placing a hair from the patient's head between two slices of bread and butter which were given to a dog. Both of these cures are based on the ancient belief in the transferance of disease from man to an animal.

For whooping cough, that distressing ailment so common among children, the charms and remedies were many, and varied in different counties. In Cheshire, it was customary to hold a frog for a few minutes inside the child's mouth, while in Norfolk, the sufferer was made to drink some milk which a ferret had lapped. In Suffolk, some of the hair of the eldest child in the family was cut into small pieces then placed in milk and was given to those suffering from the cough. In other counties it was customary to pass the child three times under the stomach and three times over the back of a donkey, or to hold a spider over his head and say :

"Spider as you waste away,
Whooping cough no longer stay."

The spider had then to be placed in a bag and hung over the mantelpiece.

A method of curing croup and whooping cough common in the villages of Oxfordshire, was to go alone into the fields and find a branch of wild rose or blackberry which had bent to the ground and rooted like a bow. "Take the child nine mornings and pass it nine times through the arch and it will be cured."

Curing by passing a child through a cleft in a tree, was one of the most common methods of averting the evil decrees of Destiny, and symbolised the idea of being born again or re-entry into life and so effecting a physical change in the body.

Another remedy, which seems to partake of the nature of a water cure, was to gather nine star stones (quartz) from running water, taking great care not to interrupt the free passage of the water. In a quart of water taken from the stream, in the direction it runs, the stones, having been made red hot, were placed. The water was afterwards bottled and doled out to the sufferer, a wineglassful for nine mornings.

There were many popular charms to cure warts, and to cause them to disappear many believed it was only necessary to steal a piece of beef and rub it over the part and then throw it away. Other remedies were to rub the warts with eel's blood or to prick them with a thorn from a gooseberry bush.

One might also try the following : "When the moon is at the full, take an empty dish outside the door and go through the pretence of washing, then look to the moon and say ' In the name of Father, Son and Holy Ghost, I wish the wart away.' " Or again : " Take a string and make an equal number of knots to the warts, lay the string under a stone, and whoever treads on the stone will attach to himself the warts ! "

In Oxfordshire and Buckinghamshire, a popular charm to cure warts was to go out alone and find a black slug. Rub the underside on the warts and impale the slug on a thorn and as it dies the wart will disappear.

To dispel the ringworm, one or all of the following are recommended :

" Ringworm white
    Ringworm red,
    I command thou wilt not spread ;
    I divide thee to the east and west,
    Or the north and to the south,
    Arise in the name of the Father, Son, and Holy Ghost."

Another, was to let the person affected take a little ashes between the forefinger and thumb three successive mornings, before taking any food, and holding the ashes to the part affected, say :

" Ringworm, ringworm red !
    Never mayst thou spread or speed.
    But aye grow less and less
    And die away among the ase (ashes)."

A further charm was to put three sticks in the fire and when red hot, pass them round the ringworm, one after another, repeating the following words :

" Ringworm, ringworm, don't spring or spread any more ; go thee (thy) ways down to the dirt."

A cure for shingles used in Surrey was to procure the " coombe," a kind of lichen, that gathers on old bells exposed to the damp and rub the parts affected with it.

There is an ancient charm practised in Cornwall to heal a scald or burn, in which nine bramble leaves are to be gathered by the sufferer and put into a bowl of spring water. Each leaf is then to be passed over the affected part and the following lines repeated to each leaf :

> " Three ladies came from the East
> One with fire and two with frost.
> Out with thee fire and in with thee frost.'.

It is noticeable that many of the old charms, as they were passed from one county to another by word of mouth, became altered and so we find the same charm when used in Somersetshire was phrased as follows :

> " In the name of the Father, Son and Holy Ghost.
> There were three Angels came from East and West
> One brought Fire, and another brought Frost,
> And the third it was the Holy Ghost.
> Out Fire, in Frost, in the name of the Father, the Son, and
> of the Holy Ghost, Amen."

This form of words required a triple repetition, and at the end the part injured was blown over thrice.

For a sore caused by a burn the following charm was used :

> " Here comes I to cure a burnt sore ;
> If the dead knew what the living endure,
> The burnt sore would burn no more."

Here, likewise, the charmer blows his breath three times upon the burnt place.

The following charm for healing sores and gunshot wounds was much in vogue in Scotland in the early seventeenth century :

> " Thir sairs are risen through God's wark,
> And must be laid through God's help.
> The Mother Mary, and her dear Son,
> Lay thir sairs that are begun."

In some places, as at Marston St. Lawrence,
Northamptonshire, a notion was once prevalent that
rain on Holy Thursday (Ascension Day) was " holy
water " coming straight from Heaven, and so
possessed of a powerful efficacy, especially in all
diseases of the eyes.

For a sprain, it was customary to apply to an
individual practised in what was called " casting the
wrested thread." This thread was spun from black
wool, and nine knots being cast on it, it was tied
round the sprained leg or arm. While the operator
is thus employed, he mutters to himself in a manner
not to be understood by the bystanders, nor even by
the person he is operating upon, the following
doggerel :

> " The Lord rade (rode)
> And the foal slade (slipped)
> He lighted
> And she righted.
> Set joint to joint,
> Bone to bone,
> And sinew to sinew,
> Heal in the Holy Ghost's name."

In the West of England it was customary to pass
scrofulous children naked through the Men-an-tol, or
holy stone, on the down, near Lany and then draw a
grave three times against the sun, and it was said a
speedy cure was sure to follow. Children were also
wont to be passed through the hopper of a corn mill
for a cure of the whooping cough. The hag or holy
stone—a stone with a hole in it, suspended every
night at the head of the bed, was esteemed an excellent remedy for the nightmare, inasmuch as it prevented witches sitting upon the stomach, which was
thought to be the source of the complaint. Such a
stone tied to a stable key was believed to cure horses
and cattle of all manner of diseases.

In Cornwall, toads were worn as a charm against quinsy, fits and other diseases.

Another recipe for the cure of quinsy was to take some dust from the floor where the patient was, and having moistened it with spittle, to rub it on the neck.

Less obnoxious, but equally ineffectual were the powders, ointments and potions made of the scrapings of certain stones.

It is stated that in the Welsh churches of Penmynydd, a fourteenth-century tomb, and at Clynnog, the stone columns have been seriously damaged by the depredations of the inhabitants, who have scraped them away to use the scrapings as a cure for sore eyes. It is also on record that a piece of one of the statues adorning the west front of Exeter Cathedral, has been knocked off within the last half of the present century, with the view to its use (by a mixture with lard) as an ointment for the supposed cure of sores. As it was called Peter's stone it was probably the figure of that Saint which was thus mutilated.

A man is said to have walked from Teignmouth, a distance of at least eighteen miles, and to have flung stones at the figures until he brought down the arm of one of them to use for the same purpose.

St. Blaise is the patron saint of diseases of the throat and his martyrdom is celebrated on February 3rd, so to remove a bone that has stuck in the throat, the sufferer is adjoined to call upon God and remember St. Blaise. Another method of getting rid of a stoppage in the throat, was to " hold the suffering person by the throat and pronounce the words, ' Blaise, the martyr and servant of Jesus Christ commands thee to pass down '."

A ceremony called the " blessing of the throats " is still performed at St. Ethelreda's, Ely Place, Holborn, on February 3rd every year, with the invocation of the protection of St. Blaise, and is largely attended by persons suffering from throat ailments.

This traditional rite of early Italian origin, was introduced into England about a century ago by the Fathers of Charity. The sufferers come forward to the altar and while kneeling, lighted tapers are crossed under the chin of each, touching the throat, while the following prayer is repeated by the officiating priest : " By the intercession of the Blessed Virgin Mary, and through the merits of the Blessed Blaise, the martyr, may our Lord deliver you from all ills of the throat."

In Ireland at the present day the reading of a portion of the Gospel of St. John is esteemed an infallible cure for a sore throat. In fact, the reciting of the first fourteen verses of this Gospel, called " In Principio," from the opening words, was esteemed of singular and exceptional power in exorcising, in what has been called the demon-theory of disease. Accordingly, Durandus informs us " that a Gospel will expel a devil sua virtute, because devils hate nothing so much as a Gospel," while in the Life of St. Hugh, the Carthusian Bishop of Lincoln, we read of the practical application of the fact by his curing a demoniac by the reading of this chapter, " In Principio," over him.

Many superstitious customs are associated with cramp, a name which centuries ago was generally applied to severe pain, not only in the limbs but in any part of the body, and a complaint which appears to have been very common.

An everyday cure was to remove the sufferer's shoe and turn it upside down, then to rub the painful part while repeating the following words :

" I spread the pain in the name of the Father, and of the Son and of the Holy Ghost. If it is a pain, in the name of the Lord, I spread it out of the flesh, out of the sinews, out of the bones."

In Lancashire, placing the shoes at bedtime just peeping from beneath the coverlet or carrying a piece of sulphur in the pocket, was believed to prevent attacks of the painful malady.

From time immemorial, great faith has been placed in a ligature or garter tied round the limb to cure cramp in the leg, and in Cornwall, it was customary to use eel skins for this purpose. Another method of relieving the pain was to prick the part affected with a pin, then immediately light a candle and stick the pin into it. When the flame reached the pin the pain vanished, while another cure was to place the best poker under the bed at night before lying down.

A bone from a hare's foot was also credited with curative powers, and according to a couplet of the seventeenth century :

> " The bone of a haire's foote in a ring
> Will drive away cramp when as it doth wring."

From the time of Edward the Confessor, the English sovereigns were believed to have the power of procuring an efficacious blessing on certain rings which were worn as a cure for cramp.

Cramp rings were usually made of iron, lead or bronze, and some were believed to be specially efficacious if fashioned from the hinge, handle or nails from a coffin.

Royal cramp rings were blessed by the monarchs and made from the royal offerings to the Cross on Good Friday.

In the Constitutions of the Household of Edward II,

in 1318, there is the following record: "Likewise the King must for certain offer on Good Friday 5 shillings which he is accustomed to receive in person from the hand of the chaplain to make rings of them to give for medicine to divers persons."

Down to the time of Queen Mary, between 1553 and 1558, there was a regular office of the "Blessing of the Cramp rings" which took place on Good Friday, when the rings were brought to the Queen in two basins, and "taking

A CRAMP RING
*Fifteenth century.*

them in her hands she passed them from one hand to another repeating a form of prayer."

These rings were much sought after by sufferers from cramp, their efficacy no doubt depending on the faith of the wearer in the object so hallowed by the monarch.

For erysipelas, a piece of elder, on which the sun had never shone, when cut into little pieces and hung about the patient's neck, or sewed into his shirt, was regarded as a certain cure in the northern counties, while in the Highlands, one half of the ear of a cat was cut off and the blood allowed to drop on the affected part to stop the spread of the disease.

The folk-lore associated with hydrophobia is very extensive, and the liver of a male goat, the tail of a shrew mouse, the brain and comb of a cock, pounded ants and soup made from cuckoos, were but a few of the remedies employed.

In Devonshire, to cure the condition commonly called "a white swelling or white leg," to which women are subject, bandages are placed round the limb affected and while they are being rolled, the following charm is repeated nine times, each time being followed by the Lord's Prayer:

" As Christ was walking, He saw the Virgin Mary sitting on a cold marble stone.  He said unto her, ' If it is a white ill thing, or a red ill thing, or a black ill thing, or a sticking, crackling, pricking, stabbing, bone ill thing, or a sore ill thing, or a swelling ill thing, or a rotten ill thing, or a cold creeping ill thing, or a smarting ill thing, let it fall from thee to the earth in My name, and the name of the Father, Son and Holy Ghost.'  Amen."

Many other quaint charms might be enumerated, but those selected are sufficient to show how superstition was closely associated and intermixed with the art of healing among the people in times gone by.

# CHAPTER XIII

## THE FOLK-LORE OF FAMILIES—FATAL CURSES AND SPELLS

THERE are several old families in Great Britain, the members of which in times long since gone by, have been associated with terrible curses or spells. Some of these have been handed down for centuries by tradition, in connection with certain acts of injustice or great wrong supposed to have been perpetrated by an early ancestor.

Generally, such curses appear to have taken the form of the gradual extinction of the family name through the lack of male issue, an instance of which may be taken from the story of the old Scottish family the M'Alisters, which is told as follows :

Centuries ago, M'Alister Indre, one of their chiefs and a courageous fighter, during a fray with a neighbouring clan captured the two sons of a widow and hanged them out of hand before her door.

The heart-broken mother denounced the iniquitous act which was only laughed and scoffed at by the chief as he rode away.

But, says the narrator, as the crimson and setting rays of the sun fell on the lifeless bodies of her two sons, her eyes meeting those of M'Alister before he rode off, she cried in grief, " I suffer now but you shall suffer always. You have made me childless but you and yours shall be heirless for ever. Never shall there be a son to the house of M'Alister."

Burke observes, it was in the reign of Queen Anne

that the hopes of the house of M'Alister flourished for the last time and they were blighted for ever, for while espousing the cause of the Pretender the young heir of the family was taken prisoner and put to death.

He had secretly left his young wife and joined the army at Perth and he was the last hope of the house of M'Alister to carry on the line.

Sir Walter Scott in one of his ballads in the *Minstrelsy of the Scottish Border*, records the fateful story of the " Curse of Moy." The curse is said to have originated in a feud between the clans of Chattan and Grant.

The Castle of Moy, the early residence of Mackintosh, the chief of the clan, stands on the edge of a small gloomy lake called Loch Moy, among the mountains of Inverness-shire. Here, on a rocky island, is said to have been the dungeon in which prisoners taken by the former chiefs of Moy were confined.

One night, after a scene of great festivity to celebrate the birth of an heir, the poet relates that

> " In childbed lay the lady fair,
> But now is come the appointed hour,
> And vassals shout, ' An heir ! an heir ! ' "

The curse which had long lain over the House of Moy seemed at last about to be broken. Many years had passed without the prospect of such an event, and it was no wonder there was feasting and revelry in the gloomy towers of Moy. But just when the festivities were at their height, a mysterious, pale and shivering form suddenly appeared to the company who defiantly exclaimed, " 'Tis vain ! 'tis vain ! " All eyes were at once turned to the apparition, who with a mocking gesture cast a look of withering scorn on the frightened faces round her as she uttered the words, " No heir !  No heir ! "

Consternation ensued as the wraith with uplifted hand signified that she had a message to tell.

> " For the blast of Death is on the hearth,
> And the grave yawns wide for the child of Moy."

She then related a tale of treachery and cruelty committed by a chief of the House of Moy in earlier days, and how a curse had been put on the family that its name should perish for ever off the earth.

" A son may be born, but that son shall surely die," was the curse uttered by Margaret, who had been deceived and betrayed by a member of the family when he had violated his promise which he had solemnly pledged her, and thus she pronounced the fatal words of doom.

> " She pray'd that childless and forlorn,
> The chief of Moy might pine away,
> That the sleepless night and the careful morn,
> Might wither his limbs in slow decay.

> " But ne'er the son of a chief of Moy
> Might live to protect his father's age,
> Or close in peace his dying eye,
> Or gather his gloomy heritage."

This curse had been laid on the chief of Moy, who not content with slaying the girl's father and lover but had ravished her also.

The wraith departed and the revels of the frightened clan ceased, for " despair had seized on every breast."  The last hope of the House of Moy had gone, for :

> " Scarce shone the moon on the mountain's head
> When the lady wept o'er her dying boy."

Another curious spell called the " Idiots curse " was associated with the family of Barcroft in Lancashire.

According to tradition, one of the heirs was of weak intellect and was kept in chains by a younger brother in a dark cellar at Barcroft Hall. He was most cruelly treated and eventually starved to death. Long before his death, the younger brother who was determined to have the estate, had circulated a report that the real heir was dead and he made himself master of the Hall. But during one of his lucid intervals, the wretched prisoner pronounced a curse on his brother and his heirs, to the effect, that the name should perish for ever and that the property should pass out of the hands of the family.

The curse was fulfilled when Thomas Barcroft, who had starved his brother to death, died in 1688, without male issue and the estate passed into the hands of strangers.

The " Curse of Mar " goes back to a much earlier period and has been attributed to Thomas the Rhymer by some, and by others to the Abbot of Cambuskenneth, but in any case it is said to have been laid prior to the elevation of the Earl in 1571 to be the Regent of Scotland. It ran as follows :

" Proud chief of Mar, thou shalt be raised still higher, until thou sittest in the place of the king. Thou shalt rule and destroy and thy work shall be after thy name, but my work shall be the emblem of my house and shall teach mankind, that he who cruelly and haughtily raiseth himself upon the ruins of the holy cannot prosper.

" Thy work shall be cursed and shall never be finished. But thou shalt have riches and greatness, and shall be true to thy sovereign and shalt raise the banner in the field of blood. Then, when thou seemest to be highest, when thy power is mightiest, then shall come thy fall ; low shall be thy head amongst the nobles of the people. Deep shall be thy moan among the children of dool (sorrow). Thy lands shall be given to the stranger and thy titles shall be among the dead. The branch that springs from thee shall see his dwelling burnt in which a king is nursed—his wife a sacrifice in that same flame ; his children numerous but of little honour, and three born and grown who shall never see the light. Yet shall thine ancient tower stand ; for the brave and true cannot be wholly forsaken.

" Thou, proud head and daggered hand, must dree thy weird, until horses shall be stabled in thy hall and a weaver shall throw shuttle in thy Chamber of State. Thine ancient tower—a woman's dower— shall be a ruin and a beacon, until an ash sapling shall spring from its topmost stone. Then shall thy sorrows be ended and the sunshine of royalty shall beam on thee once more. Thine honours shall be restored, the kiss of peace shall be given to thy countess, though she seek it not, and the days of peace shall return to thee and thine.

" The line of Mar shall be broken but not until its honours are doubled and its doom is ended."

The main features of this prophetic utterance according to the chroniclers were thus fulfilled. In 1571, the Earl was raised to be Regent of Scotland and the guardian of James VI. As Regent, he commanded the destruction of Cambuskenneth Abbey and took its stones to build himself a palace at Stirling. It never advanced farther than the façade, which was popularly known as " Mar's work."

In 1715, the Earl of Mar raised the banner of his sovereign, the Chevalier James Stuart, son of James VII. He was defeated at the Battle of Sheriff-Muir, his title being forfeited and his lands of Mar

confiscated and sold by the Government to the Earl
of Fife. His grandson and representative, John
Francis, lived at Alloa Tower, where a fire breaking
out in one of the rooms, Mrs. Erskine was burnt and
died, leaving, besides others, three children who were
born blind and who lived to old age.

At the beginning of the nineteenth century, this
remarkable curse was to be further fulfilled, for
upon the alarm of the French invasion, a troop of
cavalry and yeomen of the district took possession
of the Tower and for a week fifty horses were
stabled in the great hall.

In the year 1810, a party of visitors were surprised
to find a weaver plying his loom in the grand old
Chamber of State.

Between the years 1815 and 1820, an ash sapling
might have been seen on the topmost stone of the
building, and many of those who " clasped it in
their hands wondered if it really was the ' twig
of Destiny' and if they should ever live to see the
prophecy fulfilled."

In the year 1822, George IV visited Scotland and
sought out the families who had suffered by sup-
porting the Prince of the Stuart line. Foremost of
all was the Erskine of Mar, grandson of Mar who
had raised the Chevalier's standard, and to him the
King restored the Earldom.

John Francis, the grandson of the restored Earl,
likewise came into favour, for when Queen Victoria
accidentally met his Countess in a small room in
Stirling Castle and ascertained who she was, she
detained her and after conversing with her, kissed
her.

Although the Countess had never been presented
at St. James's, yet in this remarkable way, " the

kiss of peace was given to her, though she sought it not."

Thus, after the curse had worked through three hundred years, the " weird dreed out and the doom of Mar was ended."

Another strange curse was associated with Sherborne Castle.[1]

Tradition states that Osmund, one of the knights of William the Conqueror, who had been given the castle and barony of Sherborne as a reward, in the decline of his life determined to give up his temporal honours and devote himself to religion.

With this object he obtained the Bishopric of Salisbury to which he gave certain lands, but annexed to the gift the following conditions : " Whosoever shuold take those lands from the Bishopric or diminish them in great or small, should be accursed, not only in this world but in the world to come, unless in his lifetime he made restitution thereof."

This curse was fulfilled more than once in an extraordinary way.

Upon Osmund's death, the Castle and lands fell into the hands of the next Bishop, Roger Niger, who was deprived of them by King Stephen. On his death they were held by the Montagues, all of whom, as long as they kept the lands, were subject to grievous disasters, and in the end the male line became extinct.

Two hundred years later, the lands reverted to the Church, but in the reign of Edward VI, the Castle of Sherborne was conveyed by the then Bishop of Sarum to the Duke of Somerset who was afterwards beheaded on Tower Hill.

Sir Walter Raleigh then obtained the property

[1] " Family Romance "—Sir J. Bernard Burke, 1835.

from the Crown and he ultimately lost his head.
Prince Henry then took possession but died shortly
afterwards and Carr, Earl of Somerset, the next
holder, fell into disgrace.

The latter, having discovered a technical flaw in
the deeds in which Raleigh had settled the estate
on his son, he solicited it and obtained it. When
Lady Raleigh appealed to King James against the
injustice, the only answer she could get was, " I
mun have the land. I mun have it for Carr."

Lady Raleigh then fell on her knees before the
King, and prayed to God that He would punish
those who had thus wrongfully exposed her and her
children to ruin, thus re-echoing the curse that had
been uttered centuries before, and so it proved.

Carr did not enjoy the possession of Sherborne
for long, for he was committed to the Tower for
the murder of Sir Thomas Overbury, but when
released later, he was restricted to his house in the
country, where, in constant companionship with the
wife for the guilty love of whom he had murdered
his friend, he passed the remainder of his life.

Cowdray Castle, the principal seat of the Montagues, was given by Henry VIII to Sir Anthony
Browne, his standard-bearer. At a great festival
given in the great hall of the monks of Battle Abbey
on Sir Anthony taking possession of the estate,
it is said that a venerable monk stalked up the
hall to the dais where the knight sat. There he
denounced him and his posterity for usurping, the
possessions of the Church, predicting their destruction by fire and water, a fate which was eventually
fulfilled. One of the last Viscounts was drowned in
1793, and about the same time Cowdray Castle was
destroyed by fire. Curiously enough since then,

Battle Abbey, which a few years ago was occupied as a girl's school, was burnt out.

Another curse associated with the name of one of the supporters of the Stuart cause concerned Colonel Stephen Payne, who took a prominent part in striving to uphold their fortunes, and had wooed and won his wife amid the battles of the Rebellion.

The Duke of York had promised to stand god-father to their first child if it should prove a boy, but when a daughter was born instead, the Colonel, in a rage, is said " to have formally devoted in succession his hapless wife, his infant daughter, himself and his belongings, to the devil."

According to the story, the midwife, Douce Vardon, announced to her master, that not only would his daughter die in infancy, but that neither he nor anyone descended from him would ever again be blessed with a daughter's love.

A few days afterwards, the child, whose involuntary coming had been the cause of the " Payne curse," died. When at length a son was born to the family, he was sponsored by the Duke of York by proxy. " But," says the narrator, " six generations of the descendants of Colonel Payne have come and gone since the utterance of the midwife's curse and they have never yet had a daughter born to them."

Scottish families in particular appear to have been destined to suffer from curses, and another may be instanced in one that is supposed to be associated with the Lairds of Fyvie.

Some time prior to the thirteenth century, a chief of the clan seized and appropriated certain lands that belonged to the Church, upon which, the

following curse, said to have been recorded by
Thomas the Rhymer of Erceldoune, was put on the
family :

> " Fynin's riggs and towers,
> Hapless shall your mesdames be,
> When you shall hae within your bounds,
> From harryit (pillaged) kirlands stanes three . . .
> Ane in the oldest tower,
> Ane in my ladie's bower,
> And ane below the water's yett,
> And it ye shall never get."

Thus, since the ancient curse that Fyvie should
not descend in the male line, but few sons have been
born to the Lairds of Fyvie.

The estate passed from the Gordon to the Forbes-
Leith family, and in 1901 the first Lord Leith lost
his only son in the Boer War.

There are said to be three " weeping " stones,
one in the castle, one in the River Ythan which
flows beneath the castle, and the third elsewhere,
and until these three are brought together it is said
the curse will persist.

In Cumberland, the story of the " Quaker's
curse," which has come down from the seventeenth
century, is still told.

It concerns one Francis Howgill, a noted Quaker,
who was accustomed to travel about the country
preaching and by his inflammatory language caused
serious rioting to break out at Bristol.

On his return to Kendal where he belonged, he
was committed to Appleby gaol for refusing to take
the Oath of Allegiance. During his imprisonment, he
was permitted by the magistrates to visit his home
at Grayrigg on private affairs, and while there called
on a Justice of the Peace named Duckett who lived
at Grayrigg Hall. He was a well-known persecutor

of the Quakers and was instrumental in committing Howgill to gaol.

The magistrate was surprised at Howgill's visit and remarked " What is your wish now, Francis ? I thought you were in Appleby gaol."

" No," replied Howgill, " I am not but I am come with a message from the Lord. Thou hast persecuted the Lord's people but His hand is now against thee, and He will send a blast upon all thou hast, and thy name shall rot out of the earth and this thy dwelling shall become desolate and a habitation for owls and jackdaws."

By a strange coincidence, Howgill's prophecy or curse was fulfilled, for all Mr. Duckett's children died without leaving any issue, and some of them became so poor they had to beg from door to door.

Grayrigg Hall, which passed into the hands of the Lowther family, fell into ruin and only its extensive foundations were left in 1777 and they became the home of " owls and jackdaws."

Later, even the old stones of the place were removed and a farmhouse was built on the site of the dwelling, which according to the " Quaker's curse " had become desolate and blasted.

That it was thought such curses could be removed, is evident from the following invocation culled from a manuscript of the fifteenth century now in the Bodleian Library :

" To relieve one who has been cursed.

" Say, in the name of God ye father, and his Son the Holy Ghost three persons one Trinity, is to comfort one of the ill-worked on my body, that has disturbed my body with evill payne from the wickedness. In the name of God. Amen."

# CHAPTER XIV

## THE FOLK-LORE OF DEATH AND BURIAL

**M**ANY curious superstitions and customs have been associated with the final stages of life from remote times, for the mystery attached to death has ever evoked a certain sense of fear and dread among human beings.

The idea underlying such omens, signs and portents, appears to have been derived from the early belief, that the gods in some manner or other, at times, revealed to man an indication of future happenings.

This knowledge to a certain degree was at first confined to soothsayers and magicians, but as time went on, it became popular property and traces of it are still to be found in the folk-lore of the people.

Prognostications or omens of approaching death or fatalities are common to all races, for it can be readily understood, that the mind when racked with anxiety through the presence of sickness or impending death, becomes over-sensitive to sounds and sights.

Thus it was thought that the howling of a dog at night was owing to his being conscious of spirits hovering around a house, ready at the moment of death, to bear away the soul of the departed.

The falling of an old tree, cocks crowing in the night, the neighing of a horse at night-time and birds flying against a window, were all regarded as omens of death.

In some parts of the country, if an ox or a cow breaks into a garden, it is thought to be an omen of death, and in Scotland when anyone is dangerously ill and unlikely to recover, it is a common saying, " The black ox has trampled upon him."

In Lancashire there is a popular notion, that to build or even to rebuild a house is always fatal to some member of the family, and generally the one who may have been the principal designer of the plans of the building.

This idea appears to have arisen from the belief that if a man once started on a building his life would cease when it was completed.

In connection with this, the story is told of the owner of an estate in Wales who firmly believed that if building work on it stopped, his life would come to an end. He therefore started to build a huge wall around his park and kept men employed on it for years so that the work should not cease. One winter, there was a long and heavy frost which prevented the men from continuing with their job, and before they could resume their labours the old proprietor of the estate died.

There was an early belief in the existence of the power of prophecy at a period which precedes death. This idea probably took its origin in the supposed fact, that the soul became divine in the same rate as the connection with the body was loosened. " At the hour of death the soul is in the confines of two worlds and may possibly at the same time possess a power which is both prospective and retrospective."

Shakespeare shows his acquaintance with the belief in *Richard II* (Act II, Sc. 1) when he makes the dying Gaunt, in alluding to his nephew, exclaim :

> " Methink I am a prophet new inspired,
> And thus expiring do foretell of him."

He makes a further reference to it in *Henry IV*, Part I (Act V, Sc. 4), when the dying Percy says:

"O! I could prophesy,
But that the earthy and cold hand of death
Lies on my tongue."

The ancient Hebrews apparently held this belief, for we read in Genesis (Chap. xlix) how Jacob called his sons and said, " Gather yourselves together, that I may tell you that which shall befall you in the last days. And when Jacob had made an end of commanding his sons, he gathered up his feet into his bed and yielded up the ghost and was gathered unto his people."

In Lancashire and other parts of the North of England, this power of foretelling before death is still believed by many country folk.

The tolling of the Passing- or Soul-bell as it is sometimes called, is said to date from about the seventh or eighth century. According to an Ordinance made in the seventh year of the reign of Queen Elizabeth, " When anye Christian bodie is in passing, that the bell be tolled and that the curate be speciallie called for to comforte the sicke person ; and after the time of his passinge to ringe no more, but one shorte peale ; and one before the buriall and another shorte peale after the buriall."

The origin of the Passing-bell is said by some to have been intended to drive away any demon that might seek to take possession of the soul of the deceased, but Grose declares " it was anciently rung for two purposes ; one to bespeak the prayers of all good Christians for a soul just departing ; the other to drive away the evil spirits who stood at the bed's foot and about the house, ready to seize their prey or at least to molest and terrify the soul in its passage."

The ancient custom of watching the body after death, called in the North of England the " Lake-wake," is said to have originated from the idea that it might be carried off by some of the agents of the invisible world, or exposed to the danger of prowling animals. Later, it degenerated in Ireland and the North of Scotland into an orgy with feasting, dancing and drinking, till, says Maria Edgeworth, " In Ireland the Wake was but a midnight meeting, held professedly for the indulgence of holy sorrow but usually is converted into orgies of unholy joy."

In Scotland and some parts of Northumberland it was customary to place a pewter plate of salt on the breast of the dead person or sometimes salt and earth, the latter being regarded as an emblem of the corruptible body and the salt as a symbol of the immortal spirit.

In Leicestershire, the salt is said to be used with the idea of preventing air getting into the body and so causing it to swell, as well as to prevent putrefaction.

Herrick alludes to this belief in his *Hesperides* in the following lines :

" The Body's salt the Soule is, which when gone,
The flesh soone sucks in putrifaction."

There has long been a belief in some of the northern coast towns, that deaths mostly occur during the ebbing of the tide, and observations were carried out some years ago in a seaport, with the object of finding out if there was any truth in the tradition or not, but the results were found to be negative.

Dickens alludes to the belief in *David Copperfield*,

when Mr. Peggotty remarks to the dying Barkis,
" People can't die along the coast except when the
tide's pretty nigh out."

" He's a going out with the tide—he's a going
out with the tide."

The ancient Greeks buried their dead from east
to west, a custom which was afterwards carried out
by the Christians, but in some parts of the country
there is a strong prejudice against burial " without
the sanctuary," that meaning the north side of the
church or in a remote corner of the churchyard.
This idea is said to have arisen from the former
custom of setting apart the northern part of a
churchyard for the interment of unbaptised infants,
excommunicated persons and suicides.

Moresin says, " Those who had suffered capital
punishment, laid violent hands on themselves or
the like, were buried towards the north ; a custom
that had formerly been of frequent use in Scotland."

There is a peculiar idea said to be still prevalent
in Norfolk and East Anglia, that if the dead body
of a person has been carried across private land,
there is ever afterwards a public right of way.

In Yorkshire it was customary for mourners to
stick a pin in each private gate through which they
passed in order to pay toll to the landlord.

There is a curious old custom which it is said
still survives in some parts of Wales, Herefordshire
and Shropshire, arising from the belief, that sin
could be transferred from the original sinner after
death to another person. For this purpose, certain
poor people known as " Sin-eaters " were hired for
small sums to attend at funerals. The relations of
the dead prepared the sin-eater a meal on the coffin,
and he was thus supposed to eat the sins of the

deceased and so to make his journey in the other world easier.

In connection with this custom, Bagford, in a letter printed in Leland's *Collectanea* in 1714, states : " Within the memory of our fathers in Shropshire, in those villages adjoyning Wales, when a person dyed, there was notice given to an old Sire (for so they called him) who presently repaired to the place where the deceased lay, and stood before the door of the house, when some of the family came out and furnished him with a cricket on which he sat down facing the door. Then they gave him a groat, which he put in his pocket ; a crust of bread which he ate, and a full bowle of ale which he drank off at a draught. After this he got up from the cricket and pronounced with a composed gesture, the ease and rest of the soul departed, for which he would pawn his own soul."

In another account recorded in a manuscript in the British Museum, the " Sin-eater " is described as a " Long, leane, ugly, lamentable poor raskal. When the body was brought out of the house and layd on the bier, a loafe of bread was brought out and delivered to the sinne eater over the corpse, as also a mazar bowle of maple full of beer which he was to drinke up and sixpence in money ; in consideration whereof he took upon him, *ipso facto*, all the sinnes of the defunct and freed, him or her, from walking after they were dead. This custome alludes methinks, something to the scape goate in the old Jewish laws who should bear upon him the iniquities of the Children of Israel unto a land not inhabited."

Aubrey mentions a woman in Hereford, who for many years before her death, kept a " mazard bowle for the Sinne-eater."

Certain birds, such as the raven with its raucous croak, the crow and the swallow, are said to presage misfortune and death, while the owl and the magpie have also evil reputations. Some declare that if one hears the cuckoo's first note when in bed, bad luck is sure to await the hearer or his family, and to catch a sparrow and to keep it confined in a cage is also said to bring misfortune to a house.

Certain fruit trees and plants are also associated with death omens.

Thus, when an apple or pear-tree blooms twice in the year, it is said to forecast a death in the family, and if green broom is gathered when in bloom, it is a sign that the father or mother will die within the course of the year.

In Yorkshire, should a child gather germander, speedwell or eye-bright, it is believed that its mother will die during the year, while to bring the first snowdrop of the year into a house is said to cause bad luck to those who live in it. To dream that a tree is uprooted in one's garden is regarded as a death warning to the owner, and if a branch of yew is accidentally brought into a house at Christmas, it is looked upon as an augury that a death will occur in the family before the end of the year.

The yew is called by Shakespeare in *Richard II*, " the double fatal yew, because its leaves are poisonous and its wood is employed for instruments of death," thus alluding to the tradition, that yews were planted in churchyards for the purpose of furnishing bow-staves and arrows for the archers who made the English dreaded in the battles of the Middle Ages, and that its leaves, when eaten, often prove fatal to cattle.

# CHAPTER XV

## THE FOLK-LORE OF SKULLS AND BONES

THE strange and curious lore associated with skulls and bones is chiefly connected with their use in folk-medicine, although with the former there are also some legends of a peculiarly ghostly character. Certain bones, like the astragalus of the hare, were not only carried in the pocket as a charm against rheumatism, but when powdered were also swallowed with water for their diuretic properties. The knuckle-bone of the sheep was credited with the same virtues, while the foot-bones of a pig in some parts of the country were worn to prevent rheumatism.

The bone of a stag's heart, a white irregular piece of bone sometimes found in the heart of the hart or an ox, which often took the shape of a cross, was used as a remedy in heart troubles and was also given to women to prevent abortion. The jaw-bone of a pike, after being dried and powdered, was given to cure leucorrhœa and was also said to facilitate and give an easy childbirth.

Certain fish bones like the " whale's ear stone," a bone said to be found near the ear of a whale, were believed to possess peculiar remedial properties, while the spine of the lamprey and lizard's bones made into a kind of broth, were given to children to strengthen their bones.

The blade-bone of a sheep has been used for divination from a period of great antiquity and in

Persia and Turkestan it is still employed for that purpose.

One method of practising it, is to put the shoulder-blade of a sheep on the fire until it cracks in various directions. When it is cool it is carefully scrutinised, and a long split, length-wise, is reckoned as the " way of life," while good or evil fortune is indicated by the cross cracks on the right and the left.

In Scotland, for divination, the blade-bone when stripped is carefully inspected for any spots that may be seen in the semi-transparent part of the bone, and the discovery of a dark one is said to signify misfortune, while a black one is believed to foretell death.

Camden alludes to the practice in Ireland and says, " The Irish look through a blade-bone of a sheep and if they see any spot in it darker than ordinary, it foretells that somebody will be burned out of the house."

Drayton observes in his *Polyolbion*, " By th' shoulder-blade of a ram from off the right side par'd, which usually they boile, the spade-bone being bar'd, which when the wizard takes and gazes thereupon ; things long to come foreshows, as things long agone."

Pepys mentions in his *Diary*, that he wore a hare's foot to avert the plague, and seems to have placed more faith in the amulet than in all the vaunted remedies that were recommended for that terrible scourge.

The popular custom of two people " wishing " on linking their little fingers, probably arose from the same idea as that of breaking the wishing-bone of a fowl.

In the sixteenth and seventeenth centuries, nearly

every part of the human frame was employed in medicine, from the skull and the moss that grew upon it, to the nails from the fingers and toes.

Bechler in his *Parnassus Medicinalis*, 1663, tells us, that " Powdered human bone in red wine will cure dysentery. The marrow and oil distilled from bone is good for rheumatism. Prepared human skull is a sure cure for the falling sickness. Moss grown on a human skull is a hæmostatic and human fat properly rubbed into the skin restores weak limbs ; the wearing of a belt of human skin facilitates labour and mitigates pain, while water distilled from human hair and mixed with honey promotes its growth and prevents baldness."

The Spirit of Human Skull was highly prized as a remedy for epilepsy, especially when it was prepared from " the unburied skulls of criminals." Charas, a French chemist who lived for some time in England about the middle of the seventeenth century, says, " The London druggists sell skulls of the dead upon which there has grown a little greenish moss called Usnea, because it resembles the moss which grows on the oak. These skulls mostly come from Ireland, where they frequently let the bodies of criminals hang on the gibbet till they fall to pieces."

The market-price of skulls in London varied in his time from eight to eleven shillings each.

In making certain preparations, it was important that the skulls used should be those of persons who had died a violent death. Thus we find in a recipe to make the *Magistry of Human Skull*, written in 1738, it is directed to " Calcine the skull and powder finely but the Magistry is only a dead head of no virtue unless you employ the skull of a young man who died a violent death."

Culpepper, quoting from Paracelsus, states, that the " small triangular bone in the skull of a man called *Os Triquetum* so absolutely cures the Falling Sickness that it will never come again."

Human skulls and bones were prepared in various ways for use in medicine. Sometimes they were calcined and administered in powder and given in cases of dysentery, while the marrow and oil extracted from them were employed as an embrocation for rheumatism.

The Spirit or Essence of Human Skull, which was prepared by distillation from broken pieces or filings of the bone and spirit of wine and sage, has a place in history, for Charles II who devoted his leisure to experiments in chemistry in his laboratory at Whitehall, was greatly interested in it.

He is said to have purchased the secret of its preparation from a Doctor Goddard for a sum of £1500. Goddard who was professor of physics at Gresham College called it " Goddard's Drops," but it was afterwards often known as " King Charles' " or the " English Drops."

When Dr. Martin Lister was in Paris in 1698, he was summoned by the Prince of Conti to see his son and was requested to bring with him some of " King Charles' Drops," which were regarded as a specific for the disease from which he was suffering.

Curiously enough, the Spirit of Human Skull was one of the last remedies to be administered to the King in his fatal illness, for when all others had failed, the thirteen doctors in attendance ordered forty drops of the famous panacea in which he was so interested, to be given to the dying monarch.

The fundamental idea underlying the belief in the remedial virtues of these substances was, that the principal parts and organs of the human body were furnished with a volatile salt, which when separated out by distillation, possessed properties capable of healing many of the diseases to which man was liable.

Paracelsus, the famous physician of the sixteenth century, devised a preparation of skulls as a remedy for epilepsy which he called *Confectio Anti-Epileptica* and directed it to be made as follows.

Three human skulls were to be taken from men who had died violent deaths and had not been buried. These were to be dried in the air, reduced to coarse powder and gradually heated in a retort. After being distilled three times, eight ounces of the distillate were to be mixed with three drachms each of musk, castoreum and honey and again distilled. To the resulting liquid, four scruples of liquor of pearls and one scruple of oil of vitriol were to be added, and of this one spoonful was recommended to be taken in the morning, fasting, by those suffering from epilepsy.

The connection of the skull with epilepsy or " falling sickness," which was at that time attributed to the brain, is obvious.

In several parts of the country, certain skulls have long been preserved which, according to tradition, have peculiar supernatural powers. Some of them are said to emit screams if any attempt is made to bury them, or should they be removed from their habitations, terrible consequences ensue.

One still preserved at Wardley Hall, Worsley, an ancient house about seven miles from Manchester, is usually kept in a little locked recess in the staircase wall and the occupiers of the building will never allow it to be removed. It is said to invariably

punish the individual who dares to even attempt to
remove it and according to tradition, when it has
been removed and thrown in the neighbouring pond
or buried, it was sure to return, so that in the end,
each succeeding tenant of the house was fain to
endure its presence rather than to be subject to
the terrors and annoyances consequent upon its
removal.

There are two stories concerning the origin of this
gruesome relic which are worth quoting. One states,
that it is the skull of one Roger Downes whose
family lived at Wardley, and who is described as
being one of the most dissolute frequenters of the
Court of Charles II. He is said to have been killed
in a drunken brawl on London Bridge, his head
being severed from his body by a watchman with
a bill. The body was thrown into the Thames
but the head was packed in a box and sent as a
*memento mori* to his sister at Wardley, where it has
been kept ever since and none of the later tenants
have been allowed to remove it.

Roby in his *Traditions of Lancashire* after relating
the story, says, " the skull was removed secretly at
first but it invariably returned to the Hall and no
human power could drive it thence. It hath been
riven to pieces, burnt and otherwise destroyed, but
on the subsequent day it was seen filling its wonted
place."

Thomas Barritt, a Manchester antiquary of the
last century, who paid a visit to the skull says :
" Some years ago, I and three of my acquaintances
went to view it and found it bleached white with
weather that beats in upon it from a four square
window in the hall. The tenants never permit it to
to be glazed or filled up. Time out of mind hath a

superstitious veneration been paid to it, and there is a tradition, that if removed or ill-used some uncommon noise and disturbance always follows to the terror of the whole house.

" However, one of us who was last in company with the skull, removed it from its place into a dark part of the room and then left it and returned home.

" The night but one following, such a storm arose about the house of wind and lightning as tore down some trees. We hearing of this, my father went over in a few days to witness the wreckage the storm had made. Yet all this might have happened had the skull never been removed."

Another and more authentic story is related by H. Vaughan Hart-Davis in his *History of Wardley Hall*, who states, that the skull cannot have been that of Roger Downes as he was buried in the family vault at Wigan in 1676. The coffin was opened about the end of the eighteenth century and his skeleton was found in perfect condition, with the exception of the skull, the upper portion of which had apparently been sawn off just above the eyes.

He believes that the skull, still preserved in a niche on the staircase landing at the Hall, to be that of Edward Ambrose Barlow, a Benedictine monk, who ministered as a priest in private and secret in the chapels of Wardley and Morley.

When preaching in the private chapel at Morley Hall on Easter Sunday, April 26th, 1641, the place was besieged by a Protestant mob armed with clubs and swords, and Barlow was made a prisoner and sent with an escort of sixty armed men to Lancaster.

Having confessed to his priesthood, he was

sentenced to be hanged, drawn and quartered, which sentence was duly carried out on the 10th of September. Francis Downes of Wardley Hall, a fervent Roman Catholic, secretly secured the head which had been impaled at Lancaster Castle and hid it.

In 1745, Matthew Morton, a later tenant of the Hall, while making some internal alterations in the building, discovered a box hidden in a wall which contained the skull which he kept in an upper room, and since then it has been carefully preserved on the staircase.

The weird stories that were afterwards woven round the relic, are said to have been due to the act of a servant who when cleaning the place where the skull was kept, and thinking it was useless, threw it out of the window into the moat.

The same night, a terrible storm arose and the master of the house attributed it to the indignity done to the skull, so he at once had the moat drained and the skull recovered and returned to its place where it yet remains.

Another skull to which strange traditions are attached, is preserved in an old farmstead called Bettiscombe House in Dorsetshire. This skull, which is said to be that of a negro, a faithful servant of an early possessor of the property who had lived abroad, is believed to have extraordinary powers.

According to one story, when it is removed from the house, the building itself rocks to its foundations and the person who takes it away will certainly die within a year. If any attempt is made to bury it, the skull is said to give forth terrible screams and for this reason it has long been known locally as the "Screaming Skull." Various tenants have occupied the house and although the furniture has been changed again and again, the skull still remains a grim inhabitant of the house.

Another story states that the negro servant was murdered, but declared before his death, that if his body was not taken to his native land for burial, his spirit would never rest. This was not carried out and after he was buried in the churchyard at Bettiscombe the trouble began.

Terrible screams were heard proceeding from the grave, the doors and windows of the house rattled and creaked, strange sounds were heard and there was no rest in the place until the body was exhumed.

Several attempts were afterwards made to re-inter the negro's remains but directly this was done, the disturbances and noises began again.

In the course of time most of the bones disappeared until nothing but the skull was left, which was kept in the house a relic of the grim tradition.

A visitor who saw it in 1883, states, she "climbed the fine old staircase till she reached the top of the house, when inside a cupboard near the roof, she saw the skull grinning at her. It was very old and weather-beaten and certainly human. The lower jaw was missing and the forehead was very low and badly proportioned."

In an old farmhouse at Tunstead near Chapel-en-le-Frith in Derbyshire, another curious skull is preserved which is locally called "Dickie."

John Hutchinson writing in 1809 of its "very singular pranks and services," says, "It is believed that if the skull be removed from the house every thing on the farm will go wrong ; the cows will be dry and barren, the sheep will have the rot, the horses will fall down and break their knees and other misfortunes will happen. Hundreds of the inhabitants of the locality for miles round have full and firm faith in its mystical performances."

He traced the skull to have been on the premises for nearly two centuries during all the revolutions of owners and tenants in that time.

There is a local tradition, that the skull is that of a young woman of wealth, a co-heiress, who lived in the district centuries ago. She was murdered and in her dying moments declared that her bones should ever remain in the place.

"Twice within the memory of man," says Hutchinson, "the skull has been taken from the premises; once on building the present house on the site of the old one, and another time when an attempt was made to bury it in Chapel churchyard. But there was no peace nor rest! It had to be re-placed."

There is a farmhouse near Turton Tower in Lancashire known as "Timberbottom" or "The Skull House," which became the abiding place of two skulls, for there was a tradition that if any attempt was made to remove them, the tenants would never have peace.

Many years ago, they are said to have been buried in the graveyard at Bradshaw Chapel, but they have always had to be exhumed and restored to their place in the farmhouse. At one time, an effort was made to get rid of them by throwing them into the adjacent river, but all to no purpose, for they had to be fished up and returned to their old quarters before the spirits of their owners would rest in peace.

Yet another skull with similar traditions was the preserved at Burton Agnes Hall in the East Riding of Yorkshire. It is said to have been the skull of Anne

Griffiths, the daughter of Sir Henry Griffiths, who was in possession of the Hall in the time of Queen Elizabeth.

Anne, with her two sisters, were co-heiresses of estate, and one night when walking in the grounds, she was attacked by two ruffians and so maltreated that she died from the injuries she received. In her last moments, she implored her sisters to have her head severed from her body after death and to preserve it within the walls of her home ever afterwards.

" Never let it be removed," she begged, " and if my desire is not fulfilled, my spirit shall render the house unhabitable for human beings."

Her body, however, was interred in the churchyard and soon afterwards extraordinary happenings occurred in the Hall, while inexplicable noises, groans and shrieks that went on nightly made sleep impossible for the inmates.

After a time, the sisters consulted the vicar and told him the story, and he advised that the grave should be opened and the head removed and brought to the Hall. When this had been done, all the noises ceased and quietness was restored.

There is a story that a later owner of the Hall, desirous of getting rid of the relic, had it buried in the garden. Upon its removal, however, everything went wrong on the estate and it was eventually dug up again and restored to its place in a cupboard and walled in, after which all is said to have gone well, and " no longer were dismal cries heard in the night nor accidents take place at day."

At Higher Chilton Farm at Chilton Cantelo in Somersetshire, the skull of a former owner named Theophilus Brome, who died in 1670, is preserved, although his body is buried in the churchyard. It is said that when any attempt has been made to bury it or if it is removed, strange and unaccountable noises are heard in the house.[1]

It is difficult to account for the origin of these strange legends so curiously alike, but it is significant that, according to the traditions, the owners of the skulls mostly died violent deaths, and the idea that the restless spirit of a murdered person would return to disturb the living if their dying wishes had not been complied with, goes back for thousands of years.

[1] Further particulars of these and other curious skulls will be found in *The Mystery and Lure of Apparitions*. C. J. S. Thompson, London, 1930.

# CHAPTER XVI

## THE FOLK-LORE OF SAILORS AND FISHERMEN

FEW occupations are associated with more superstitious beliefs than that of the sailor, and all round our coasts among the fisher-folk, some curious customs connected with the craft still survive.

Sailors are firm believers in omens of good or bad import. Among those that presage misfortune are the loss of a water-bucket or a mop when at sea, and to sneeze on the left side of the vessel is regarded as a very bad omen.

On the east coast of Scotland, at the beginning of the herring season, the crew of the boat try to seize the first herring drawn on board to see if it is male or female. If it is a female, it is said to be a good omen for the season, but on the other hand, should it be a male, it is believed to be a bad one.

If some one calls after a fisherman as he is leaving his cottage for his boat, it will bring him bad luck, and similar misfortune is augured should anyone cross his path. Should either of these incidents happen, it is customary to make a cross on the ground with a knife and spit on it while uttering a charm to avert the evil.

In the Island of Lewis it was formerly a custom to offer a sacrifice to a sea deity named " Shoney " to ensure good fishing, and in the Firth of Forth, if anyone cried to a fisherman " Brounger's in your headsheets," as he was starting out, he would strongly resent it and in former times would have turned his boat three times round in the water to avert the omen, as " Brounger was believed to be the god of the storm and tempest."

When a fishing boat is being built it is customary to nail a horseshoe or a small piece of rowan tree into it to avert the evil influence of witches. It is considered unlucky to break up an old boat and although a vessel may have been wrecked and cast ashore, it is often allowed to lie and go to pieces on this account.

Scottish fishermen say it is unlucky to meet a minister on the way to their boats and they have great aversion to taking a parson on board their craft. They also have a strong dislike to pigs, hares and rabbits, and as an antidote to the bad luck they are supposed to bring, they shout " Cold iron " or take hold of some iron implement at once.

Whistling is always supposed to be followed by wind and in this belief, fishermen's wives are careful not to blow the meal off any oatcake they may be baking, if they wish to avoid a hurricane which may blow their husbands' boats out to sea.

The lowing of a cow heard after the setting of the nets is considered an ill omen, and sometimes they are drawn up and re-set to avert the evil.

On some parts of the coast it was formerly a common custom to stick a coin into a cork-float or into the beam of a trawl, as a sacrifice to the " sea god " to bring good fishing, and the first fish of the season was always nailed to the mast as a thank-offering if success resulted.

It is said that some American sailors will never start on a voyage unless there is a mascot of some kind on board, such as a monkey or an animal of one kind or another.

It is considered lucky to carry a little salt in the pocket when embarking on a voyage, and in the Isle of Man a sailor will rarely go aboard his ship without his salt.

In former times, English sailors are said to have attributed some peculiar virtue to the third wave, which makes the loudest noise, but they dreaded the ninth wave and made the sign of the cross when they saw it.

Anything in the shape of a heart was esteemed as a charm by sailors, as it was believed to avert the tempests and storms caused by demons. Thus, when starting on a voyage a wife or sweetheart often presented her man with a heart-shaped pin-cushion,

A HEART CUT OUT OF A PIECE OF BROWN CLOTH STUCK WITH PINS AND NAIL-PARINGS FOUND AT WESTMINSTER
*Pitt-Rivers Museum.*

stuck full of pins, to bring good luck. Besides the caul already referred to, in South Devon sailors often carry the " Merry Thought " bone of a fowl as a charm against drowning, and on the Yorkshire coast the small T-shaped bone from a sheep's head is carried for the same purpose.

On the Kentish coast and also in Devonshire, a small piece of sea-worn coal is given sailors to carry to bring good luck, a custom which may have had its origin in the ancient belief among the Romans that a piece of jet when carried promoted good health.

On the Norfolk coast, fishermen often carry small pieces of rounded amber which they may pick up, as a charm against rheumatism, a belief which doubtless arose from the early use of oil of amber as an embrocation for the same complaint.

Certain sea-shells have always been used as charms and in some fishing villages, necklaces of shells worked into some recognised pattern are still made and worn to bring good luck to their wearers.

There is an ancient tradition among seamen, that no one should pare his nails or cut his hair on board ship except in a storm, also that the man who wears the clothes of a fellow-sailor who has died at sea before the termination of the voyage, will be dogged with ill luck.

Sir Thomas Browne states that a " Kingfisher hanged by the bill showeth us what quarter the wind is by an occult and secret property, converting the breast to that point of the horizon from whence the wind doth blow."

Sailors often forecast the weather from the appearance of certain fish. Thus, Pennant says, " the appearance of the dolphin and the porpesse are far from being esteemed favourable omens by seamen, for their boundings, springs and frolics in the water are held to be sure signs of an approaching gale."

Another writer declares that " When dolphins persue one another in fair and calm weather it foreshews wind and from that part whence they fetch their frisks, but if they play such when the seas are rough and troubled, it is a sign of fair and calm weather.

" Cuttles, with their many legs, swimming on the top of the water and striving to be above the waves, do presage a storm.

" Sea-urchins, thrusting themselves into the mud

or striving to cover their bodies with sand, foreshews a storm.

"Cockles and most shell-fish, are observed against
a tempest to have gravel sticking hard unto their
shells, as a providence of Nature to stay or poise
themselves and to help weigh them down, if raised
from the bottom by surges.

"Fishes in general, both in salt and freshwaters
are observed to sport most and bite more eagerly
against rain, than at any other time."

There is an old tradition, that a dead body on a
ship causes it to sail slower and many sailors believe
it will bring misfortune to the vessel and its crew.

In a curious old book entitled, *A Helpe to Memory
and Discourse*, printed in 1630, this superstition is
alluded to in the form of question and answer, as
follows :

"Q. Whether doth a dead Body in a shippe
cause the shippe to sayle slower and if it doe, what
is thought to be the reason thereof ?

"A. The shippe is as insensible of the living as
of the dead ; and as the living make it goe the
faster, so the dead make it not goe the slower, for
the dead are no Rhemoras to alter the course of her
passage, though some there be that think soe and
that by a kind of mournful sympathy."

Although sailors have ever been renowned for
their bravery and courage, they are often firm
believers in ghosts and apparitions, and many are
the stories of phantom ships and mysterious vessels
that are said to have been encountered in the
Southern Seas.

The tradition of the *Flying Dutchman*, that
phantom ship that struck terror into the hearts of
the most intrepid mariners, is well known, and as

recently as 1911 the crew of the *Orkney Belle*, a large whaling steamer, declared that they met with a ghost-ship.

The story as told by the second mate is as follows :

" One evening when we were about five miles from Reikjavik, Iceland, I was standing on the bridge with the Captain and a thin mist swirled over everything.

" Suddenly it thinned, leaving visibility easy, when to our surprise a sailing vessel loomed practically head on.

" The Captain signalled dead slow and the carpenter bawled from the deck ' *The Flying Dutchman.*'

" The strange vessel slid slowly alongside, within a stone's throw and we noticed her sails were billowing, yet there was no wind at all. She had a high poop and a carved stern. All our crew rushed to the side but not a soul was to be seen on this strange vessel. Then three bells sounded as from a silver bell, when suddenly this strange craft heeled over starboard and disappeared into the fog."

According to traditions such ships have wandered the seas for centuries and a poet thus refers to the ancient legend :

" 'Tis the phantom ship, that in darkness and wrath,
    Ploughs evermore the waste ocean path,
    And the heart of the mariner trembles in dread,
    When it crosses his vision like a ghost of the dead."

Children are deemed to bring good luck to a ship but to throw a cat overboard or drown one at sea, is said to court dire misfortune.

" I look upon sailors to care as little what becomes of themselves as any set of people under the sun," says a writer in 1767, " yet no people are so much terrified at the thoughts of an apparition.

"Their sea songs are full of them; they firmly believe in their existence and honest Jack Tar shall be more frightened at a glimmering of the moon upon the tackling of his ship than he would be if a Frenchman was to clap a blunderbus to his head."

St. Nicholas is the patron saint of sailors, as according to a legend, he saved from a storm the ship in which he sailed to the Holy Land and also certain mariners who invoked his aid, and thus we find many churches dedicated to him within sight of the sea.

In some of these, especially in the harbours round the Mediterranean coast, we find the walls covered with votive offerings in the form of pictures, carvings or models of ships, sometimes representing the dangers they have escaped, placed there by sailors who have suffered shipwreck, in gratitude to the saint for the protection he has given them and in accomplishment of the vows they made at the height of the storm. This custom dates from Roman times, as it is recorded that Bion, the philosopher, was shown several of these votive offerings hung up in a Temple of Neptune near the seaside.

# CHAPTER XVII

## THE FOLK-LORE OF ANIMALS

AMONG domestic animals, cats, especially black ones, have always been associated with witchcraft. The black cat was the usual familiar of the witch and consequently intimately connected with many superstitious practices.

There is a legend common in the northern counties that :

"Whenever the cat or the horse is black,
The lasses of lovers will have no lack."

And there is another couplet that runs :

" Kiss the black cat, an' 'twill make ye fat ;
Kiss the white one, 'twill make ye lean."

The tradition that cats have nine lives is an ancient one and in a book called *Beware of the Cat,* printed in 1584, it is stated that " it was permitted to a witch to take on her catte's body nine times."

In Gay's Fable of *The Old Woman and her Cats,* one of them thus upbraids the Witch :

" 'Tis infamy to serve a hag ;
Cats are thought imps, her broom a nag ;
And boys against our lives combine,
Because, 'tis said, your cats have nine."

" The conceit of a cat's having nine lives hath cost at least nine lives in ten of the whole race of them," says Trusler. " Scarce a boy in the street but has in this point out done even Hercules himself, who was renowned for killing a monster that had but three lives."

The connection of the cat with witches was no doubt the reason for the persecution and ill-treatment of the animal in the seventeenth century.

The hair of a black cat was supposed to have curative properties, and a well-known charm in Cornwall and some parts of Devonshire to cure a stye on the eye, is to stroke the eye from the nose outward with the tail of a black cat, repeating with each stroke :

> " I toke the queff that's under the 'ee,
> Oh qualyway,
> Oh qualyway."

In the Isle of Man, where tailless cats are said to flourish, considerable lore is associated with them. There is an old legend that the cats once had a king of their own and they are believed to be on intimate terms with the fairies and elves and other beings of the invisible world.

A cat sneezing was considered a lucky omen to a bride who was to be married next day, and they had a popular reputation for foretelling wet weather. Melton says, that " When the cat washes her face over her eares wee shall have great store of rain, and when sitting with their tails to the fire or washing their paws behind their ears it betokens a change of weather."

If the cat's fur looks bright it is likely to be fine, but when they are found licking their feet and trimming the hair of their heads or whiskers, it presages rainy weather.

Other animals associated with weather-lore and regarded as omens of rain are young horses when seen rubbing their backs against the ground ; sheep, bleating, playing or skipping ; oxen, licking themselves against the hair and pigs dragging hay or straw to any place. A cow turning up her tail against a hedge is said to foretell rain, an action which puzzled an early poet who thus asks a solution :

> " A learned case I now profound,
> Pray give an answer as profound ;
> 'Tis why a Cow, about half an hour
> Before there comes a hasty shower,
> Does clap her tail against the hedge ? "

There has long been a popular notion that the howling of a dog by night presages death and in connection with this superstition, Alexander Ross says, " that Dogs by their howling portend death and calamities is plaine by historie and experience."

" It may be," says another old writer, " that they scent death even before it seizes a person." Certainly dogs are often aware of the coming of a person they know, long before they see them, and they have been known to crouch and whimper at the door of a room in which a sick person is lying out of a sense of sorrow. They have also been known to stand and howl over the bodies of their masters when they have been killed or met with an accidental death, and from this it is probable the superstition originally arose.

The superstition that a hare seen running across the road is a sign of ill-omen is an ancient one. Borlase tells the story, that when Boadicea had harangued her soldiers before a battle against the Romans, she opened her bosom and let go a hare which she had there concealed that the augurs might thence proceed to divine. The frighted animal made such turnings and windings in her course, as according to the then rules of judging, prognosticated happy success.

On the other hand, in the seventeenth century, a

hare crossing the way was regarded as a sign of ill luck and Ramesey says in 1668, " If an hare do but cross their way, they suspect they shall be rob'd or come to some mischance forthwith."

" The hare," says an early historian, " was used by the ancient Britons for the purposes of divination and they were never killed for the table."

" Although it was regarded as unlucky if a hare crossed the path, it hath anciently been accounted good lucke if a wolfe crosse our way," says a writer in 1633. " Our ancestors in times past as they were merry conceited, so they were witty ; and thence it grew that they held it good lucke if a Wolf crost the way and was gone without any more danger, but ill luck if a Hare crost and escaped them, that they had not taken her."

Pliny says it was customary to fasten the heads of wolves on the gates of towns to put away witchery, sorcery and enchantment.

The connection between weasels and witchcraft is widespread and is said to have originated in early times in Thessaly,. which was said to be the favourite haunt of witches. " One of their practises was to take the form of weasels and bite off the ears and noses of dead bodies prepared for burial in order to use them in their concoctions." Since then, the squeaking of a weasel is said to be a portent of death and was at one time greatly dreaded.

There is a belief still common among farmers, that when beasts eat greedily and more than they are used to do, it indicates foul weather. Donkeys rubbing their ears or braying more than usual presage rain, and hogs crying and running uneasily up and down with litter in their mouths, shew a storm to be near at hand.

There is an old legend that the hyæna, in some countries, has the power of casting a spell over any solitary wayfarer it meets so that he is forced to follow the animal to its den, crying, " My father. My father ! " as he does so. The victim's only hope is, that on entering the lair he may strike his head against a rock so as to draw blood which will break the spell.

The recognised method of saving a person bewitched by a hyæna is to let some of the victim's blood.

The hyæna is said to be able to exert its hypnotic power on animals as well as men, so hunters have a strong aversion to look into the eyes of the animal.

# CHAPTER XVIII

## THE FOLK-LORE OF BIRDS AND INSECTS

MANY superstitious legends are associated with birds as harbingers of good or bad fortune, and in the part they play in the system of natural divination so common in country districts.

The Cumberland dalesmen believe that when rooks build their nests higher in the trees than usual, the summer will be a long and good one, while swallows, when they come to our shores earlier than April, are said to presage warm and fair weather.

It is considered lucky for swallows or martins to build their nests in the eaves of a house, especially near a window, and most unlucky to destroy one.

In ancient times they were regarded as sacred to the household gods and therefore honoured and preserved, their advent being welcomed by a solemn anniversary song.

As a bird of omen there is an old story, that " Swallows lighted upon Pirrhus' tents and lighting on the mast of Mark Antony's ship sayling after Cleopatra to Egypt, the soothsayers did prognosticate that Pirrhus should be slain at Argos in Greece and Mark Antony in Egypt." It is well known that when swallows are seen to fly low, rainy weather is likely to follow, and the same is said of birds in general that frequent trees and bushes. "Thus," says

George Smith, "sparrows in the morning early, chirping and making more noise than ordinary they use to do, foretell rain," and another old writer states that "miseries and unnatural wars have been forewarned by armies of swallows and martins fighting against one another."

The kingfisher is said to be an harbinger of good luck to the one who sees it and to kill one, even accidentally, is believed to bring misfortune. There is a beautiful legend associated with this brilliantly coloured bird, that when Noah freed the birds from the Ark, the kingfisher flew away first, and was thus privileged to dye his breast with the rose-red of the setting sun and to carry on his back, for all time, the reflection of the azure sky.

Of other weather-lore connected with birds, the woodpeckers' cry is said to indicate wet weather, but buzzards or kites soaring very high, forecast hot weather and fine days. Cranes soaring aloft and quietly in the air, presage fair weather, but " if they make much noise as consulting which way to go, it foreshews a storm that's near at hand."

Herons, when observed flying up and down in the evening as if doubtful where to rest, are said to denote that bad weather is approaching.

The peacock, in spite of its beautiful plumage, has a bad reputation, and its tail feathers, in particular, were said to bring ill luck. This idea is said to have originated from the fact that peacocks were the sacred birds of Juno, the patron goddess of women, and either the robbery of these birds of their tails was thought to offend the goddess or else the use of the plumage sacred to Juno. The resemblance of the tip of the feather to the human eye, was believed to attract the influences of evil.

Thomas Lupton in his book of *Notable Things*, 1660, says, " The peacock by his loud and harsh clamor, prophesies and foretells rain and the oftener the cry, the more rain is signified ; Paracelsus states, that if a peacock cries more than usual or out of his time, it foretells the death of some in that family to whom it doth belong."

The robin redbreast is reverenced in some countries because the colour of its feathers is supposed to have been due to a drop of Sacred Blood, and like the wren it had Divine associations. Thus the couplet :

" A Robin and a Wren
Are God Almighty's cock and hen."

It was said that if any person killed a robin or destroyed its nest, he would either break a bone or meet with some other misfortune within the course of the year.

The feeling of general kindliness to robins is said to be largely due to the old story of the " Babes in the Wood," and children have always been taught to feed them, especially in cold and wintry weather.

Throughout the centuries, poets have sung of this little bird who in ancient times was regarded as sacred to the household gods and was considered as a guest who should never be sent empty away.

Thus, Thomson wrote :

" The Red breast, sacred to the household gods,
Wisely regardful of th' embroyling sky,
In joyless fields and thorny thickets leaves
His shiv'ring mates, and pays to trusted man
His annual visit."

The belief that ill luck will follow the killing of a

robin is embodied in the following lines by J. H. Pott,
written in 1780 :

> " For ever from his threshold fly
> Who, void of honour, once shall try,
> With base inhospitable breast,
> To bar the freedom of his guest ;
> O rather seek the peasant's shed,
> For he will give thee wasted bread,
> And fear some new calamity,
> Should any there spread snares for thee."

The charitable action of the robins in covering
the bodies of the " hapless babes " with leaves, is
thus alluded to in Percy's *Old Ballads*.

> " No burial this pretty pair
> Of any man receives,
> Till Robin Redbreast painfully
> Did cover them with leaves."

Drayton also wrote of

> " Cov'ring with moss the dead's unclosed eye,
> The little Redbreast teacheth charitie."

In Reed's *Old Plays*, the Robin and the Wren are
thus mentioned :

> " Call for the Robin Red breast and the Wren,
> Since o'er shady groves they hover,
> And with leaves and flow'rs do cover
> The friendless bodies of unburied men."

Pope in one of his poems also alludes to

> " Robin Redbreast till of late had rest,
> And children sacred held a Martin's nest."

In early times the wren was said to have been
the augur's favourite bird, and the Druids represented
it as the king of the feathered tribes. The superstitious respect shown to this little bird is said to
have been the reason why the first Christian

missionaries took an animus against it, and caused it to be hunted and killed by the Irish peasants on Christmas and St. Stephen's Days.

According to a chronicler, " The bird when caught was carried about hung by the leg in the centre of two hoops crossing each other at right angles, and a procession made in the village of men, women and children singing an Irish catch importing him to be the king of all birds."

Another curious story as regards wren-hunting is given by Aubrey as follows : " At the battle fought in the north of Ireland between the Protestants and Papists in Glinsuly, County Donegal, a party of the former would have been surprised by the Irish had it not been for several wrens who awakened them by dancing and pecking on their drums as the enemy was approaching.  For this reason the Irish mortally hate these birds, calling them the ' Devil's Servants ' and killing them wherever they catch them ;  they teach their children to thrust them full of thorns ; you'll see sometimes on holidays, a whole parish running like madmen from hedge to hedge, a wren-hunting."

The owl has had a reputation for bringing bad luck from early times, and many allusions are made in the works of the ancient historians to the misfortunes and calamities presaged by this bird of ill-omen.

According to Virgil, " The solitary owl foretold the tragical end of Dido, Lampridius and Marcellinus ;  among other prodigies which presaged the death of Valentinian, the Emperor, mention an Owle which sate upon the top of the house where he used to bathe and could not thence be driven away with stones."

Rome itself once underwent a lustration because an owl strayed into the Capitol, as it was thought to be a messenger of death. Butler thus alludes to the incident in his *Hudibras :*

> " The Roman Senate when within
> The city walls an Owl was seen,
> Did cause their clergy with lustrations
> (Our Synod calls them humiliations)
> The round-fac'd prodigy t' avert
> From doing town and country hurt."

Macaulay commenting on the superstition of the Romans with regard to auguries from birds says, " On their silence, singing, chirping, chattering and croaking, on their feeding or abstinence ; on their flying to the right hand or left—was founded an art ; which from a low and simple beginning, grew to an immense height and gained a surprising degree of credit in a deluded world."

This dread of the owl continued throughout the Middle Ages, for Bartholomew Glanvil writing in the fourteenth century states : " Of the Oule, Divynours telle that they betokyn evyll ; for if the Owle be seen in a citie, it signifyeth distruccion and waste, as Isidore sayth, The cryenge of the Owle by nyght tokeneth deathe, as divinours conjecte and deme."

Chaucer in the *Assembly of Foules* also alludes to

> " The jelous Swan, ayenst hys deth that singeth
> The Oule eke, that of deth, the bode bringeth."

Shakespeare in *Julius Cæsar* (Act I, Sc. 6) has the following lines :

> " The Bird of Night did sit
> Ev'n at noon-day upon the market-place
> Houting and Shrieking."

Smith in his *Pastorals* (1770) makes a further allusion to the common superstition as follows :

" Within my cot, where quiet gave me rest
Let the dread Screech Owl build her hated nest,
And from my window o'er the country send
Her midnight screams to bode my latter end."

The tawny owl was stigmatised a messenger of death and the screech owl, at midnight, in the country, was reckoned as alarming as a band of robbers.

Bourne says " the owl is a most abominable and unlucky bird which sends forth its hoarse and dismal voice as an omen of the approach of some terrible thing ; that some dire calamity and great misfortune is at hand."

But in spite of all the evil things recorded about owls, as weather forecasters their reputation was favourable as an old writer tells us, that " Owls whooping after sunset and in the night, foreshews a fair day to ensue."

Crows have been reputed to be birds of ill-omen from early times, and like ravens with their melancholy croak, they have ever been associated with death and misfortune.

When seen flying in a great flock, crows were believed to presage a famine or great mortality and Ramesay states, that " if a crow fly but over the house and croak thrice, how do they fear, they, or some one else in the family shall die."

" Some will defer going abroad, though called by business of the greatest consequence, if, happening to look out of the window they see a single crow," says Duncan Campbell in his *Secret Memoirs*

Shakespeare thus alludes to the raven in *Othello* :

> " . . . O it comes o'er my memory
> As doth the raven, o'er the infected house,
> Boding to all."

And Gay in his pastoral, *The Dirge*, mentions,

> " The boding Raven on her cottage sat,
> And, with hoarse croakings, warn'd us of our fate."

The ancient Greeks regarded ravens as sacred to Apollo, the great patron of augurs, and they were called the companions and attendants of that deity. Cicero is said to have been forewarned by the noise and fluttering of ravens about him that his end was near. Bartholomew Glanvil writing in the fourteenth century says, " As divinours mene the Raven hath a maner of virtue of meanyng and tokenynge of divination," and we find down to the nineteenth century that the raven was accounted the most prophetical of all birds.

Magpies were considered to be ominous or otherwise according to the number seen together, thus to see first one and then no more is said to be unlucky, but to see two, denotes a marriage; three, a successful journey; four, an unexpected piece of good news, and five, that you will shortly be in a great company.

According to an old couplet :

> " One for sorrow, two for mirth
> Three for a wedding and four for a birth."

The prognostic of sorrow is said to be averted by turning three times round. " By the chattering of magpies they know they shall have strangers in the house," says Nathaniel Home, " and by the flying and crying of ravens over their houses, especially in the dusk evening, and where one is sick, they conclude death."

A single magpie seen flying to the right means that good luck awaits the observer, but if it flies to the left, bad luck is portended.

There is a tradition that the blackbird was once white, but one very cold winter he took refuge in a chimney and so became blackened with soot. In Italy, certain days are still known as " blackbird days," meaning the days during which the bird was imprisoned in the chimney. Nowadays, a white blackbird or albino, which is occasionally met with, is said to be the harbinger of misfortune to the observer.

Storks, in the countries they frequent, are believed to bring peace and happiness to the houses on which they build their nests and they are welcomed by the inhabitants. Their care for their young is said to account for the tradition that they were very gentle with infants and were the carriers of babies to the house.

The sprightly little yellow-hammer was formerly held in dislike on account of the tradition that it hatched out serpents from its scrawly-marked eggs, and in some parts of Wales, the eggs when found by the village boys were destroyed in case they should hatch out snakes. Another prejudice against the yellow-hammer was on account of the legend that it had been inoculated with one drop of the devil's blood and was therefore unlucky.

There is a tradition in Boston, Lincolnshire, that should a cormorant be seen on the steeple of St. Botolph's church some disaster may be expected to the town.

Curlews with their mournful cries are called

" Gabriel's hounds," and by some, they are supposed to be lost souls tossed hither and thither by
the winds. The circling plover is also said to be
connected with the soul of the lost, a tradition which
dates from early Christian times, when it was
believed that the souls of the Jews who were present
at Calvary were condemned to enter the bodies of
birds who were ever restless and flying.

Sea-mews, when they make a greater noise than
usual in the morning, are said to augur stormy and
blustering weather, and their bodies are said to be
possessed by the souls of drowned sailors. The
stormy petrels known to sailors as " Mother Carey's
chickens," are said to be sent to warn seamen of
danger, *Mater Cara*, or the dear mother, being the
ancient protectress of all sailors at sea. The soul
of King Arthur, according to an old legend, became
the abode of a chough, while the kingfisher was said
to harbour the souls of the beautiful Greek Halcyone
and her Royal husband who was drowned.

The folk-lore of birds has thus been summarised
in verse :

> " Bird melodious or bird fair,
>     Be absent hence !
> The crow, the slanderous cuckoo, nor
> The boding raven, nor chough hoar,
>     Nor chattering pie,
> May on our bridehouse perch or sing
> Or with them any discord bring,
>     But from it fly."

" Of the cuckoo," says Werenfels, " if the superstitious man has a desire to know how many years
he has to live he will enquire of the bird," and
Sir Thomas Browne remarks, " it is common for
those who are unmarried, to count the number of
years yet allotted to them of single blessedness, by

the number of the cuckoo's notes which they count when they first hear it in spring."

In several of the southern counties some curious superstitions are associated with bees, and there is a belief in many places that when bees remove or go away from their hives, their owner will die shortly afterwards. Should a bee-keeper die, it was the duty of the kinsfolk to go round the hives, tap three times on each and say, " Bees, bees, bees, your master is dead and you must work for ——," the name of the new owner being mentioned. This ancient custom was called " telling the bees."

John Molle, writing in 1621, says, " It is believed that bees die in their hives if the master or mistress of the house chance to die, except the hives be presently removed to another place."

In Devonshire, at one time, no bee-keeper would sell a swarm of bees for money but would only part with them by barter, such as a sack of corn or perhaps a small pig, which was considered the equivalent value of a Maytime swarm, and they were never removed but on a Good Friday.

It is also considered very unlucky for bees to swarm upon a dead tree. If the bees swarm high upon the trees, it is regarded as an omen that the price of grain will be high, but should they swarm low, the value is likely to be less.

There is an old belief that when swarming begins, if a noise is made with a gong or bell or by knocking the fire-irons together, the bees will settle close by their old hives and not wander far afield. It is stated that in some of the old monasteries, the bee-keeping monks used to sound the monastery bell as soon as the bees began to swarm, because they believed that the wings of the queen bee were so sensitive, that the vibrating sounds had the effect of making her want to settle and so gather the whole swarm around her.

It is customary in some parts of Devonshire when a farmer dies, to turn the bee-hives round at the moment when his body is being carried from the house, and in certain districts, the hives are put into mourning and crumbs of the funeral biscuit offered to the bees.

The custom of putting the hives in mourning is thus mentioned by Whittier in *Telling the Bees* :

> " Under the garden wall
> Forward and back
> Went drearily singing the chore-girl small,
> Draping each hive with a shred of black."

Borlase tells us, that in his time, in Cornwall, " the spirit Browny is invoked when the bees swarm, as they think that their crying Browny, Browny, will prevent their returning into their former hive and make them pitch and form a new colony."

As weather omens, when bees do not wander far from their hives, they are said to presage the approach of a rainy or stormy season.

The little lady-bird, with its brightly spotted back, has the reputation of being able to indicate the abode of a lover and is thus used by the curious. When one is caught, it is to be thrown into the air while the following lines are repeated :

> " Fly away east, fly away west,
> Show me where lives the one I like best."

# CHAPTER XIX

## THE FOLK-LORE OF PLANTS AND FLOWERS

IN ancient times, primitive man invested both trees and plants with a personality and certain trees in particular came to be endowed with peculiar mystic and sacred properties and were regarded with reverence and awe. They were believed to be the abodes of deities and spirits, and to injure them was considered a wrong to the invisible beings who resided in them.

Even among savage races, there was a widespread belief that trees had souls and special honour was paid to some as being the embodiment of the spirits of the woods.

Certain trees, like the oak, which was sacred to Thor, were regarded as holy and acts of sacrifice and worship were paid to them, while it was considered an act of sacrilege to mutilate them.

There are still some curious survivals of this tree-soul doctrine, and Thorpe tells us, that in West-phalia, the peasantry are accustomed to announce formally to the nearest oak any death that may have occurred in the family, with the words, " The master is dead. The master is dead." Lubbock observes, that there was an oak copse at Loch Siant in the Isle of Skye, held so sacred, that no persons would venture to cut the smallest branch of it.

The Wallachians are said to have a superstition that every flower has a soul, and that the water-lily is the sinless and scentless flower of the lake which blossoms at the gates of Paradise to judge the rest, and that she will inquire strictly what they have done with their odours.

Holes in the trunks of trees were believed to be the doors through which the special spirits of the trees passed, hence one reason for the belief that various diseases may be cured by contact with them. The lime, the pine and pollard ashes were regarded with special veneration when a hole was found in them, and in Somersetshire and Cornwall it is still believed, as already mentioned, that a rickety child passed through the aperture would be made strong and healthy.

It is little wonder that considerable lore should be found associated with plants and flowers and that many became connected with magic and witchcraft.

Certain blossoms were also said to possess magical influences and in the East, the beautiful golden mimosa is credited as an efficacious charm against all kinds of malignant powers such as the " evil eye."

The mountain-ash, or rowan, has a host of super-stitions connected with it, and in early times it was regarded as being the embodiment of the lightning from which it was sprung. Its leaves, twigs and particularly its bright red berries, were all employed as charms.

Red was the witches' colour and also sacred to Thor, and so in the Highlands and in Ireland, farmers frequently tie a piece of red worsted or red cloth round their cows' tails to prevent them from being ill-wished. The Highland dairymaids often carry a little cross made from rowan twigs bound together with red worsted, to prevent witches injuring their cattle or turning the milk.

They have an old saying :

" Rowan-ash, and red thread
Keep the devils from their speed."

Both the hazel and the white-thorn were regarded as lightning shrubs, and in Ireland it has long been considered as unlucky to cut down the white-thorn,

ROWAN TREE CROSS TIED WITH
RED WORSTED

Used as a charm in Scotland and as a protection
from witchcraft.

*Pitt-Rivers Museum.*

as it is said to be under the protection of the fairies who resent any injury done to it. In some parts of the country, hazel twigs are placed in the window-frames during a thunder-storm as a protection against lightning, and spring-wort is believed to possess the same property. St. John's wort and the elder were also said to have the power of protection against the fatal effects of lightning, and the presence of holly planted near dwellings and the house-leek growing on the cottage roof, are said to be due to the same belief.

Rue had a widespread reputation with witches and was also largely employed in magical rites. Like some other plants, it was regarded as being equally efficacious in counteracting the evil effects of witchcraft, and when worn together with agri-mony, or maiden-hair, was believed to prevent spells and to indicate the presence of a witch.

Rosemary has ever been highly esteemed for its magical and medical properties, while it also formed

a frequent ingredient in love-charms.  Its association
with love is expressed in the following lines :

> " Who passeth by the rosemarie
> And careth not to take a spraye,
> For woman's love no care has he.
> Nor shall he though he live for aye."

" Rosemary," says Roger Hacket in 1607, " is for
married men, the which by name, nature and
continued use, man challengeth as properly belonging
to himself.  It helpeth the brain, strengtheneth the
memory and is very medicinal for the head.  Another
property is, it affects the heart."

Probably on account of its persistent odour, it
has long had the reputation of being an aid to
memory.  Thus, in the *Handefull of Pleasant Delites*,
printed in 1584, we have the lines :

> " Rosemary is for remembrance
> Between us day and night,
> Wishing that I might alwaies have
> You present in my sight."

Shakespeare alludes to the tradition in *Hamlet*
(Act IV, Sc. 5), where Ophelia remarks :

> " There's rosemary—that's for remembrance,
> Pray you, love, remember ; and there's pansies—
> That's for thoughts."

The great dramatist makes a further allusion to
the magical power of pansies in *Midsummer Night's
Dream* (Act I, Sc. 2), where Oberon says :

> " Fetch me that flower—the herb I show'd thee once ;
> The juice of it on sleeping eyelids laid,
> Will make man or woman madly dote
> Upon the next live creature that it sees."

Both rosemary and bay were used at weddings as
well as funerals in bygone times, the former being
dipped in scented water and the leaves of the latter

gilded, a practice to which Herrick thus alludes in *Hesperides* :

> " This done, we'll draw lots who shall buy
> And guild the Baies and Rosemary."

The wild flower commonly called " Bachelor's buttons " so common in our hedgerows, was supposed to have a magical effect on the fortunes of lovers. Gerard in his *Herbal* thus accounts for the origin of the popular name. " Now the similitude that these flowers have to the jagged cloth buttons antiently worn in this kingdom, gave occasion to our gentlewomen and other lovers of flours in these times, to give them their current designation."

Lavender, like rosemary, was also associated with affection and remembrance. Thus, Dryden in one of his *Eclogues* writes :

> " Some such flowers as to his hand doth pass,
> Others such a secret meaning bear ;
> He, for his lass, him lavender hath sent,
> Showing his love, and doth requital crave ;
> Him, rosemary, his sweetheart, whose intent
> Is that he should her in remembrance have."

The wild flower popularly called " Lady's mantle " was at one time much sought after by women, on account of its reputation for " restoring feminine beauty however faded, to its early freshness." The wild tansy also, when soaked in butter-milk for nine days, was said to make the complexion very fair.

The hawthorn and fumitory were believed to have an almost magical effect on the skin, and concerning the former, there is an old rhyme which runs :

> " The fair maid who the first of May,
> Goes to the fields at break of day,
> And washes in dew from the hawthorn tree
> Will ever after handsome be."

It was necessary to gather fumitory at the time of a wedding and when the flowers were boiled in water, with milk and whey added, they were regarded by rustic maidens as an invaluable wash for the complexion.

The flowers of St. John's wort, dedicated to St. John the Baptist, who is celebrated on Midsummer Day, were believed to act as a special protection against witches. They had to be gathered on Midsummer Eve, at midnight, and were either worn on the person or hung up over the door to prevent the witches from entering the house. Sometimes they were placed in the window to prevent the witches from looking in and thus casting their evil spells.

This belief is universal throughout Europe, and in the Landes district of France it is still customary in the villages to make a cross of St. John's wort and fasten it on the front door, but it must be renewed every Midsummer Day to be effective.

Mugwort, which had been gathered on Midsummer Eve, when kept in the house, was also believed to be a protection from misfortune and disease. Vervain or verbena, the four-leaved clover, and wild thyme were other flowers associated with witchcraft and magic. The Romans made their bridal wreaths of verbena which had to be gathered by the bride herself, and it was regarded as of special value in making love-philtres. At the present day, it is customary in country places in Germany to present a bride with a wreath of verbena.

The flowering fern which blooms at midnight and soon afterwards seeds, was famous among the flowers to be gathered on Midsummer Eve. Whoever caught the bloom of the seed was said to be endowed with miraculous powers of divination, for " it was revealed to him where hidden treasure was to be found and he could also render himself invisible."

There are many traditions connected with the aspen, whose trembling leaves are said to have been caused through a curse having been cast on the tree, when unlike other trees it failed to pay homage to the Holy Child.

> " Only the aspen stood erect and free,
> Scorning to join the voiceless worship pure,
> But see ! He cast one look upon the tree,
> Struck to the heart, she trembles ever more."

There is an old legend, that an aspen leaf placed under a woman's tongue when she is asleep will make her speak. Gasynhill alludes to it in the lines :

> " Some say the woman had no tongue,
> After that God did her create,
> Until the man took leaves long
> And put them under her palate ;
> An aspen leaf of the devil he gat
> And for it moveth with every wind,
> They say women's tongues be of like kind."

Further mention of the tradition is made in an old Scottish ballad :

> " This night in her first sleep,
> Under her tongue then lay
> Of quaking aspen leaf."

The branches of the ash are supposed to have been used by witches on their rides through the air, but their evil influence might be counteracted by eating the buds of the tree on St. John's Eve.

Ash leaves, when used in the following manner, were said to have the power of causing a lover or future husband to appear to a love-sick maiden.

After plucking an even ash leaf, while holding it in her hand, she was to say :

" The even ash leaf in my hand,
    The first I meet shall be my man."

She was then to put it in her glove and repeat :

" The even ash leaf in my glove,
    The first I meet shall be my love."

Finally, she was to slip it in her bosom and repeat the words :

" The even ash leaf in my bosom
    The first I meet shall be my husband."

After that, she was to take a walk and the future husband or lover would appear to her.

A similar charm was carried out with a clover leaf in Cambridgeshire, the leaf being placed in the right shoe. After this was done, the following lines were to be repeated :

" A clover, a clover of two,
    Put it into your right shoe ;
    The first man (or woman) you meet,
    In the field, street or lane,
    You'll love him (or her) or one of his name."

Foxgloves, popularly called " witches' bells," were so named because the witches were said to be fond of decorating their fingers with the bell-shaped flowers.

The elder was believed to possess remarkable powers and according to an old tradition, " any baptised person whose eyes were anointed with the green juice of its inner bark, was able to see witches in any part of the world."

It was employed in magical rites on account of its influence in warding off evil spirits and even the devil himself. Those standing in the magic circle were recommended to carry elder-berries which had been gathered on St. John's Night, in their hands, " for by so doing, they might be able to obtain the mystic fern-seed which would endow them with the strength of thirty or forty men."

Woodbine was a favourite plant with Scottish witches, who are said to have effected magical cures by passing their patients nine times through a garland of its twining tendrils.

Coles, in his *Adam in Eden*, mentions some curious lore of the seventeenth century associated with certain plants. He tells us, that if " a footman takes mugwort and put it into his shoes in the morning, he may goe forty miles before noon and not be weary. The seed of flea-bane strewed between the sheets causeth chastity. The seeds of docks tyed to the left arme of a woman do helpe barreness. Calamint will restore freshness to smelling meat, if it be laid amongst it while it is raw, and the often smelling of basil breedeth a scorpion in the brain."

Much curious lore is connected with moon-wort (*Botrychium lunaria*), which in former times was believed to have the power " to open locks and to unshoe horses that trod on it." Coles declares, that " it will open the locks wherewith dwelling houses are made fast, if it be put in the key-holes, as also it will loosen the locks, fetters and shoes from those horses' feet that goe on the places where it groweth." He tells the story of how the horses of the Earl of Essex, on being drawn up in a body on White Down near Tiverton in Devonshire, lost their shoes, because moonwort grew upon the heath.

Du Bartas thus alludes to the tradition in his *Divine Weekes :*

> " Horse that feeding on the grassy hills,
>     Tread upon moonwort with their hollow heels,
>     Though lately shod, at night go barefoot home,
>     Their maister musing where their shoes become.
>     O moonwort ! tell me where thou hidst the smith,
>     Hammer and pinchers, thou shodd'st them with ?
>     Alas ! what lock or iron engine is't,
>     That can thy subtle secret strength resist,
>     Still the best farrier cannot set a shoe
>     So sure, but thou (so shortly) canst undo."

Withers in referring to the moonwort in 1622, says :

> " There is an Herb, some say, whose vertue's such
>     It in the pasture, only with a touch,
>     Unshoes the new-shod steed."

The laurel, like the bay, has been regarded as a defence against lightning from Roman times and Leigh referring to Tiberius Cæsar says : " He feared thunder exceedingly and when the aire or weather was anything troubled, he ever carried a chaplet or wreath of Lawrell about his neck, because that is never blasted with lightning."

The leaves of the laurel were also said to reveal the hidden future by their crackling, when burnt by girls to win back their errant lovers.

Herrick thus alludes to the tradition that the daffodil foretells the future :

> " When a Daffadill I see,
>     Hanging down her head t'wards me,
>     Guesse I may what I must be ;
>     First, I shall decline my head ;
>     Secondly, I shall be dead ;
>     Lastly, safely buried."

Of plants illustrating the doctrine of signatures, which by their external character were believed to indicate the particular diseases for which Nature had intended them ; besides those already mentioned, the herb-robert may be taken as an example, which on account of the beautiful red hue assumed by its fading leaves was called a " Stauncher of blood."

Lungwort, as its name indicates, because of its spotted leaves, was believed to be efficacious in chest complaints, and carpenter's herb or self-heal for healing wounds, on account of its corolla being shaped like a bill-hook. The rose was used by the Greeks as an ingredient in their love-philtres and the petals thrown on the fire were believed to bring good luck.

In some countries the dark roses are associated with blood, doubtless due to the similarity of colour, and if a woman wishes to have rosy cheeks she is told to bury a drop of her blood under a rose-bush. An old charm employed against hæmorrhage of all kinds in some parts of Germany ran as follows : " On the head of our Lord God there bloom three roses ; the first is His virtue, the second is His youth, the third is His will. Blood, stand thou in the wound still, so that thou neither sore nor abscess givest."

The walnut was employed for diseases of the brain on account of its likeness in shape to the whole head ; the common nettle for the nettle-rash ; heart-ease in cases of heart trouble, and owing to the woody scales of pine-cones bearing a resemblance to the teeth, pine leaves boiled in vinegar were used as a remedy for toothache.

Spleen-wort had a reputation for curing ailments of the spleen, while the yellow bark of the berberry-tree was a popular remedy for jaundice and was known in some parts of the country as the " jaundice-berry."

Quaking grass, when dried and kept in the house, was believed to prevent ague and also, on account of its constant trembling, the aspen was employed as a remedy for the same disease.

Thus, the origin of the use of some of the herbs employed in folk-medicine may readily be traced.

The apple tree is still held sacred in some of the fruit-growing districts of England and is associated with many mystic legends. In Devonshire, it was formerly customary for the farmer and his men to take a large jug of cider to the orchard and there, encircling one of the best bearing trees, they drank the following toast three times :

> " Here's to thee, old apple tree,
> Whence thou may'st bud, and whence thou may'st blow !
> And whence thou may'st bear apples enow !
> Hats full ! caps full !
> Bushel—bushel—sacks full,
> And my pockets full too ! Huzza ! "

In Cornwall, the villagers sometimes used to walk in procession to the principal orchards and selecting a large tree, they would sprinkle it with cider and place cakes and roasted apples in its branches, then salute it with a form of prayer in which it was implored to be fruitful during the ensuing year. It was then toasted in the following words :

> " Health to thee, good apple tree,
> Well to bear pocket-fulls, hat-fulls,
> Peck-fulls, bushel bag-fulls."

At each cupful of cider drunk the men set up a shout.

" Watsail," says an old writer, " a drinking song sung on ' Twelfth-day Eve,' and throwing toast to the apple trees in order to have a fruitful year, seems to be a relic of the heathen sacrifice to Pomona."

# CHAPTER XX

## THE LORE OF AMULETS

THE belief that certain objects, natural or artificial, composed of metals, stone, clay or other materials, sometimes possess occult powers capable of protecting those who carry them from danger, disease or evil influences, is found among savage, semi-civilised and civilised races throughout the world and has existed from time immemorial.

The word amulet, which was formerly used to describe such objects that were worn round the neck or about the person, to prevent disease or to defend the wearer from danger or misfortune, is now often employed as synonymous with talisman, whereas the meaning is entirely different, The latter was originally applied to seals or magical signs engraved on stone or metal, which were also used for protection from evil and bodily harm.

The use of amulets goes back to prehistoric times, and in ancient Egypt their employment was universal both by the living and in connection with the dead.

The Arabs have a legend, that when Pharaoh's army had been drowned in the Red Sea, the Egyptians elected a woman called Dalūkah as queen, because she was wise and prudent and also skilled in magic.

During the course of her reign, she filled Egypt with her temples and with figures of animals. In the temples, she collected all the secrets of Nature and all the attracting and repelling powers which were contained in minerals, plants and animals. She performed her sorceries, at the moment in the revolution of the celestial bodies when they would be amenable to a higher power. Thus, the figures of the gods and men sculptured or painted on the walls and the hieroglyphic inscriptions, were supposed, at one time, to be magical figures and formulæ intended to serve as amulets and talismans.

This ancient legend is interesting in connection with the common use of amulets in Egypt from a very early period.

Sir Ernest Wallis Budge tells us that their use for the dead probably arose from the idea of guarding them from savage animals, serpents, worms and decay.

SACRED TALISMAN OR SEAL
Consisting of divine names to cure all diseases and heal all griefs.
*From a manuscript of the sixteenth century.*

Each member of the body was placed under the special protection of some amulet, in the form of a deity, animal or other shape. In the earliest times, certain formulæ or prayers were recited over the amulets by the priests before being worn by the living or placed on the dead, and "words of power" were inscribed on them afterwards.

Pieces of green schist, in various forms, were the first to be employed for this purpose, which at a later period came to be engraved with figures of animals, and afterwards amulets fashioned in carnelion, precious stones, gold, silver, and other materials, shaped in various forms came to be used.

Authorities state, that over 275 different varieties of amulets have been discovered in Egypt and these have been roughly classified as follows : 1. Amulets to give confidence and faith. 2. Amulets for a double purpose. 3. Amulets of similars.

The amulet of the heart was directed to be made in the form of a scarab, for the scarab was believed to possess remarkable powers, and if the proper " words of power " be written upon it, it acted not only as a protection of the physical heart but also gave new life to him to whose body it was attached.

The scarab was the type and symbol of the god Khepera and the idea of life has been associated with it from remote times.

In Egypt and the Sudan, the insect itself, when dried and powdered, then mixed with water, is swallowed by women against sterility, and for driving away the effects of any kind of sorcery and incantations, the head and wings of a large scarab are boiled and laid in oil. They are then warmed up and stewed in the oil of the Apent serpent, then again boiled and afterwards swallowed.

The popularity and faith in the scarab as an amulet is testified by the innumerable specimens fashioned in all kinds of materials that have been found in Egypt.

Among the various forms of Egyptian amulets, mention may be made of the " Eye of Horus," used to confer on the dead the power of seeing out of the coffin and on the living strength, vigour, protection from danger and good health. The " buckle " worn as a protection against evil influence; the " tet " to give the dead person power to reconstruct the body and become a perfect spirit in the underworld ; the vulture as a protective amulet ; the " papyrus sceptre " to give the dead vigour and renewed youth in the next world ; the " Ankh " which was the amulet of life ; the god Nefer, to bring happiness and good luck ; the " Menat " to bring joy and health to the living and power of life and reproduction to the dead.

THE EYE OF HORUS

Egyptian charm to avert the " evil eye." *Circa* 1500 B.C.

*Pitt-Rivers Museum.*

Besides these, a figure of a frog was used to symbolise fecundity and resurrection ; a crab to protect the wearer from fever ; the fish from gout and kindred diseases and a scorpion, to render the wearer invulnerable to the bites and stings of venomous reptiles and insects.

Leopard and lion-headed amulets were used as protection against wild animals and worn to promote courage, and tooth-shaped amulets were believed to promote dentition in infants and were also worn as a protection against lightning. Actual shark's teeth in metal settings have also been found in Egypt and were used as amulets.

Shells of various kinds, threaded and worn as necklaces, were regarded as a protection against the

" evil eye " ; cowries in particular, on account of their resemblance to an eye, being considered as the most powerful.

The disc of the Sun-god Rā, with its vulture wings, signified protection and was placed over the door of every great temple. Amulets in the form of a crescent, which originated from the new moon and were symbolic of the protection of the Moon-god, were worn to avert the " evil eye " as they are carried for the same purpose in many European countries to-day.

The mummified serpent was the protective amulet for the household, and was usually preserved in a bronze box and kept in the dwelling. It was also believed to be a protection against malaria. The lizard amulet was used to preserve the wearer from quartan fever ; the shrew-mouse to avert boils ; the eel against ague, and the claw of the gazelle and human-bone amulets were employed to prevent ulcers.

Amulets in the shape of a hand were used to ward off evil influences, and the clenched fist signified vigorous action and defence against malignant forces.

The ancient Babylonians and Assyrians hung amulets model-led in clay outside the doors of their houses to keep away and prevent the entrance of evil spirits, and they suspended

EGYPTIAN HAND CHARMS
Used to avert the " evil eye."
*Circa* 1500 B.C.
*Ashmolean Museum.*

tablets of gold inscribed with certain characters around the necks of their children to preserve them from harm.

The ancient Greeks, like the Egyptians, employed

various objects as amulets and had great faith in their virtues. Pliny, Galen and Dioscorides allude to their value in protecting the body from disease and Galen tells us, that the King Nechepsus, who flourished about 630 B.C., wore " a green jasper, cut into the shape of a dragon, surrounded with rays, which when applied to the region of the digestive organs strengthened that part wonderfully."

The Romans believed that many substances were endowed with occult virtues, and these might be brought under the control of any one possessed of the requisite knowledge. The *bullæ* mentioned by Plautus were amulets of gold, silver, bronze or lead. Some were in the form of a heart as the seat of life, the moon or the sun.

The meaning of the word is " water bubble," and some of the *bullæ* were made in the form of a sphere, while others were composed of two convex discs, one overlapping the other. They were used by the Etruscans as necklaces, and children were presented with them on the day of their birth to avert the " evil eye " and wore them until they reached the age of puberty. The eyes of a green lizard were also believed to possess the power of protection against the " evil eye," and human hair was said to avert danger from head wounds.

To avoid being struck by lightning, the Emperor Augustus always carried a seal-skin when a storm threatened.

Stones and metals were employed as talismans, after being subjected to some special preparation or inscribed with magical figures.

Bronze in particular was believed to have the power of driving away evil spirits. Small figures of some of the great deities, like Apollo or Jove, fashioned in gold or silver, were carried to preserve the owner from harm. Models of the phallus in silver or bronze were commonly carried to avert the "evil eye" and were sometimes worn by women as necklaces.

During the latter part of the Roman Empire, the wearing of amulets became so general, that the Emperor Caracalla made a public edict that no one should wear an amulet about his person under heavy penalties. But this did not stop the custom, for belief in amulets continued and is universal in Italy to-day. The origin of many still used may be traced to their ancient progenitors.

Among the Hebrews, there has been a general belief in amulets from early times. "They were used," says Ibn Ezra, "written on gold or silver after the manner of a charm, and sometimes took the form of miniature serpents or the crescent moon and in time of war the soldiers wore them on their wrists."

During the Middle Ages, it is interesting to note how the doctrine of signatures or similars influenced the use of amulets for curative purposes, and in the case of objects worn as a protection against disease, it is found that they frequently represented the limb or organ that was subject to attack. Thus, a stone shaped like a human foot was carried to protect the person from gout in that limb, and a mole's foot, owing to its cramped appearance, was worn as a cure for cramp. The claws and teeth of wild animals were believed to protect those who carried them from being attacked by savage beasts, and a piece of quartz, which had a resemblance to a molar tooth, was worn to prevent toothache.

Meteoric fragments, popularly called thunderbolts, were considered to be a protection against lightning, while prehistoric stone axes, arrow-heads, iron pyrites, belemnites and other objects of mysterious origin turned up in the soil, were employed for the same purpose.  Pieces of wood shaped like acorns were carried in the pocket during thunderstorms to avert danger from lightning, an idea which probably arose from the belief that the oak tree was particularly likely to be struck, and a piece of a child's navel-cord placed in a ring was supposed to prevent pains in the head or colic in the stomach.

Coral necklaces were originally worn on account of the belief that they would prevent bad dreams and allay the nightly fears of children.  A piece of rope cut from the halter that had hanged a criminal was said to cure ague, and chips from a gibbet on which one or more persons had been executed or exposed, if worn next to the skin or round the neck in a bag, were believed to prevent an attack of the same complaint.

Among physical amulets, a dried frog worn in a silk bag round the neck has long had the reputation of preventing attacks of epilepsy, and legs torn from the body of a living toad were highly esteemed as cure-alls.

In some parts of the country, within recent times, men called "toad-doctors" used to visit the fairs selling toads' legs in little bags, for which they often obtained six or seven shillings, as amulets to prevent sickness.

A Scottish medical man tells the story, that his father, who was born in 1821, knew a man whose only son was a victim of epilepsy, a disease once very common in the Highlands.  He was told that the dried brains of a suicide was an infallible remedy for the complaint.  So he went off at midnight and alone, to a wild spot on the shores of the Bay of

Cromarty, where he knew that a person who had committed suicide had been buried. He extracted the brains which he took home and carefully dried them on a hot iron plate, and gave the ashes to his son with an extraordinary result, so much so, that the fame of the cure spread over the country and people came from far and near to see if they could obtain some of the strange remedy.

In early times, epileptics were believed to be possessed by evil spirits and such amulets afforded a means, by which people thought they could defend themselves from their attacks and by their extraordinary nature drive them from the body.

Written amulets usually consisted of some cabalistic characters or a few words written on a piece of skin or parchment. This was either enclosed in a small case of metal or leather and worn suspended from the neck, or bound against the body. It was not uncommon for the physician of the fifteenth century to write his prescription in mysterious characters, and hang it round the neck of the patient, or bind it over the part nearest the seat of the complaint. Of written amulets perhaps the most popular was Abracadabra, which when written on a piece of parchment in the following manner, was said to protect the wearer from most diseases :

```
A B R A C A D A B R A
  A B R A C A D A B R
    A B R A C A D A B
      A B R A C A D A
        A B R A C A D
          A B R A C A
            A B R A C
              A B R A
                A B R
                  A B
                   A
```

This word is said to be compounded of the three Chaldæan words for the Holy Trinity.

In India, the belief in amulets is common to all races. Among the Buddhists, their use is universal and nearly every man, woman and child wears an amulet round the neck or on the breast.

They are usually enclosed in a box of silver or copper and consist of a picture of a deity, relics of a saint, or a written charm or prayer. The box is often ornamented with turquoise, which is also believed to have the property of averting the " evil eye." Among the Hindus, the claws, teeth, fat, milk and skins of certain animals are believed to confer upon the wearers the courage, agility and cleverness of the animals from which they have been taken. Perforated stones hung round the neck are believed to ward off goitre, and old flint implements and celts are highly valued as a remedy for stomach pains and inflamed eyes, if a little is scraped off and swallowed in water or applied to the part. Certain precious stones are also believed to possess similar virtues. The turquoise is especially valued for its occult properties, and one is often inserted as a charm in the forehead of the images of Buddha. In northern India, if a man bathes while wearing a turquoise, the water it touches is believed to protect him from boils. Copper is regarded as a sacred metal by the Hindus, and rings of that metal are worn to drive away the demon that causes sciatica.

Among the substances used as amulets which have come down from Vedic tradition, plants, roots and herbs play an important part.

These amulets are prepared with elaborate ceremony and the wearer is invested with the object by a priest with solemn ritual.

Certain native woods from sacred trees are believed to have special properties. Against diseases in general, a *varana* amulet, an amulet of barley, an amulet of chips cut from ten different holy trees, glued, and bound together with gold wire, are used.

For constipation, gall-nuts and camphor are carried ; to prevent worms in a child, the root of reed grass is employed, while the head of a stalk of *munja* reed is used to cure excessive discharges.

To endow the wearer with wisdom, an amulet consisting of the tongues of three birds, the parrot, crow and lark, are used and to promote longevity, an amulet of ivory and elephant's hair bound with gold wire. A miniature model of a ship or boat is worn to ensure a safe voyage and a ring of copper, silver, gold or iron, worn on a finger of the right hand is believed to be a protection from sorcery. An amulet made from the skin of a black antelope is employed to promote virility, and to bring prosperity an amulet consisting of four pieces of *khadira* wood, each fashioned in the shape of a plough and put on a string, is worn.

The Tibetans employ amulets and charms very extensively, as might be expected among a people who are so highly superstitious, but they are mostly of ancient Vedic or Hindu origin.

When worn on the person, the charm is generally stitched up in a piece of cloth, or carried as an amulet in a box of metal often decorated with coral or turquoise. They have implicit faith in their charms, and the objects used are those most dreaded by evil spirits. They often take the form of miniature images of the chief Buddhist deities or saints, modelled in metal or clay, sacred symbols, the eight lucky emblems, relics of holy Lamas, consecrated barley, earth, and small pebbles from holy shrines, as well as incense and musk.

In China, the priests sell small metal plaques stamped with magical characters, or write them on small pieces of skin or parchment, which are worn as amulets to protect the wearer from sickness and accident. Buttons stamped with the image of certain deities who have power to avert evil influences, are also used on the clothes.

The talismans and charms employed by the Arabs are chiefly of Gnostic or Hebrew origin. Solomon's ring, which was said to possess a variety of occult virtues is celebrated in Arabian legends. His seal and the hexagonal star are also believed to have powerful magical properties both by the Arabs and the Abyssinians. One of the most popular amulets is the open hand, which like the *mani fico* in Italy is frequently carried to avert the " evil eye." The symbolism of the hand raised, palm outwards, to repel some threatened evil, is obvious, and the five fingers are believed to represent the five most sacred persons, viz., Muhammad, Ali, Fatima, Hasan and Husain.

HAND OF FATIMA

Used as a charm in Persia, Arabia, Syria and Algeria to avert the " evil eye."

*Pitt-Rivers Museum.*

In Persia, written charms and talismans are carried in wallets or wrapped up in pieces of decorative material and secreted on the person or attached to the arms. Women often carry them enclosed in boxes of gold or silver.

In Abyssinia, the charms mostly used are of Coptic origin, and consist of magical texts or prayers written on a long narrow strip of parchment or leather. At the top, a crude picture of the arch-angels, Michael or Gabriel, with sword in hand is sometimes drawn. The inscription may take the form of several secret signs or a spell composed of " words of power."

These scrolls, when rolled up tightly, are either worn suspended from the neck or kept in the house.

Among the Russians in the Middle Ages, plants and herbs played a prominent part as amulets. There was a distinct order of wise men or magicians who were regarded as experts, and each had his own secret herb book which was handed down to his successor.

Pieces of roots, twigs and leaves of certain plants were carried as amulets to ward off various diseases. Stones, belemites, bones and the claws of certain animals were also believed to be endowed with occult properties, while such curious objects as " snakes' horns " and " eagle stones " were very highly prized on account of the difficulty in obtaining them.

The Polar Eskimos near Cape York, Greenland, in order to endow their children with strength, sew into their boys' caps the skin from the roof of a bear's mouth, and to make them wary and cunning, a piece of a fox's head is sewn into their clothes.

The beaks and claws of certain birds are believed to afford protection against disease and death, and a piece of navel-cord is worn as an amulet to promote health in a child and assure longevity.

The Greenlander fastens an eagle's beak to his whaling harpoon to bring good luck, and the Alaskan attaches a tern's bill to his seal-spear with the same object.

The Iroquoise Indians carry miniature canoes as a safeguard against drowning, and small clubs are used as war charms.

In Southern Peru and Bolivia, the Indians believe that tapir's claws will prevent sickness, and the teeth of poisonous snakes fixed on leaves or stuck in the tubes of rushes, are regarded as specifics for headache and also able to prevent blindness.

Underlying most of the American Indian belief in the power of amulets, is the conception of what is called "*manitou.*" Thus, if an Indian experiences a peculiar thrill at the sight or sound of an object, it becomes invested by him with a sacred character and is recognised as "*manitou.*"

The mystic thrill is often actively sought by means of fasts to induce visions, and many amulets used by the Indians are the direct outcome of this and are chosen on account of their being "*manitou.*"

# CHAPTER XXI

## THE LORE OF TALISMANS, MASCOTS AND HEALING-STONES

AS already shown, amulets were chiefly used
or worn for the purpose of protection, in the
belief that some unseen power was resident
in the material object ; whereas the talismans, which
usually consisted of certain symbols or characters
in various combinations either written on parchment or engraved on metal, were carried or worn to
shield the owner from danger and for their help in
bringing good fortune. They were also supposed to
be able to ward off the attacks of evil spirits, and
for this purpose, the ten names of the deity written
on parchment were regarded as being specially
potent and effective.

In some cases, their occult power was believed to
be derived from the stars and constellations. Thus, a
shield written or drawn on parchment marked with
characters drawn from the Tetragrammaton and
made under certain constellations, was carried as a
defence against disease, lightning and tempests. In
others, the power was more of a magical character.
Thus, a certain sign, together with the figure of a
man drawn wearing a coat of mail, was said to give
understanding and memory and to aid against the
attacks of evil spirits.

The custom of placing figure-heads in the bows
of ships originated in Roman times, when it became
customary to put the statues of certain deities such

as Mars, Apollo or Mercury, in the poops of their vessels to preserve them trom tempests and ship-wreck.

A writer of the sixteenth century states, " The custom of mariners setting up these figures against shipwreck is very ancient.  The ship of Alexandria that Paul sailed in, had the images of Castor and Pollux or according to the Arabs, the Gemini, and that which took Hippocrates when he made the journey to Abdera, bare the figure of the Sun."

But some of these talismans were used, not so much for the avoidance of shipwreck, as for the turning away of some disaster or accident and the procuring of good fortune.

The influence of astrology in the Middle Ages is shown in the descriptions handed down as to how certain talismans were made.

Each planet had a table or square consisting of an arrangement of names, figures or numbers, which were supposed to both give and receive power. This table or certain symbols from it, written or engraved, formed the talisman.

Saturn's table engraved on a plate of lead and carried on the person was said to bring good fortune, to help childbirth and make a man powerful. Jupiter's table engraved on a silver plate was believed to bring favour and love to him who wore it, or if graved on coral, it was said to render the owner proof against witchcraft.

The table of Mars was much sought after by soldiers, for when graved on a sword or armour, it made him who carried it valiant in battle and terrible to his adversaries. When cut in carnelion, it was believed to stop bleeding from a wound. The table of Venus engraved on silver was said to bring good fortune and the love of women, while that of Mercury engraved on tin or brass, was believed to bring him who carried it what he desired. The Moon engraved on silver brought cheerfulness and took away ill-will, and when travelling, it expelled enemies and evil things from its owner.

In the Middle Ages, certain precious stones that were supposed to be the abodes of spirits or influenced by the planets, were frequently employed as talismans. When a knight was leaving his castle to join a Crusade or take part in some adventurous expedition, his lady would sometimes give him a precious talisman to protect him from harm and render him invulnerable in battle. Certain jewels that were believed to be endowed with occult powers, were often used with the object of protection and to bring good fortune to the wearer.

The special properties of some stones are thus described. A diamond was believed to endow the wearer with courage, and to make him more fearless than careful. A jacinth had the reputation of being able to strengthen the heart, and was often worn close to the region of that organ. A sapphire was supposed to sharpen the intellect, and was also worn as a preventive against the bites of venomous animals. An emerald was believed to possess the quality of preventing giddiness and strengthening the memory, and a ruby was used as an amulet to ward off plagues and pestilences. The amethyst was supposed to promote temperance and sobriety, and caused the wearer to abstain from strong drinks and from taking too much sleep. The chrysolite was said to ward off fevers, and the onyx, worn round the neck, was supposed to prevent an attack of epilepsy. The opal was believed to cure weak eyes, and the topaz to cure inflammation and keep the wearer from sleep walking. Lapis-lazuli, worn as a jewel, was said to make the wearer fortunate and rich, while amulets of jasper resisted fevers and dropsy. A piece of bloodstone was often carried by those engaged in warfare, so it could be applied to a wound to stop bleeding.

The belief in talismans survives to-day in the use of mascots in the Army and among sports clubs, as well as in the figures and devices displayed on the bonnets of motor cars and on aeroplanes.

Meaningless as many of these objects are, their use is inspired by the same idea, viz., to ward off misfortune or accident and to bring good luck to those who carry them. Faith in the mascot is the common idea, and with that faith its followers believe they will succeed and conquer all difficulties.

A similar notion surrounds the regimental mascot that usually takes the form of a living creature and is really the spiritual helper in animal form.

The Roman legions carried serpents upon poles before them, and at a later period, the shields and helmets of warriors were decorated with emblems of animals or mystic characters, to protect them from invisible foes and aid them in battle.

Well-known instances of animal mascots exist in the goat of the Royal Welch Fusiliers, the Shetland pony of the Argyle and Sutherland Highlanders, and the Irish wolf-hound of the Irish Guards which is aways decorated with shamrock on St. Patrick's Day.

All these are but survivals of the belief in talismans so general centuries ago.

Certain stones and pebbles of mysterious origin have long been believed to possess talismanic and other extraordinary properties, and among them was the toadstone, which for centuries has had a reputation as a protection against witchcraft and poison.

When it came near a liquid containing poison or was placed on a person who was bewitched, it was said to sweat or change colour.

When powdered it was sometimes swallowed as a remedy for fevers or the bites of venomous reptiles.

The so-called toadstones varied in colour, some being dark grey and others of a light brown colour. They were sometimes set in silver and worn as a ring, which was handed down in families from one generation to another. They were supposed to be found in the heads of very old toads, from which they had to be extracted when they were dying. In reality, some were artificially made of fused borax or other material, and others were the fossilised teeth of the ray. Their traditionary virtues were derived from the toad itself, which was credited with many medicinal properties and was used as a remedy for plague and smallpox.

Aubrey gives a process for preparing the toad for internal use, in which " twenty great fatt toads are directed to be stewed slowly, while alive, in a pipkin on the fire. The calcined remains are again heated, and then finely powdered." Sir Kenhelm Digby speaks of their virtues, and recommends " toads for quinsy, bleeding at the nose, and, above all, a most valuable remedy in king's evil and scrofula."

Another famous stone greatly valued in the past was the bezoar, which was renowned throughout the world as an antidote to all poisons and credited with occult properties.

Bezoar stones were calculi found in the intestines

of Persian wild goats, cows, a species of ape and other animals, and varied in size from that of a small egg to a hazel nut.

Some are of a yellowish-white colour while others are brown or greenish-grey, according to the animal from which they are obtained.

Those most highly valued were the Oriental brought from Persia which were sometimes sold for ten times their weight in gold.

Another variety was the Occidental which are said to have been obtained from the llamas of Peru. Similar stones obtained from the monkey were brought from Brazil, while the Indian porcupine furnished another kind of a pale purple colour.

They were not only valued as antidotes to all poisons but scrapings from the stones were given internally for heart weakness, palpitation, colic, jaundice, fevers and plague. During an epidemic of plague in Portugal in the seventeenth century, bezoar stones were lent to sufferers at about the equivalent of ten shillings a day, and only a little over a century ago, a Shah of Persia presented the Emperor Napoleon with three which were said to be of great value.

Goa stones, which were artificial bodies made by the Jesuit missionary fathers who settled in Goa in the East Indies in the seventeenth century, were said to be chiefly composed of powdered precious stones, musk, ambergris and gold leaf. They also were believed to be endowed with remarkable powers, scrapings being given in wine to counteract the effects of poisons and inhaled to prevent infection from disease.

Lemnius tells us of another stone " the bigness of a bean, found in the gizzard of an old cock which makes him that wears it, beloved, constant, bold and valient in fighting and in sports."

Aetites, commonly called the "Eagle stone," was regarded as a charm of great value especially by women, who believed it would prevent miscarriage.

These stones, which were about the size of a walnut, were of a light brown colour and according to tradition, were only to be found in eagles' nests. Analysis has shown them to be composed of an argillaceous oxide of iron deposited around a nucleus of some other material.

Lemnius writing in 1658, says, " Being bound to the wrist of the left arm, by which from the heart the ring finger next to the little finger an artery runs, and if all the time the woman is great with child, this jewel be worn on those parts, it strengthens the child and there is no fear of abortion or miscarriage." This tradition arose from the belief that an eagle could not hatch her eggs without the assistance of the stone.

Lupton referring to the eagle stone says, "it brings love between man and wife and if a woman have a painfull travail in the birth of her child this stone tyed to her thigh brings an easy and light birth."

In some parts of Scotland and Ireland there is a belief, that certain small stones or pebbles have the property of imparting remarkable curative properties to water in which they have been immersed.

They are supposed to be especially effective in cattle diseases and are locally known as "murrain stones " on account of the healing power of the water in which they have been dipped, when sprinkled on cattle suffering or likely to be affected by that disease.

The most famous of these stones was known as

the " Lee Penny " that has come down for centuries
as an heirloom in the ancient Lockhart family.  Sir
Walter Scott records its story in *The Talisman* and
tells how Saladin, the Saracen King disguised as a

physician, cured Richard Cœur de
Lion of a dangerous fever by means
of a talisman which is thus described.

" Know then that the medicine
to which thou Sir King, and many
a one beside, owe their recovery is
a talisman composed under certain
aspects of the heavens when the
Divine Intelligences are most propitious I am but the poor admini-
strator of its virtues.  I dip it in a

THE LEE PENNY

cup of water, observe the fitting hour to administer
it to the patient and the potency of the draught
works the cure."

Sir Walter, at the conclusion of the book, states
that the Soldan sent the talisman as a nuptial present
to the young Earl of Huntingdon and it was bequeathed by him to a brave knight of Scotland, Sir
Simon of the Lee, in whose ancient and honoured
family it is still preserved.  Its virtues are still
employed for stopping blood and in cases of canine
madness.

Scott also recounts the tradition held by the
Lockhart family as to how the talisman was acquired
by them.

From this it appears, that Sir Simon Locard was
a companion of the " good Lord Douglas," when
that staunch comrade of the Bruce set out for
Palestine to deposit his dead master's heart in the
Holy Sepulchre.  As is well known, Douglas, in his
ardour to wage war against the Infidel, turned

aside to help the Spaniards against the Moors, and perished in battle. In the course of this or a later campaign in Palestine, Sir Simon Locard made captive a powerful Moorish emir, for whom he demanded a high ransom. It is related, that in delivering the treasure, the emir's mother or wife inadvertently exposed a curious stone which she hastily endeavoured to conceal. The shrewd Sir Simon incontinently suspected that it must needs be a prized possession, and under pressure, the woman explained that it had power in arresting hæmorrhages and healing wounds. Thereupon, Sir Simon, who seems to have been less gallant towards the fair than on the field, insisted that the talisman should form part of the emir's ransom, and it was very reluctantly handed to him with directions as to its mode of application. When Sir Simon returned from the wars, he brought the talisman with him and it still remains the property of his descendants.

The stone itself is heart-shaped and is set in the reverse of a groat of Edward IV of the London Mint, hence the name " penny."

A small chain is attached to it and it is preserved in a gold box, the gift of the Empress Maria Theresa to the famous Count Lockhart.

The method of using the " stone " or " penny " is important, for it is to be drawn once round a vessel containing the water and then dipped in it three times, or as they say " three dips and a sweil," and then the water receives its power of healing.

Down to the middle of the last century, the water in which the " penny " had been dipped was sent all over the country and had a reputation as a preventive and panacea for many diseases.

The late Sir James Y. Simpson, who was interested

in these old cure stones, states that he was once told
by an old Scottish farmer that in his young days no
byre (cowshed) was considered safe unless it had a
bottle of "Lee Penny water" suspended from the
rafters. So great was the vogue of the amulet at one
time, that ailing people and animals were brought to
Lee from all parts of the country. It frequently
happened that when a town was infested with plague,
which proved intractable to ordinary measures,
application was made for a loan of the Lee Penny.
In the reign of Charles I, the Corporation of Newcastle
(which city was then being ravaged by the pestilence)
borrowed the Penny, under the heavy bond of £6,600
It is said that the Corporation would willingly have
forfeited the bond in order to retain such an alexi-
pharmic in their midst, but the Lockharts insisted
on its restoration to them. As late as the beginning
of the eighteenth century, the stone was lent to
Baird of Saughtonhall, near Edinburgh, to cure his
lady, said to be suffering from hydrophobia. According to the account given at the time, Lady Baird was
actually in the " horrors " of rabies when the Penny
arrived, but by drinking the water medicated by the
stone, and bathing in it, she was speedily restored to
health. Towards the end of the century, belief in the
efficacy of the Penny for human diseases seems to
have sunk almost to zero, but it was still supposed
to be of value for veterinary purposes. In his *Account
of the Lee Penny*, published in 1782, Hunter states :
" It being taken and put into the end of a cloven
stick and washed in a tub full of water and given to
cattell to drink infallibly cures almost all manner of
diseases. The people come all airts (parts) of the
Kingdom with diseased beasts."

Simpson mentions several other medicinal stones

which were formerly highly esteemed in the Highlands and Lowlands of Scotland, but their use for
human beings has now practically ceased, though
they are still valued and employed for treating cattle
when sick.

In connection with the Lee Penny, when Isobel
Young was charged and convicted of witchcraft in
1629, in the evidence against her and her husband
George Smith, it transpired, that they had sent to the
Laird of Lee to borrow his curing stone for their
cattle, which had the "routing ill." This curing
stone, called the Lee Penny—being an ancient
precious stone or amulet set in a silver penny—was
preserved in the family of Lockhart of Lee. Lady
Lee, it appeared, declined to lend the stone, but
gave flagons of water in which the "penny" had
been steeped. This water having been drunk by the
cattle, was believed to have effected their cure.

Early in the eighteenth century, Gavin Hamilton
of Raploch lodged a complaint with the Presbytery
of Lanark against Sir Thomas Lockhart of Lee for
his superstitious use of "ane stone set in silver for
the curing of diseased cattell." The matter, after
the manner of ecclesiastical deliberations, was carried from court to court, but it was ultimately
adjudged with all solemnity, that "whereas the charm
was merely dipped into water which the diseased
cattle had to drink, whereas no words of incantation
were used to invoke its magical powers, and whereas
they had so far advanced in science as to know that
God had given special virtue to herbs and stones for
healing man and beast, they found no cause to
prevent its use."

During the Great War, many of the German
prisoners were found to be in possession of talismans,

chiefly consisting of written charms or cabalistic letters inscribed on paper, which they wore or carried to protect them from harm, disease or death. One of them found on a soldier read as follows :

" A powerful prayer, whereby one is protected and guarded against shot and sword, against visible and invisible foes, as well as against all manner of evil. May God preserve me against all manner of arms and weapons, shot and cannon, long or short swords, knives or daggers, or carbines, halberds, and anything that cuts or points, against thrusts, rapiers, long and short rifles or guns and such-like, which have been forged since the birth of Christ ; against all kinds of metal, be it iron or steel, brass or lead, ore, or wood."

Such talismans were probably of ancient origin and appear to have been handed down in country districts in Germany from one generation to another.

# CHAPTER XXII

## THE FOLK-LORE OF COLOURS, LETTERS AND
## NUMBERS

COLOUR has played by no means an unimportant part in folk-medicine for centuries past, and to red in particular was attributed many and peculiar virtues.

Its employment is thought to have arisen from the supposition that it was the most obnoxious colour to evil spirits, who were generally regarded as being the cause of every disease and ailment that the flesh of man is heir to. Besides this, it was considered to be a sacred and a regal colour, symbolic also of triumph and victory over all enemies. It represented heat and therefore in a manner that element itself, just as white typified the contrary element, cold.

John of Gaddesden, an old English physician who flourished in the fourteenth century, recommended that red bed coverings should be used for the cure of smallpox, with the idea that the colour induced the pustules to come to the surface of the body.

" Let scarlet red be taken," he says in his *Rosa Anglica*, " and let him who is suffering smallpox be entirely wrapped in it or in some other red cloth. This I did when the son of the illustrious King of England (Edward II) suffered from smallpox ; I took care that all about his bed be red and that cure succeeded very well."

In the *Saxon Leechdoms* there is a cure for lunacy

which reads : " Take a clove-wort and wreath it with a red thread about the man's neck when the moon is on the wane in the month of April and he will soon be healed."

A skein of scarlet silk worn round the neck was said to prevent bleeding from the nose, and as late as the first half of the last century, scarlet tongues of cloth were sold in a shop in Fleet Street, to tie about the throats of sufferers from scarlet fever.

We have a relic of this old superstition in the faith that is still placed in a piece of flannel worn to prevent rheumatism, but to be effectual the flannel must be *red*.

In early times, black and white were both used in folk-medicine and on an Assyrian clay tablet which dates from about 1500 B.C., we have the following recommendation :

> " Take a white cloth ; in it place the marint.
> In the sick man's right hand ;
> And take a black cloth,
> Wrap it round his left hand.
> Then all the evil spirits
> And the sins which he has committed
> Shall quit their hold of him,
> And shall never return."

Apparently, by the black cloth in his left hand the sufferer repudiated all his former evil deeds, while the white cloth in his right hand symbolised his trust in holiness.

In north Hampshire, a stye in the eye is treated by plucking a single hair from the tail of a *black* cat on the first night of the new moon and rubbing it nine times over the pustule.

The smearing of blood taken from the tail of the same animal over the parts affected, was used as a cure for shingles, and an ancient cure for convulsions was a piece of flesh cut from a *white* hound, baked with meal.

Colours form an important part in the ceremonial of the Roman Catholic Church, and the vestments used for the Mass vary in colour according to the nature of the day. Thus, red is worn when martyrs are celebrated, gold on festive occasions, violet on fast days, white to celebrate virgins, and green on days that have no specific character.

Customs regarding colour in wearing apparel vary in different parts of the country, but at christening ceremonies it was formerly a general custom for boys to be decked with blue ribbons, while girl babies were adorned with pink.

With respect to weddings and the colour, if any, to be worn by the bride or her maids, there is an old saying :

> " Green is forsaken,
> And yellow is forsworn,
> But blue is the prettiest colour that's worn."

The antipathy to green as a colour for any part of a bridal costume is still very marked in the northern counties. In the south it is said :

> " Those dressed in blue
> Have lovers true
> In green and white
> Forsaken quite."

Another rhyme runs :

> " Blue is true, yellow's jealous,
> Green's forsaken, red's brazen,
> White is love and black is death."

The popularity of blue is universal and the phrase " true blue " has come to be synonymous with fidelity. In the Near East, it is regarded as the most

powerful colour to avert the " evil eye," and the
majority of the charms worn for that purpose are
blue. It was essentially the colour of lovers as
illustrated in the following lines :

> " If you love me, love me true,
> Send me a ribbon and let it be blue ;
> If you hate me, let it be seen,
> Send me a ribbon, a ribbon of green."

In Leicestershire it is said that a bride should
wear

> " Something new,
> Something blue,
> Something borrowed."

while in Lancashire the saying is thus varied :

> " Something old, something new,
> Something borrowed and something blue."

How did belief in luck arise ? There are various
suppositions in answer to this question, for what we
call luck is really the absence of misfortune. To be
lucky is to be fortunate or to be habitually favoured
by fortune, that may or may not be due to skill or
design.

Some say that the idea arose when primitive man,
who believed that the supernatural world was bent
on his destruction, managed to live and attain some
degree of comfort by appeasing the evil spirits that
beset him, he deemed himself a fortunate or " lucky "
being.

If, on the other hand, he was stricken by disease
or came to want, he was out of favour with the
supernatural world and was an " unlucky " being
afflicted by misfortune.

Thus, a person was considered lucky if he attained
wealth, power, health and comfort, or on the other

hand, failure of design, poverty and ill-health indicated his misfortune or ill-luck.

Luck was not confined to persons, for in early times it was also applied to certain days and numbers. Grose says, that " many persons have certain days of the week and month on which they are particularly fortunate and others in which they are generally unlucky, and these days vary in different persons."

Friday has long been under opprobrium and it is a day on which no new work or enterprise should be begun.

Stow observes, that Thursday was noted as a fatal day to King Henry VIII and his posterity, and in later times the superstitious believed that certain letters were also fraught with good or evil fortune in a person's destiny.

An ingenious writer contends that the letter M was fateful to the Emperor Napoleon Buonaparte, which he illustrates as follows :

" Marbœuf first recognised his genius at the Military College, Marengo was his first great victory, Morlier was his best general, Moreau betrayed him, Murat died for him, Marie Louise shared his fortunes, Moscow marked the turn in those fortunes, and Metternich beat him in diplomacy.  His first battle was Montenotte, his last Mont St. Jean.  He stormed Montmartre, took Milan, Marmont deserted him. His right hand man was Montesquieu and his last resting-place in France, Malmaison.  He surrendered to Captain Maitland and his companions at St. Helena were Montholon and Marchand.

" His marshals were Massena, Mortier, Marmont, Macdonald, Murat and Moncey, and no fewer than twenty-six of his generals had names beginning with the letter M."

"Napoleon III," he contends, "had the same letter of fate, for he married the Countess of Montijo, his most intimate friend was Morny and his tutor Moreith of Montelimar. His greatest military successes were the capture of the Malakoff and the Mamelon tower. His greatest battle was Montebello and MacMahon won Magenta for him. He drove the Austrians out of Marignano and made his triumphant entry into Milan. He was repulsed before Mantua, in his last war driven back to the Moselle and his fate was settled by Moltke at Metz."

Grafton in his *Manuel* (1565), records the following unlucky days according to the opinions of astrologers: "January 1, 2, 4, 5, 10, 15, 17, 29. All these are very unlucky. February 26, 27, 28, unlucky; 8, 10, 17, very unlucky. March 16, 17, 20, very unlucky. April 7, 8, 10, 20, unlucky; 16, 21, very unlucky. May 3, 6, unlucky; 7, 15, 20, very unlucky. June 10, 22, unlucky; 4, 8, very unlucky. July 15, 21, very unlucky. August 1, 29, 30, unlucky; 19, 20, very unlucky. September 3, 4, 21, 23, unlucky; 6, 7, very unlucky. October 4, 16, 24, unlucky; 6, very unlucky. November 5, 6, 29, 30, unlucky; 15, 20, very unlucky. December 15, 22, unlucky; 6, 7, 9, very unlucky."

In Scotland, that day of the week upon which the 14th of May happens to fall, is believed to be unlucky throughout the remainder of the year, and formerly none would marry or do business on it.

In an account of the *Perillous Dayes of every Month* an old writer observes: "In the change of every moon be two dayes in the which, what so ever thing is begun, late or never, it shall come to no good end, and the dayes be full perillous for many things. In January when the moon is three or four dayes old. In February 5 or 7. In March 6 or 7. In April 5 or 8. May 8 or 9. June 15 or 25. July 3 or 13. August 8 or 13. September 8 or 13. October 5 or 12. November 5 or 9. December 3 or 13."

In the seventeenth century, when bleeding was regarded as a panacea for nearly every ill, it was forbidden to let blood on six days of the year as " being perillous of death." These were January 3rd, July 1st, October 2nd, August 1st and the last days of April and December.

Sir John Sinclair in his *Statistical Account of Scotland*, 1793, states : " Lucky and unlucky days are by many anxiously observed. None choose to marry in January or May. Some things are to be done before the full moon, others after. In fevers, the illness, is expected to be more severe on Sunday than on the other days of the week and if easier on Sunday, a relapse is feared.

At Kirkwall and St. Ola, in many days of the year the fishermen will neither go to sea in search of fish nor perform any sort of work at home."

From a very early period, certain numbers have been believed to have a mystic significance and were regarded by magicians as important when casting spells.

The number 7, so frequently mentioned in the Old Testament in connection with Jewish ceremonial, is still regarded as a divine and lucky number. The Pythagoreans called it the vehicle of human life, and it was venerated in religion and as the number of blessedness and rest. " It works wonderful things," says a writer of the sixteenth century. " Thus the seventh son can heal distempers and can foresee the future."

In Yorkshire, there is an old belief that the seventh son of a seventh son is a born physician, having an intuitive knowledge of the art of curing all disorders, and the same idea prevails in Wales.

In the northern counties, it is said, if any woman has seven boys in succession, the last should be bred to the medical profession as he would be sure of being successful.

The peculiar powers attributed to certain numerals are thus recorded in a manuscript of the sixteenth century.

One, was regarded as the father of numbers and signified harmony. It was a fortunate and prosperous number.

Two, was the number of intellect and the mother of numbers. It was generally held to be an evil number bringing trouble and unhappiness. Three, was a holy number and has ever been looked upon as lucky. It was the number of the Trinity and signified plenty and fruitfulness. Thus we say, three times running is lucky and the third day was venerated in ancient times.

Four, was regarded by Pythagoras as the root and foundation of all other numbers, and over it his followers swore their most solemn oaths. It was the square number, and the number of endurance, firmness of purpose and will.

Five, was a peculiar and magical number of importance to the magicians, and the pentacle, with its five points, was regarded as a powerful talisman against the approach of evil spirits. It was also believed to be the number and symbol of justice and faith.

Six, was regarded as the perfection of numbers. It was sacred to Venus and regarded as the ideal

number of love.   In six days the world was made
and it is called the number of man, because on the
sixth day he was created.

Seven, was the most highly esteemed among sacred
numbers and was believed to be particularly lucky.
The Pythagoreans called it the vehicle of human
life, for there were seven days, seven planets, seven
metals, and the seven ages of man.   It is called
the number of an oath by the Hebrews and was so
used by Abraham.

It has been termed the number of Royalty and a
royal salute is thrice seven or twenty-one guns.

" Are there not some who cure by observing number ? " says an old writer on witchcraft.   " Balaam
used magian geometricam.   There are some witches
who enjoin the sick to dip their shirts seven times
in south running water.   Elisha sent Naaman to
wash in Jordan seven times.   Elijah on the top of
Carmel sends his servant seven times to look for
rain.   When Jericho was taken, they compassed
the city seven times."

Eight, was regarded as the number of justice and
fullness, but was also a number of attraction.

Nine, was a number of power, wisdom, mystery
and protection, and was used by the early priest-
physicians to cure sickness.   It was the product of
three and connected with intellectual and spiritual
knowledge.

Ten, was a holy and divine number, but eleven
was of evil reputation and signified violence and
destruction.   Twelve was a divine number, wherein
heavenly things were measured.   Thus, there are
twelve signs of the Zodiac, twelve months in the
year, twelve tribes of Israel, twelve prophets, twelve
apostles and twelve stones in Aaron's breastplate.

It was further esteemed as the number of time and experience.

Of all numerals, however, thirteen was regarded as the most abhorrent and fraught with ill-luck. It signified death, misfortune and general destruction. The Romans considered it most unlucky and an evil omen for thirteen people to sit down in a room together. Later its bad repute was attributed to the fact that thirteen was the number at the Last Supper, Judas being the thirteenth, and numerous stories are related concerning this superstition and the misfortunes which have followed it.

The common belief that should thirteen persons sit at a table, one of them will die before the year is out, still exercises a wide influence in our social life. On Friday, May 13th, 1927, it was stated in the press of that date, that " social functions were almost at a standstill," and recently a daily paper thought it well to report that the Imperial Airways aeroplane " Horatius " was struck by lightning thirteen minutes after it had left Croydon Aerodrome and there were thirteen passengers on board.

Many superstitions are associated with other numerals such as number forty, which was revered and held in veneration in ancient times for its connection with the life of Christ, but sufficient have been mentioned to show the curious powers that have been attached to colours and numbers from the beginning of our era.

# CHAPTER XXIII

## THE FOLK-LORE OF DRINKING AND DRINKING VESSELS

THROUGHOUT the ages many curious customs have been associated with drinking and drinking vessels, some of which have survived and are carried on to-day.

Fermented liquors were known to the ancient Babylonians and Egyptians at least three thousand years ago, and there are many allusions to intoxication in the Old Testament scriptures, but the lore of drinking customs is more directly connected with the ceremonies associated with the act of drinking.

In the early centuries, to convert the skull of an enemy into a drinking cup was a common practice and many references are made to this grim custom by the classic historians.

Warnefrid in his *De Gestis Longobard* tells us that "Albin slew Cuminum and having carried away his head converted it into a drinking vessel, which kind of cup is called Schala."

Livy, Herodotus and Diodorus Siculus mention the same custom among the Scythians and Gauls, and Ragnar Lodbrog, in his death-song, consoles himself with the thought, "I shall soon drink beer from hollow cups made of skulls."

In the Middle Ages, the word skoll or skull came to be applied to the drinking of a health, for as Calderwood states, "Drinking the king's skole meant the drinking of his cup in honour of him," which, he adds, "should always be drank standing."

Both the Greeks and Romans, in ancient times, had many customs attached to drinking, and at their banquets the wine-cup was never raised to the lips without first invoking a blessing from one of their deities, and at the conclusion of the feast another cup was drunk to their good genius.

The Romans drank to the healths of their Emperors and of friends who were absent, and at their great banquets, first elected a master of the table, who after having drank his first cup to the most distinguished guest, handed a full cup to him, in which he would acknowledge the compliment. It was then passed round by the company, always from left to right and presented with the right hand, but sometimes each guest had his own cup which was replenished with wine directly it was emptied.

In Greece, the wines of Cyprus, Chio and Lesbos were much esteemed, the latter being especially mentioned by Horace in the lines :

> " Beneath the shade you here may dine,
> And quaff the harmless Lesbian wine."

He also alludes to Falerian, a strong rough wine that had to be kept for ten years before it was fit for drinking, and was then mixed with honey to soften it.

Homer refers to a famous wine of Maronea of Thrace, which was sometimes mixed with twenty times the quantity of water before drinking it, but it was customary with the Greeks to dilute most of their wines with water in the proportion of three of the latter to one part of wine.

The Anglo-Saxons drank chiefly ale and mead, and wine is referred to as the drink of elders and wise men. William of Malmesbury in describing the customs of Glastonbury tells us that the monks had mead in cans and wine in their grace-cup.

That wine was appreciated in this country in the twelfth century, is evidenced by the following description of what a good wine should be, given by a writer of the period. He says, " It should be clear like the tears of a penitent so that a man may see distinctly to the bottom of the glass ; its colour should represent the greenness of a buffalo's horn ; when drunk it should descend impetuously like thunder ; sweet tasted as an almond ; creeping like a squirrel ; leaping like a roebuck ;

ANGLO-SAXON DRINKING CUPS

strong like the building of a Cistercian monastery ; glittering like a spark of fire ; subtle like the logic of the schools of Paris ; delicate as fine silk and colder than crystal."

The principal wine drunk in England in the thirteenth and fourteenth centuries was Malmsey, a sweet wine prepared from the Malvasia grape and imported from Candia. Although it would appear to be far from a refreshing liquid in which to bathe, according to the records of the expenses of Mary, Queen of Scots during her captivity at Tutbury, we find a weekly allowance of Malmsey granted to her for a bath.

Clary was another wine favoured in the time of Edward IV and was prepared by infusing the herb of that name in spirit. It was said to possess stomachic properties, was believed to be an excellent cordial and was used as a remedy for hysteria.

In the fifteenth century, compound drinks came into vogue and in the monastic records we find reference to spiced liquors, such as raisin wine with comfits and flavoured with cinnamon. Among these, Hypocras was a favourite, which was usually served hot at the commencement of a banquet and also at wedding feasts.

It was sometimes prepared by infusing pepper, ginger, cloves, grains of paradise, ambergris and musk in brandy, to which sugar and red wine were added.

Sir Walter Raleigh was the inventor of another cordial compound which he called " Cordial Water." It consisted of strawberries infused in brandy, sweetened to taste and diluted with water.

It was not until 1531, we first hear of Sack, a name originally applied to the vintages of Candia, Cyprus and Spain. It was evidently a full-bodied wine, for Sir Launcelot Sparcock in the *London Prodigal* says :

> " Drawer, let me have sack for us old men ;
> For these girls and knaves small wines are best."

The sack of Shakespeare's time is thought to have been a lighter wine, similar to our sherry, and all the Elizabethan poets are agreed on its stimulating properties. Thus, one sings :

> " Sacke will make the merry minde be sad,
> So will it make the melancholie glad.
> If mirthe and sadnesse doth in sacke remain,
> When I am sad I'll take some sacke again."

The custom of pledging, is said to have come down from the time when the Danes held sway in the land.

" For," says an old writer, " it was common with these ferocious people to stab a native in the act of drinking with a knife or dagger, hereupon people would not drink in company unless someone present would be their pledge or surety that they would receive no hurt whilst they were in their draught."

Henry, in referring to the subject, says: " If an Englishman presumed to drink in the presence of a Dane without his express permission, it was esteemed so great a mark of disrespect that nothing but his instant death could expiate.  Nay, the English were so intimidated that they would not adventure to drink even when they were invited, until the Danes had pledged their honour for their safety, which introduced the custom of pledging each other in drinking."

To prevent excess in drinking, in Anglo-Saxon times, Dunston, Archbishop of Canterbury, ordained that pins or nails should be fastened into the drinking cups and horns, at stated distances, and whosoever should drink beyond these marks at one draught, should receive severe punishment.  This doubtless gave rise to the custom of pin-drinking or " Nick the Pin " as it was called, in which the drinker was not allowed to drink below the pin or peg placed inside his cup.

Later, this developed into the peg-tankard which was an ordinary shaped mug, having in the inside a row of eight pins, one above another from top to bottom.  It usually held two quarts, so that there was a gill of ale between each pin.  The first person who drank was to empty the tankard to the first peg or pin, the second was to empty to the next pin and so on, making them all drink alike or the same quantity.

The whistle-tankard was another variety of drinking vessel, which was constructed with a whistle attached to the brim which could be sounded when the cup required replenishing. From this the saying " If you want more you must whistle for it," is said to have originated.

To drink to the nail or to drink " supernaculum," as it was called, an ancient custom in England, meant emptying the cup or tankard and then pouring the drop or two that remained at the bottom upon the person's nail that drank it, to show that he was no flincher.

The custom is thus alluded to in *The Winchester Wedding*, 1792 :

> " Then Philip began her health,
>     And turn'd a beer-glass on his thumb ;
>   But Jenkin was reckoned for drinking
>     The best in Christendom."

Health drinking in the seventeenth century, if we are to believe Barnaby Richin in 1619, developed into an elaborate ceremonial. Describing the method in his time, he tells us that the proposer " First uncovering his head, hee takes a full cup in his hand and settling his countenance with a grave aspect, hee craves for audience ; silence being once obtained hee begins to breathe out the name peradventure of some honourable personage, that is worthy of a better regard than to have his name polluted amongst a company of drunkards ; but his health is drunk to, and hee that pledgeth must likewise off with his cap, kisse his fingers and bowing himselfe in signe of a reverent acceptance. When the leader sees his follower thus prepared, he soups up his broathe, turnes the bottom of the cup upwards and in ostentation of his dexteritie, gives the cup a phillip to make it cry Twango.

" The cup being newly replenished to the breadth of an haire, he that is the pledger must now begin his part and thus it goes round throughout the whole company."

The custom of drinking healths was in later times commonly called " toasting," a word of which the origin is uncertain. There is evidence to show, that pieces of toast were sometimes put into the beverages of the seventeenth century with nutmeg or other spice, to give the liquor a flavour.

The Earl of Rochester alludes to this in the lines :

> " Make it so large that, fill'd with sack
> Up to the swelling brim,
> Vast toasts on the delicious lake,
> Like ships at sea may swim."

Again, in 1720, Warton thus writes of Oxford ale :

> " My sober evening let the tankard bless,
> With toast embrown'd and fragrant nutmeg fraught,
> While the rich draught, with oft repeated whiffs,
> Tobacco mild improves."

Concerning the origin of the word in its present sense, a story is told in an old volume of the *Tatler* from which it may be gathered that the term had its rise from an incident that occurred at Bath in the time of Charles II.

" It happened that on a public day, a celebrated beauty of those times was in the Cross Bath and one of the crowd of her admirers took a glass of the water in which the fair one stood and drank her health to the company. There was in the place a gay fellow half fuddled, who offered to jump in and swore though he liked not the liquor he would have the ' toast.' He was opposed in his resolution, yet this whim gave foundation to the present honour which is done to the lady we mention in our liquor who had ever since been called a ' toast '."

From other allusions in poems and plays of the seventeenth century, it was evidently a practice to put toast into ale with nutmeg and sugar. Thus we have in an old song, " Put a browne tost in the pot," and in another in 1613 :

> " Will he will drinke yet but a draught at most
> That must be spiced with a nut-browne tost."

The popular phrase " no heel-taps," in connection with toasting, had its origin in the command that no liquor was to be left in the bottom or heel of the glass after drinking the toast. Bannatyne alludes to the phrase in 1780, and says, " Having it seems a little more than was proper in the bottom of his glass he was saluted with the call ' no heel-taps '."

Some of the old " heel-tap " glasses of the eighteenth century had toasts to fair ladies engraved around the rims.

Upsie-Freeze was another old term applied to drinking, and we find reference to it both in Masinger's plays and Brathwayte's verses. The former tells us of " Upsy freesy tipplers " and the latter writes :

> " Where either called for wine that best did please,
> Thus helter skelter drunke we Upsefrese."

Another game connected with drinking was the Scottish " Hy-Jinks " which according to Allan Ramsey, " Thus the quaff or cup is filled to the brim, then one of the company takes a pair of dice and after crying ' Hy-jinks ' he throws them out ; the number he casts up points out the person must drink, he who threw beginning at himself number

one, and so round till the number of the persons
agrees with that of the dice, then he sets the dice
to him or bids him take them.  He on whom they
fall is obliged to drink or pay a small forfeiture in
money ;  then throws and so on, but if he forgets
to cry ' Hy-jinks ' he pays a forfeiture into the
bank."

The term " Hob-nob," which formerly signified a
request to drink a glass of wine with the proposer,
is said to have originated as follows :  " In the days
of Good Queen Bess, when great chimneys were
common, there was at each corner of the hearth a
small elevated projection called the hob and behind
it a seat.  In winter time, the beer was placed on
the hob to warm and the cold beer was set on a
small table said to have been called the nob ;  so
that the question, ' Will you have Hob or Nob '
seems only to have meant ' Will you have warm or
cold beer.' "

In the early centuries, the drinking cups were often
fashioned of gold or silver and elaborately decorated
with precious stones or chased in beautiful designs
by master craftsmen.

A notable example is the Howard Grace Cup, now
in the Victoria and Albert Museum, which is made
of ivory set in gold with an inscription round the
edge, " Drink thy wine with joy," and on the lid
are engraved the words, " Sobrii estote," with the
initials T.B. interlaced with a mitre.  Many other
fine Grace and Loving-cups are in the possession of
our City Companies and are used to adorn their
tables at their feasts and banquets.

Heywood, writing on drinking cups in 1635, says:
" Some are of Elme, some of Box, some of Maple,
some of Holly ;  mazers, broad-mouthed dishes,

noggins, whiskins, piggins, crinzes, ale-bowles, was-
sell-bowles, tankards and kannes from a bottle to
a pint.

"Other bottles we have of leather small-jacks,
besides the great black-jacks and bombards at the
court, from which the Frenchmen used to say that
Englishmen drank out of their boots.

"We have besides cups made of horns of beasts,
of cocker-nuts, of gourds, of the eggs of ostriches, and
others made of shells of divers fishes.

"Come to plate, every taverne can afford you flat
bowles, prounet bowles, beakers, and private house-
holders in the cities can furnish their cupboards
with flagons, tankards, beere cups, wine bowles,
some white, some percell guilt, some guilt all over,
some with covers, others without of sundry shapes
and qualities."

Of the phrases associated with drinking in his time
he mentions "to drinke upse-phreese, supernaculum,
to swallow a snap-dragon or a raw egg, to see that
no lesse than three at once be bare to a health."

In the eighteenth century curious names were
often given to the favourite cups compounded of
beer, for which several taverns were noted. Thus
we had Humptie-dumptie, Clamber-clown, Stiffle,
Blind Pinneaux, Old Pharaoh, Three-threads, Knock-
me-down, Hugmatee and Foxcomb, all of which
were very similar in composition.

Like the cocktails of to-day, other compound
drinks had their special names, such as Cock-ale,
Stepony, Stitchback, Northdown and Mum, while
one hostelry in Fleet Street which was called the
"Heaven," was renowned for its claret-cup, a drink
that was compared by those who affected it with the
name of the tavern.

The Grace-cup or Loving-cup in former times was filled with a compound of wine and spices or sack. It was handed round the table before the removal of the cloth, and no one was allowed to drink therefrom until the guest on either side of him had stood up ; then the person who drank rose and bowed to his neighbours, a custom that is said to have originated in the precaution to keep the right or dagger-hand employed.

# CHAPTER XXIV

## THE LORE OF GAMES—SUPERSTITIONS OF THE THEATRE

OF our popular outdoor national games which have survived the centuries, football is probably the oldest.

It was originally associated with Shrove Tuesday and played in the streets or fields on that and other holidays. As far back as 1533, in the records of the city of Chester, there is an account of " the offering of ball and foot-balls that were put down and the silver bell offered to the Maior on Shrove-Tuesday."

In the streets of our villages or towns and even in the City of London as late as the seventeenth century, football contests took place between the townsfolk and were watched with keen interest from the windows of the neighbouring houses.

In Scotland, football has always been popular, although James I described it as " too rough a game and meeter for laming than making able."

From other accounts, such contests often developed into a free fight among the contestants, for Stubbs describes it as " a bloody and murthering practise rather then a fellowly sport or pastime," and broken bones and even deaths were not uncommon.

In the time of the Commonwealth, the Puritans set their faces against the game and for some years it languished, but it was too deeply rooted in the English people to be extinguished and in the eighteenth century it was revived with renewed vigour.

It was played with the most primitive rules, and Misson describes it as " a useful and charming exercise played with a leather ball about as big as one's head, filled with wind.

" This is kick'd about from one to t'other in the streets by him that can get at it and that is all the art of it."

Towards the end of the eighteenth century, both men and women played in some of the Scottish contests. In Inverness-shire it is stated that on Shrove Tuesday there was formerly " a standing match at foot-ball between the married and un-married women in which the former were always victors."

From another account we learn that in the parish of Scone, every year on Shrove Tuesday, the bachelors and married men drew themselves up at the Cross of Scone on opposite sides. A ball was then thrown up and they played from two o'clock till sunset.

The rules of the game at that time are interesting. ' He who at any time got the ball into his hands, ran with it till overtaken by one of the opposite party, and then, if he could shake himself loose from those of the opposite side who seized him, he ran on. If not he threw the ball from him, unless it was wrested from him by the other party, but no person was allowed to kick it."

The object of the married men was to put it three times into a small hole in the moor, the dool or limit on the one hand ; while that of the bachelors was to drown it, which meant dipping it three times into a deep place in the river, the limit on the other. The side which could effect either of these objects won the game.

Football was prohibited in Scotland by James II in 1457 and again in 1481 by James IV.

For the last two centuries it has been a popular game among the colliers and miners in the North of England, and at the time of a wedding it was formerly the custom for a party to watch the bridegroom coming out of church after the ceremony, in order to demand money for a football, a claim that admitted of no refusal.

In Cumberland, a football match was often associated with a cockfight and good players and sporting birds were sought for with great diligence.

At Bromfield, when the cockfight was ended, the football was thrown down in the churchyard and the point then to be contested was, which side could carry it to the house of his respective captain, perhaps a distance of two or three miles. Every inch of ground was keenly contested and the ball was presented to the conquering side.

The modern development of the game, whose popularity is now universal, does not come within our scope, but its past history, such as is known, is not without interest to its exponents at the present day.

Cricket, which is essentially an old English game, has also got an interesting past, for in one form or another it dates back to the fourteenth century.

In a manuscript written in 1334, now in the Bodleian library, there is a drawing of a woman represented as bowling to a man who is holding a bat in his hand prepared to strike, and there is a record that, in 1350, John Parish of Guildford enclosed a plot of land for the purpose of playing cricket, but it is probable at that time it was little more than a game of bat and ball.

The game is mentioned in the time of Queen Elizabeth, in a dispute about the enclosure of a piece of ground, and in 1611 there is an allusion to it in Cotgrave's *Dictionary* with reference to a " cricket-staff or the crooked-staff wherewith boys play cricket."

In 1694, in Chamberlain's *Angliæ Notitia*, there is a statement that, " they will go in the evening to

BAT AND BALL, OR CRICKET
*From a manuscript of the fourteenth century.*

foot-ball, stool-ball, cricket, prison-house, wrestling and cudgel playing," and in 1699, the game of cricket is again mentioned.

From all accounts, the county of Kent appears to have been the original home of cricket, for according to an old writer it is " a game most usual in Kent with a cricket-ball, bowled and struck with two cricket-bats between two wickets."

The first print illustrating the game as then played by the " Gentlemen's Club, White Conduit House, which shows wickets, stumps, batsmen and fielders," was published in 1784.

Lord's cricket ground, still the scene of many important matches, owes its name to Thomas Lord, who was one of the attendants at the White Conduit Club at the close of the eighteenth century, and he subsequently established the Marylebone Club at Lord's.

The popularity of cricket has never waned in England, and the love of the game, the name of which has become synonymous with fair play and Englishmen all over the world, has spread to most of our Dominions across the seas. A poet thus sings its praise:

> " Hail cricket ! glorious manly British game,
> First of all sports, be first alike in fame."

Golf or goff is also of respectable antiquity, and Strutt considered it the most ancient of all games played with a ball that required the assistance of a club or bat. In the reign of Edward III, he tells us, " The Latin name Cambuca was applied to this pastime and it derived the denomination no doubt, from the crooked club or bat with which it was played. The bat was also called a bandy from its being bent and hence the game itself is frequently written in English as bandy-ball."

It has been played in Scotland, which may be called the home of the game, since 1457, the ball used at that time being stuffed very hard with feathers and it has never lost its popularity in the North.

It became a fashionable game among the nobility in England at the beginning of the seventeenth century and was favoured by Prince Henry, the eldest son of James I. A story is told by a contemporary writer, that at one time when " playing at Goff, a play not unlike pale-maille, while his schoolmaster stood talking with another and marked not his highness, warning him to stand further off ; the prince thinking he had gone aside lifted up his golf club to strike the ball ; meantime, one standing by said to him, ' Beware that you hit not Master Newton,' wherewith he, drawing back his hand, said, ' Had I done so, I had but paid my debts '."

The popularity of golf is now world-wide and poets have sung its praises and extolled the glory of its champions on both sides of the Atlantic.

The few superstitions associated with our national games are chiefly based on a firm belief in the

A GAME OF GOLF
*From a manuscript in the Bodleian Library. Circa 1500.*

principle of luck, which is exemplified in the mascots carried by football teams and displayed by their adherents on one side or the other at our great matches.

Their object presumably is to avert misfortune, to inspire faith in their teams and to aid them to victory.

Like those who go down to the sea in ships, actors and those connected with the theatre are often superstitious and many curious customs are associated with the theatrical profession.

How some of them have arisen it is difficult to trace, while others, such as it being regarded as unlucky to open a " show " on a Friday or the thirteenth of a month, are obviously of a general character and not specially connected with the theatre.

Like the sailor's belief that whistling on board ship is unlucky, so it is considered of evil portent to whistle in an actor's dressing-room, and those who inadvertently do so are made to go outside and turn round three times.

For a lady to start knitting on the side of the stage is regarded as unlucky, and it is supposed to be equally so should anyone wish an actor or actress " good luck " on the first night or before a performance.

The fact that it is regarded as unlucky to wear either peacock feathers or a green costume on the stage is but the adoption of a general superstition.

Most theatres boast of a cat or two and they are generally encouraged and protected, for if one should walk on the stage before the curtain goes up it is considered a lucky omen, but on the other hand, if pussy makes her appearance during a scene in the play, it is believed to be a sign of coming misfortune.

At one time it was considered unlucky to have real flowers on the stage in a setting, while to hum " I Dreamt that I Dwelt in Marble Halls " or " The Dead March," was to court disaster.

Probably on account of the prominent part witches play in *Macbeth*, together with the supposed compounding of their magical concoctions, some actors evince a strong dislike to playing in the drama and to repeat lines from the incantation scene is believed to invite ill-luck.

Yellow is a colour generally avoided by actors and tabooed on the stage, while it is said that the conductor of a theatrical orchestra will not even allow a yellow clarionet to be played in the band on account of the ill-repute of that colour.

The ladies of the chorus have their own superstitions, and if a heel comes off a girl's shoe, or if
she stumbles during a dance, it is said to be a lucky
omen.  To make up with a new set of grease paints
on an opening night, or to look into a mirror over
the shoulder of another while she is making up, is
said to be unlucky, while to break a comb is an
indication of an approaching quarrel with a friend.

According to an account of actors' superstitions
in *The Scrap Book*, the " tag " (the last line of the
play) should not be spoken at a rehearsal, but for
the first time on the opening night, otherwise things
will go wrong, and it is considered an indication of a
favourable reception if a player's shoes squeak
while he is making his first entrance.  When kicking
off his shoes, should they alight on their soles and
remain standing upright, it signifies good fortune,
but should they fall over, bad luck is indicated.

Should a player stumble on making his entrance,
it is regarded that he will miss his cue or forget his
lines, and should his costume catch in a piece of
scenery as he goes on, he must retrace his steps at
once or trouble will ensue during the rest of the
performance.

It is thought to be unlucky to take a glimpse of
the house from the wrong side of the drop-curtain
when it is down, for some say that the prompt side
has an evil influence, so the peep-hole in the curtain
is generally placed in the centre.

Some actors will avoid going on a stage where a
picture of an ostrich is hanging, and trying the
handle of a wrong door, the catching of a drop-
curtain or the upsetting of a make-up box, is said
to be a forerunner of misfortune.

Good fortune is said to accompany the wearing

of certain wigs, while forgetfulness is attributed to others, and some actors will insist on wearing one to which good luck is attributed, throughout the run of a play.

Acrobats have a superstition that if when they throw their cuffs on the stage preparatory to beginning their turn they remain fastened together, all will be well, but should they come apart it is regarded as an omen of misfortune.

To open an umbrella or sunshade on the stage during a scene in a play was at one time considered to be most unlucky, and a cast consisting of thirteen characters was looked upon as inviting misfortune to any play.

Such are but a few of the superstitions that have grown up in connection with the theatre and the stage. Some have already died out and others are now only laughed at, but most old actors still have a lingering belief in many of these omens of good or ill-fortune.

# CHAPTER XXV

SUPERSTITION AND WITCHCRAFT IN EVERYDAY LIFE

SUPERSTITION has been defined as the survival of old beliefs in the midst of a new order of things, and this interpretation is certainly borne out by the belief in witchcraft which still exists amongst us.

The reason for its persistence is not far to seek, for is chiefly due to the common dread of the mysterious unknown mainly manifested through ignorance and fear.

Evidence points to the fact, that some people are as credulous now as their progenitors were centuries ago, and superstition under various names is as rife to-day as it was in bygone times.

The eagerness to obtain a glimpse of the future may be gathered from the advertisements of fortune-tellers, seers, crystal-gazers, and prophets who claim to prognosticate the future. They still flourish and find their dupes in London and other large cities.

From the fact that a newspaper with a large circulation devotes columns every week to astrology, and advertising space in important dailies is taken up by the offers of persons to cast horoscopes and others who call themselves " psychologists," it is obvious that many superstitions have not died out but still form a common factor in everyday life.

The vicar of a large parish in south-east London recently expressed the view, that superstitious practices have greatly revived since the Great War, and he alleged that belief in witchcraft in England, particularly in Devonshire, Norfolk, Cornwall and Durham, exists to-day, and that people still pay visits to witches secretly at night.

He published the following letter which he had received from South Wales, detailing the case of a mother and two children who had been under the influence of a witch for five years. " The witch ill-wished the mother and she has been ill since. Doctors cannot help her, she cannot go out of doors, and all her friends have deserted her. The children are feeling the effects of the curse and the home has been broken up."

He goes on to state that " it seems impossible but it is nevertheless a fact, that in so-called Christian England there are many believers in witchcraft, as well as many people practising as ' black ' and 'white' witches who prosper by their ill-gotten gains."

Belief in the agency of dreams in conveying warnings and news of the future is still widespread. Even those who openly state that the interpretation of dreams is mere amusement, often secretly fear that there is something behind their dreams and visions which has a powerful influence over their fate.

We know that belief in witchcraft in some forms still exists in the Metropolis and that many people carry holed-flints and dried potatoes in their pockets, in the firm belief that they will protect them from rheumatism and bad luck. Within recent years, a chemist's shop in the heart of the city had a ready sale for small glass tubes filled with mercury, which when enclosed in tiny wash-leather bags, were carried by business men in their pockets as a preventive of rheumatic pains.

In the East End, necklaces or strings of glass beads of various colours are sold in small shops, for placing round the necks of babies soon after they are born, in order to protect them from throat and chest troubles.

The majority of people instinctively avoid walking under a ladder that may be reared against a building in our streets, and some will not sit at a table on which three lighted candles are standing.

To look at the new moon through a window-pane or to open an umbrella in the house, is believed to bring misfortune and many " touch wood " on the slightest provocation.

Few will see two knives crossed on a table without at once straightening them, and most diners begin to feel uncomfortable when a neighbour accidentally spills some salt on the cloth.

All these relics of old superstitions still persist in spite of the efforts of the " Thirteen Club," whose members meet their guests under a ladder and by devices such as inverted horse-shoes, broken mirrors, crossed table-knives, peacocks' feathers and other portents of ill, seek to discourage them.

The old Highland belief that a sprig of white heather will bring good luck to the wearer, is still an article of faith with some of our leading politicians who are frequently seen with it in their button-holes.

In Cornwall and Devonshire there are people who still believe in the power of the " evil eye," and witches are dreaded and feared in many of the villages on account of the terrible vengeance they are supposed to be able to work on those who offend them.

The calf's heart stuck full of pins and thorns is still placed in the cottage chimney to " work an evil spell," and the belief in the power of the witch is widely prevalent in many out-of-way parts of some counties, while " charming " is still practised by professional charmers in others.

HAGSTONE WITH KEY
ATTACHED
Used to avert the " evil eye "
from cattle.
*Pitt-Rivers Museum.*

In the Midlands, many still stand in fear of the witch's power, as instanced in a case that came before the Wolverhampton police magistrate on January 17th, 1932, when a woman summoned her husband for persistent cruelty, alleging that he had struck her with a poker. When the husband was asked if he had any witnesses to call, a man came forward who said he " had seen what happened but dare not speak of what he had witnessed, because the woman was a witch and would put a spell on him." He declared that she " boiled violets in water and then cast her spells."

Cases are constantly coming to light in which considerable sums of money have been extorted by these " witches " from their victims.

In October, 1927, a gipsy woman was convicted at the Cornwall Assizes of obtaining money under false pretences and unlawfully pretending to use a certain kind of witchcraft, sorcery or enchantment. The victim, an old Cornish gardener of St. Mawes, was locally known as Paddy, and the woman acquired such an influence over him that she induced him to part with sums amounting to £500.

She pretended that an illness from which he was suffering was due to his being " overlooked by the ' evil eye,' " and that she, as a " white witch," could cure the " black magic " which was the cause of his trouble.

On her visits to him she played about with a compass over his head, making a sign on a door, and talked about the " Planets and Venus." She declared that if he did not pay her more money he would " go blind, become a bed-lier and die."

Poor Paddy said that the woman had been in the habit of visiting him and telling him that he was ill, and at last he told the police, who arrested the " white witch " and she was convicted and put out of the way of working further spells for six months.

In Norfolk and other parts of East Anglia, belief in witchcraft is by no means uncommon and the rector of a country parish recently stated, that many of his parishioners had an ingrained belief in " good and evil spells."

" The charge of witchcraft," he said, " is usually whispered against old women of dominant personality, Roman-nosed women ; and there is a common belief that if I offend 'un (the old woman) then she 'll do me a mischief."

In Wales, especially in the southern counties, many witch-doctors still practise, and according to a local medical practitioner some of them sell to their clients letters of protection against witchcraft.

Such a letter, sold to an old man in Cardiganshire about 1910, was as follows : " In the name of the Father and of the Son and of the Holy Ghost, Amen. And in the name of our Lord Jesus Christ. I will give thee protection and will give relief to thy creatures, thy cows, calves, horses, sheep and pigs, and all creatures that alive be in thy possession from all witchcraft and from all other assaults of Satan. Amen." The letter was written in English.

The story of a sacrificial offering of money to placate an evil spirit standing between a farmer and a fortune, was related before the magistrates at Llansawel in Carmarthenshire on January 25th, 1932.

CORP CREIDH

Clay figure used in witchcraft. These figures were usually placed in a stream and allowed to slowly waste away. Invernessshire, N.B.

*Pitt-Rivers Museum.*

It transpired that the farmer had received visits from two women who had driven up to see him in a saloon car. The elder of the women informed the farmer that he had a relative abroad who was going to leave him a large sum of money.

As a matter of fact he had an uncle who had emigrated many years ago.

The visitors then invited him to do some crystal-gazing and they produced a crystal ball. One of the women, after wrapping the ball in a piece of black cloth, sprinkled some common salt over it and then murmured an incantation.

The farmer was then asked to look into the crystal, and he said he saw the words " Overcome evil by good " and some other writing which he could not decipher, but on gazing at it again he perceived the figures " £500."

The woman assured him that that sum of money would come to him very soon, but an evil spirit

stood in the way and that a burnt offering was
necessary to placate it.

At her bidding, the farmer produced a pound note
and a half sovereign which he handed over, and
they were then seemingly wrapped up with great
ceremony in another black cloth, which was deposited
on a plate over which two slips of paper were superimposed in the form of a cross. The woman then
struck a match and set fire to the paper cross and
afterwards placed the bundle on the kitchen fire.

The farmer was then asked to stand on a plate,
which broke into thirteen pieces. A charm was
next produced in which he was told to wrap not
less than five pounds in notes and to conceal it
in his bed.

It was not to be interfered with until another visit
had been paid to him. After some little time, the
women called again and told the farmer that the
fortune indicated had increased to £1000, and they
guaranteed him that if five pounds more could be
" sacrificed " as a burnt offering, the whole amount
would be on the table by the coming Wednesday.

The farmer, thinking that this was too good to be
true, became suspicious and invited the police to be
present at the seance, and while the two women were
performing their mystic rites on a further offering of
two pounds, they were pounced on by the constables
and marched off to the police station.

The burnt offering snatched from the fire by one
of the policemen was found to consist only of a small
empty cigarette packet, while the " charm " was
simply a piece of tinfoil enclosed in a match-box.
The two pounds in notes which were supposed to
have been thrown into the fire, were found on the
floor at the woman's feet. One of the delinquents

was fined and the other was ordered to pay the costs.

A case in which fear of the witch's power was the predominant feature, occurred in April, 1928, at Yarmouth, when a married woman was sentenced at the Quarter Sessions to nine months' hard labour, for obtaining £88 by menaces from a widow who was her neighbour. The accused was alleged to have threatened to cast a spell over the widow so as " to fill her house with witchcraft and to put her to bed so that she could not move hand or foot."

The unfortunate woman was so terrified by this threat, that she drew her savings from time to time and handed the money to her tormentor under repeated intimidation, and even after that she paid her five shillings weekly out of her pension for over two years.

In many parts of Ireland superstition is still rife among the peasantry, and a case in which a woman brought an action for slander against two farmers and was tried at the Quarter Sessions at Dungannon, County Tyrone, on October 8th, 1927, well illustrates the credulity still existent.

The prosecutor stated that in her district, a number of people believed in the power to " blink " (bewitch) cattle, and rumours had been spread abroad that she had that power.

In consequence of the stories circulated in the neighbourhood, she and her husband had visited one of the defendants and asked him why he had made such slanderous statements.

One of the defendants in his evidence declared that the statements were true, because " the thatch of his house had cured the cattle, and he thanked goodness for it."

" Burning the thatch," he said, " was one of the recognised cures for ' blinked ' cattle, and he had burnt his under the cow's nose, and the cow had jumped to her feet and got better."

The prosecutor said she had visited the other defendant, who had said she had destroyed his cattle, on the same evening. After the cows were cured, she stated, the defendants protected the animals by tying a red rag on their tails, " and mind you," she added, " it wasn't a wee rag for you could see it a good piece away." Red they knew was the witches' colour and was used as a protection against their power.

The prosecutor gained her case and sufficient damages to clear her character.

A great deal of nonsense has recently been written concerning love-potions and philtres which it is declared are being sold not only in country districts but in many parts of London, but beyond the use of the old charms with dragon's blood and quick-silver by certain credulous women on " All Hallow-E'en," there appears to be no evidence to support these statements. A curious case of amatory interest, however, which came before the magistrates at Beverley, Yorkshire, a few months ago, shows how credulous people may still be defrauded by cunning charlatans.

The accused, a woman of middle age, was charged with obtaining by false pretences, sums to the amount of £125 from two elderly maiden sisters who were evidently anxious to find suitable husbands and secure happy married lives.

It transpired that the two ladies consulted the woman in January, 1930, who told one of them to give her something she had worn and she would soak

it in a mysterious preparation she called " Zep."
When the article which had been soaked in the fluid
was burnt, she would see the man she would marry
in the smoke.  She said that " Zep " was made in
Germany " from an animal bred in the East and
was sent to London in tubes costing from £25 to
£75."  Between January and June, 1930, the com-
plainant had parted with from two to three hundred
pounds for " Zep," and when all her money was
gone, she sold her jewellery and handed over the
proceeds, amounting to £70, for the same purpose.

She was told that " she would not see her future
husband for two years and it would take six hundred
drops of ' Zep ' to get him."

The other sister said she was told that " ' Zep '
would attract a man to her and get her happily
married.  She had paid £200 but did not get a
husband."

The sad sequel to the case was told at the hearing,
when it was stated that, the sisters, who had been
in comfortable circumstances, had sold their house,
parted with all their money to the woman who had
so cruelly defrauded them, and one was now in
domestic service while the other had to seek outdoor
relief.

It is evident from these and other cases that have
come to light in recent years, that belief in witchcraft and the occult arts has by no means died out
in this country.  It must also be admitted that
superstition, either due to an inbred fear of the
unknown or auto-suggestion, still constitutes an
element in our social system at the present day, and
in spite of educational progress, it continues to play
an important part in our everyday life.

THE author wishes to acknowledge his indebtedness to the works of Sir T. F. Thiselton Dyer, Messrs. P. H. Ditchfield, Elworthy, Krappe, Walsh, Hall and Polden for information respecting many common superstitions and old customs.

# INDEX